BACK THE
MAN
YOU FELL IN
LOVE WITH

Carolyn Bushong, L.P.C.

ADAMS MEDIA CORPORATION
Avon, Massachusetts

To Alan,
My lover, my partner, and my best friend.

Copyright ©2003, Carolyn Bushong.
All rights reserved. This book, or parts thereof, may not
be reproduced in any form without permission from the publisher;
exceptions are made for brief excerpts used in published reviews.

Published by Adams Media Corporation
57 Littlefield Street, Avon, MA 02322 U.S.A.
www.adamsmedia.com

ISBN: 1-58062-750-1

Printed in Canada.

J I H G F E D C B A

Library of Congress Cataloging-in-Publication Data
Bushong, Carolyn Nordin.
Bring back the man you fell in love with / by Carolyn Bushong.
p.   cm.
ISBN 1-58062-750-1
1. Man-woman relationships. 2. Women--Psychology. 3. Love.
I. Title.
HQ801 .B8857 2003
306.7--dc21

2002014290

CONTENTS

"Why Doesn't He Act Like He Loves Me Anymore?" • Why He Acts Cold and Rejecting • Why He Lies • Why He Tries to Act Tough (The "Manly Man" Code) • Getting Back the Man of Your Dreams • Men's Secrets

Secrets I've Learned As a Therapist • The Dysfunctional Fit • What Is Your Dysfunctional Style? • How to Develop an Equal, Healthy Relationship

"Why Can't He Just Change?" • How Women Squander Their Power • Women's "Bad" Behaviors • Five Ways to Stop Nagging

Getting Him to Hear You • It Takes a Strong Woman to Bring Out the Healthy Man in Your Mate • "How Did My Relationship Get So Out of Balance?" • Ten Steps to Becoming a "Functional" Partner • Reversing the Rejection • When You Get Your Power Back, You Are His Equal

Stop Fighting Dirty • Negotiating Fair Deals • Creating Consequences, Setting Boundaries, and Giving Ultimatums • Ten Ways to Gain Power in Your Relationships • Five Steps to Successful Negotiations

Author's Note

The cases in this book are combinations of single cases and amalgams. Each person or couple has been carefully disguised in accordance with the professional standards of confidentiality and the right to privileged communication with a therapist.

Acknowledgments

Thanks to my sister, Ruth Krueger, M.S.W., who over the years has become my closest girlfriend. We've had our disagreements, but always worked through them. One night when I stayed in her hospital room during her second bout of cancer, we were discussing our own successful relationships with our mates, and as two therapists would do, turned the idea into the concept for this book.

And thanks to my Mom and Dad, Evelyn and Roy Nordin (now divorced), who often relied on me as a child. Though they gave me too much emotional responsibility as I grew up, it indirectly built my confidence, convincing me I could be the person that would find the answers to theirs and other peoples' (including my own) relationship problems.

Thanks to my literary agent, Alan Nevins, who remained persistent in selling this book as the title and the direction kept changing. And thanks to Claire Gerus, my editor, who was able to see the importance of this project as we worked closely together exploring the direction of this book.

Also, thanks to Patty Romanowski whose way with words kept me improving my writing style. And thanks to all my office staff and typists whose computer skills kept me on deadline: Michelle Lang Treiste, Karen Evans, Shannon Chavez, and Jason Cline.

And of course, thanks to all my clients who provided me with the fascinating stories to share with you to make these techniques come alive.

Also, though not directly related to the book, thanks to Jennifer, Larry, Rick, Dave, and Spike—all great radio hosts—whose humorous comments during my relationship advice on the air, are able to lighten up the seriousness of the subject.

And last, but not least, thanks to Alan Errickson, the man I fell in love with and love even more today. Because of my fifteen-year relationship with Alan, I now know what true love is all about. Both of us came into the relationship with our own emotional baggage and issues, and we both changed—for the better. Together we learned to face issues and resolve them.

We pursued a common goal—a healthy, happy, equal relationship—and developed a strong, loving partnership that now seems effortless. Our love has not only continued, but has grown more deeply over the years.

Introduction

I grew up with a father whose ideas about relationships went no further than Archie Bunker's. The men I knew, dated, and even the one I married were just like him. The concept of an "equal" relationship entered my mind in theory and fantasy only.

After three years married to a man like my father (while I finished my master's in counseling), I divorced and vowed to never be any man's "wife" again, since I saw the role of wife as synonymous with slave. After dating (I use the term loosely) approximately 50 to 100 men over the course of nine years, I decided that men were all alike: selfish, unemotional, uncaring, and only looking for sex.

Most men had been controlling with me, like my father had been. So, I began dating younger, less successful men whom I could control (but didn't respect), soon realizing that wasn't the answer either. As I was counseling mostly women at the time, was politically involved with feminist issues, and teaching classes on assertiveness training, I kept my negative opinions about men pretty solid.

My first book, *Loving Him Without Losing You*, came from my motto to myself: "Never be dependent on any man for any reason," which I still believe. But once we women become emotionally and financially independent from men, then what? I didn't realize there was more to learn: how to remain strong within a relationship with a man, and create a truly equal relationship. Instead of fearing an intimate relationship with a man and keeping him at a distance to stay safe, I needed to use my newfound strength to help a man change his behavior toward me. But how was I to test my true strength without entering into a relationship with a man?

It wasn't until I met Alan that I really learned the rest of the formula for happiness: An equal partnership with a man who is a lover and a friend, in which neither one controls the other.

And no, it didn't just magically happen that way. It was advantageous that we already had some equality in the relationship—we were close in age, both professionals, owned our own homes, and traveled in the same social circles. Alan made more money than I did at the time, though not significantly more. I do believe because we weren't extremely out of balance financially, age-wise, or in any other way, this improved our chances for success, but wasn't necessarily the key.

I believe the key was that I was basically happy with my life and unwilling to sacrifice my personal power for any relationship. That doesn't mean that I controlled him. It means he was forced to negotiate with me. No decisions or negotiations in our relationship were based on gender, on our past relationships, on how our parents did things, or on our friends' relationships. We both discussed what we wanted, how we wanted it to work, and proceeded forward.

When my clients hear about my relationship with Alan, they say, "It's too bad there aren't more men like Alan in the world," to which I reply, "I agree, but let's call his ex-wife and see if she feels that way." In his marriage, Alan never cooked, was a workaholic who never came home, never helped raise his daughter, nagged his wife about her weight, and cheated on her. He has never treated me that way—he knows I'd never accept that kind of treatment.

I've grown too. Alan taught me that I didn't need to keep a wall of anger and resentment toward men around me to protect myself. In fact, I learned with him that the more I could be soft and loving, while still remaining strong and clear about my stand, the more he listened and changed—and the stronger the bond became between us.

You will see through my own personal examples in the following chapters of this book how I stood my ground, communicated with power, and set boundaries with consequences to get Alan to treat me the way he does today in our fifteen-year relationship.

I also use numerous client success stories of women (and men) whom I've helped find happiness in their relationships during my more than twenty-five years as a relationship counselor. I've helped a large number of women change themselves and change their men through boundary setting, which ultimately caused their men to once again act like the men of their dreams. Many have been able to create long-term, equal, happy, and passionate relationships. It is also important to me that I live my life true to my teachings, and so I've never asked my clients to do anything I haven't had the courage to do myself. The ideas and techniques presented in this book have worked in my relationship with Alan and also in the relationships of my numerous clients.

I realized (and hope you realize) that men are not inherently selfish or bad, but that we women often let them behave that way. Once women realize they can have true equality with a man, they automatically begin to behave differently. It's the change in their behavior—from acceptance of how they believe men are to a new belief that men can be equal partners—that changes the entire dynamic of the relationship.

In my second book, *The Seven Dumbest Relationship Mistakes Smart People Make,* I showed mistakes both men and women make in relationships, and how they can stop making these mistakes. Then I realized that couples often read it and still pointed the finger at their mate—"See, he does that and needs to stop"—rather than stop their own bad behaviors. Someone has to pick up the ball and start the changes—and it's usually the woman who is most passionate about changing the relationship.

So, the woman who wants to get back the man of her dreams—and turn her relationship into a positive force in her life—must accept that to have what she wants, she alone may be responsible for instigating change in the beginning. The fastest, surest way, to change her man, and to change her relationship, begins with changing herself into an equal partner who does not evoke or condone his bad behavior. She has to change, even if he is more than 50 percent responsible for their problems, and even though she and others may think that this is not fair. It is very important to remember that she is not sacrificing anything for him. In the end, she is doing this work to preserve and strengthen her relationship with her mate because it makes her happy. In each of the dozens of specific cases included, I show how each woman transformed her mate into the man of her dreams and was able to have the relationship she has fantasized about.

Chapter 1

Why He Doesn't Treat You the Way He Used To

How did the man we once saw as perfect become the man he is today—the one who never seems to listen? Never seems to know what we want? Worst of all, he never seems as emotionally connected, loving, open, and in love with us as he once was and certainly as we want him to be now. When did he start assuming you would take care of the kids, the house, and his aging parents? How did he forget our anniversary, our daughter's last recital, or our favorite color of rose? In other words, when did he stop being that great guy we fell in love with, and become this freedom-loving, self-indulgent, rebellious, inattentive guy we're living with today? Is it too late? Can we get back our loving man? Yes, we can, and I will show you how.

Romance Is Difficult

The romantic, loving relationship every woman longs for, every day—and every night—is filled with passion, excitement, devotion, and true love. Her mate adores her and respects her, is secure in himself yet regards her as a fully equal partner in the relationship. This is the very heart of a positive, healthy, adult relationship between partners who approach their relationship and each other with honesty, respect, and restraint. If these traits strike you—as they strike most women—as "unrealistic," they're not, as you will soon understand.

No matter how deeply you may love your partner, no matter how committed you may feel to a relationship, the truth is, love is hard. Most of us wish our relationships and our men could be the way they were at the beginning. When we first meet someone, he romances us, tells us he loves us, and behaves in a wonderful, loving way. The special way he treats us in the beginning of the relationship is part of why we fall in love with him in the first place.

Seven Years and No Marriage in Sight
▶ Britney and Kyle's Story

My client Britney is a bright, attractive, divorced thirty-nine-year-old banker with a classic problem: a man who will not commit. She's been dating Kyle, who is forty, for nearly seven years. Kyle is a successful businessman, popular in their social circle, handsome, and never married. Britney was attracted to him from the moment they met because he was affectionate, considerate, and attentive. However, over time, things changed, and the relationship seemed to stall. They've never lived together or seriously discussed marriage. In the past few months, Kyle has grown more distant, emotionally and even sexually.

When I asked Britney why she stays with Kyle, she said, "What can I say? I really do love him, and I know he loves me. But I don't know how much longer I can go on like this. I keep hoping I'll get the old Kyle back."

In the beginning, Kyle made Britney feel special when he told her she was different from other women he'd known. Then, after the first couple of years or so, he stopped treating her special. He was late for dates, he neglected to call for days, and would become angry and withdrawn every time they argued. Kyle became inconsiderate, self-absorbed, self-righteous, and emotionally cold. He seemed to have a negative attitude toward relationships in general, and was growing increasingly disrespectful of Britney and their relationship. Her friends and family always asked her when they were getting married. She didn't know. Maybe never. She kept buying time, trying to "understand" why Kyle was acting this way.

"Why Doesn't He Act Like He Loves Me Anymore?"

There were several possible reasons why Kyle had pulled away, but the most important one was that Britney allowed it. She was surprised when I told her she could change much of his bad behavior if she tried. I told Britney, "You can change the way he treats you, if you change your behavior toward him first. You're no longer the woman he first met either. You never would have put up with this kind of inconsiderate behavior when you were first dating. You have to become the strong, confident woman you used to be to get back the romantic loving man he was then. People—especially men—will treat you as badly as you allow them to. So if you don't accept his cold, inconsiderate behavior, he will probably change it. If you continue to allow it—or even worse, chase after him when he behaves this way—his behavior will never change."

Some men act inconsiderate and cold toward women from the start. Others were once more loving and caring (or at least very good at leading us to believe they were) but learned that cold, distant, inconsiderate behavior helped them feel less vulnerable and less threatened by women. Some men will never settle down and be warm and loving in a relationship, no matter who their mate is or what she does. Many more, however, are basically loving, caring, considerate men inside (or close enough) who revert to bad behavior when they lose respect for their mate and see that she will tolerate it. As I've said, I don't believe men are inherently "bad" or are so different from women. I do believe, however, that behind every man who has lost respect for his mate is a woman who has handed over her share of the power in the relationship.

Why is it so easy for men to avoid being loving and warm? Our culture fails to teach boys and young men how to recognize and sustain a healthy romantic relationship. We gratify or wink at attitudes and behaviors we wouldn't want to see in a man dating our own daughter or sister, for example. We accept it because "that's the way men are." Most fathers we see, perhaps including our own, do not behave like loving, caring men around their wives. Our mothers, whose powers of transformation failed on their own husbands, send us the message loud and clear: You cannot change him. Since most of our female peers have heard pretty much the same message themselves, sisters, girlfriends, coworkers, and the society at large only reinforce the "unhappily ever after." So we get confused. We assume that our need to be loved is love for him, and we start accepting behaviors from our mates we would never tolerate with friends. We make the mistake of believing that "love is the exception," and that because we love him, we need to "understand" him. Then we excuse, overlook, tolerate, and encourage the bad behavior that makes us unhappy.

When we are unable to find a loving man, we're thoroughly convinced that either he doesn't exist, or we're not good enough to attract him. If we're in a less-than-loving relationship, we believe we have no choice but to accept the man we love just the way he is, since everyone believes men cannot change. We think that simply by loving him enough, we will at least make things tolerable. Notice how easily we shoulder the full responsibility for our men and our relationships (which never change or improve either), but forego the opportunity to act responsibly in our own behavior (which has the power to change everything).

When we see a woman who seems to have found her true man, we often dismiss it as a rare exception. We may grudgingly acknowledge (if only to ourselves) that she has some secret (maybe he has some unseen "weakness," maybe she is great in bed). Tellingly, we credit the man in that relationship for his good behavior. We never consider what it is about that special relationship—and the woman's behavior behind it—that makes him want to live up to her expectations and not revert to "bad" behavior.

Instead, we find a man who treats us coldly and we place all our hope in the power of our love to make him treat us better. When our love fails to work the magic, we try to change his behavior by resorting to the repertoire we are most familiar with: nagging, bitching, whining, complaining, scolding, and withholding affection. These are all tactics we know would never work with anyone else and certainly never work when used on us. But we know of nothing else to try to make him love us. And, love being love, we would never just give up and walk away. By the time we are forced to accept that our love will not work the magic and make him treat us better, it is too late. We've convinced ourselves that we love him too much to leave. We are deeply invested, or we're probably in denial. We married him, had his children, and lost our power. We expected our love to change him, and when it doesn't, we respond in one of several ways, all equally immature and childish: We often act like victims, fearing that we are not good enough, blaming ourselves for everything wrong with the relationship, and babying him and enabling his bad behavior. Or we become controlling, and angry, always criticizing and blaming him.

Chances are, your mate learned a variation on the same lessons you learned at home. If your mother's behavior toward your father taught you how to be a helpless victim or a dominating shrew, his father's behavior probably taught him those male behaviors that have evolved so exquisitely to inspire those reactions in you. Men who act distant or unloving in relationships are products of behavior and conditioning. And so are women who act selfless and sacrificing. Is this just "how men and women are"? No. I believe that this is an example of how men and women have learned to believe that they are. These beliefs rob us of not only the opportunity but also the capacity to experience full, meaningful, and rewarding relationships that far exceed anything in a fairy tale. Whether or not your mate has never had a chance to be a loving, wonderful man before, you—by understanding and changing your behavior with him—can motivate him to change.

Why He Acts Cold and Rejecting

Little boys are taught at an early age not to express their emotions—that emotional vulnerability is a sign of weakness. "Be a big boy and stop crying!" They're also taught, of course, never to hit a woman and that confronting a woman in any way is wrong. "Don't you talk to your mother (or sister) like that!" So what is a man supposed to do when he disagrees with a woman? How is he supposed to deal with his anger? The only accepted behavior men see available to them is walking away. So they shut down, avoid, and walk away.

Men's emotional relationships with their mothers further complicate the situation. Because mothers are in a position of power, little boys learn to fear women. As a child, a boy wants to please his mom, but seldom receives anything more than criticism from her, so he feels he can never win. Because a little boy loves his mother, yet is continually scolded and reprimanded by her, he's continually put in a lose/lose situation. He learns that rather than lose, he'll choose not to play the game altogether. So, out of fear of losing, he learns to avoid. Nonparticipation becomes the behavior of choice.

Men don't think of their behavior as cold and rejecting. They have no clue how hurtful their bad behavior is to us. They're just protecting themselves. We women would never treat anyone we care about this way, so we can't understand how a man who says he loves us could behave like this. We take a man's self-protective behavior as personal rejection. But it's not. It's just a cover he uses because he's afraid of not doing it right.

Britney didn't realize that Kyle's withdrawal and coldness came from his own personal issues more than anything she did. Kyle doesn't know how to confront or work through emotional issues (especially with women), so he backs away when uncomfortable. Kyle does love Britney. However, Britney is right when she says the relationship is disintegrating. Kyle is building a case against marrying Britney. Issues aren't getting resolved, so Kyle is building a wall of resentment toward Britney that keeps him from ever wanting to make a long-term commitment.

Why He Lies

As a child, a little boy learns two major defenses to deal with women: avoid her (which we just discussed), or tell her what she wants to hear (and then do what you want). Because of this early training, men never learn to be emotionally honest or responsible with what they tell us. Instead, they often tell us what they think we want to hear: "Okay, I'll be home early." Then they come home two hours later. Then we say, "Why did you lie to me?" He says, "I didn't lie; I just got home later than I planned."

Most men display these dishonest behaviors with women without a second thought. These men fear that if they tell the truth, their wives or girlfriends will be hurt, upset, or angry. If they tell her what she wants to hear, they please her initially and then hopefully end up getting away with it, because "she'll be asleep and never know when I came home."

He Tells Her What She Wants to Hear

▶ *Allison and Sid's Story*

That's what my client, Sid, does with his girlfriend Allison. He says what he thinks she wants to hear, and then usually doesn't follow through. When she accuses him of lying, he just says he's sorry and takes his punishment. Allison asked him to come over for dinner early Monday night (which meant 5 P.M. to her), and he said okay. However, he knew he was going to start working on his boat at three in the afternoon and that it would take three to four hours to finish. When he showed up for dinner at 7 P.M., Allison was furious! Usually Sid shuts down and lets her yell at him for a while. But this time, it turned into a fight. Sid said, "You're such a bitch—always riding my ass!" She said, "I wouldn't have to be if you didn't lie to me all the time." The battle escalated and he left.

Days later, in my office, Sid was proud of himself for standing up to her (for a change). After some discussion, he realized he should have simply told Allison he couldn't come over early because he planned to work on his boat. He admitted to me that he was avoiding the confrontation. "She would've tried to talk me out of working on the boat. She probably would've said she was hurt because I'm choosing the boat over her. She would've accused me of not making her a priority." I reminded him that she said those things anyway—he didn't avoid the problem, he just postponed it. He agreed, but like a "bad little boy," he wanted to avoid the confrontation as long as he possibly could so she couldn't talk him out of working on his boat. I explained that he should have taken a stand with her, stood his ground, and still worked on the boat. He couldn't picture himself being able to still work on the boat once Allison started guilt-tripping him, crying to him that she wasn't a priority.

Sid does love Allison, but whenever there's a conflict, the little boy inside of him thinks:

- I can't win.
- I'm always disappointing her. Maybe I'm not the right person for her.
- If I do what I want, she'll think I'm a bad person because I'm not doing what she wants.

- It's best to keep her happy by telling her what she wants to hear for as long as I can.
- I do deserve her bitching, nagging, and whining. It's my punishment for not doing what she wants. But why can't she ever let it go and get over it?

Fear of hurting her, fear of being wrong, fear of being a bad person—these are the reasons Sid shuts down and acts cold and rejecting. Additionally, the more she nags, criticizes, and guilt-trips him, the more he resents her.

Allison doesn't realize that she helps teach Sid to lie to her. Reacting with her own "bad" behavior of nagging and guilt-tripping him only sends the relationship off on a negative spiral with no answers in sight, because he feels he can't win either way.

You Probably Know Him Better Than He Knows Himself

Most men are not self-aware. They don't sit around analyzing their relationships or their behaviors—or even their mates' behaviors. We women wish they did, but they don't. So we do it for them. We figure if we can understand why he is behaving the way he is, and we tell him, then he should want to change it. However, that seldom motivates him to change—and in fact, often makes him feel more criticized. There's nothing wrong with trying to figure him out as long as we don't critically throw the information in his face or use it to feel sorry for him, excusing his bad behavior.

Britney knew all about Kyle's childhood and had him all figured out, although Kyle himself didn't. Kyle's parents divorced when Kyle was ten and his mother left him with his father. Britney believed that his mother's abandonment caused Kyle to fear closeness and commitment. Britney could also tell that Kyle longed for his mother's approval by the way he talked to her on the phone,

9

never showing anger toward her (although he had told Britney he was hurt and angry his mom left him).

Britney realized that Kyle was treating her the same way he treated his mom. When upset, he never told her, he just withdrew until his anger dissipated (although he never really got over it). She surmised that he probably feared losing her the way he had lost his mom—especially if he acted angry in her presence. However, the truth is that Kyle will probably end up losing Britney because he withdraws. And, since Kyle never tells her that he's upset or what he's upset about, Britney can't even change the behavior that bothers Kyle, so he ends up building resentment toward her, which will eventually kill the relationship.

What Britney needs to do is use what she knows about Kyle in her favor instead of using it to excuse his bad behavior. Britney needs to realize that this is a personal problem of Kyle's that Kyle needs to deal with, and this is probably why he's never been married. She needs to stop taking Kyle's withdrawal personally. Then, since he fears abandonment, she needs to threaten to abandon him if he continues to withdraw from her. "The next time you pull away and won't talk to me, I'm going to refuse to see you for three days. And if after those three days are up, you still haven't told me what you were upset about, I'll not see you for another three days."

Allison also had already analyzed Sid when she first came into my office complaining about him. She knew why he was behaving the way he was, even though she didn't know what to do about it.

I tried to help Allison see that if she could get past feeling rejected and change her own whining and guilt-tripping behavior, she could play on his fears instead of playing into them. If a man avoids you and you chase after him, he will only run faster. Two things happen: One, Sid feels pressured as he did with his mom; and two, Allison begins to lose value in his eyes because she seems desperate. Sid then uses Allison's pressuring and other bad behaviors to justify dumping her.

However, if a man avoids you and you then pull further away from him, you end up playing on his deeper fear of losing you. This usually makes him come back toward you to try to win you back. This is when, and the only time when, you have enough emotional power in the relationship (and he is vulnerable enough) for him to really listen to you. Then and only then can he join you in finding solutions to your relationship problems.

Allison understood this, but her own insecurities and inability to see what she was doing kept her from following through for quite a while. Each time these fights happened, she felt so relieved that he was back that she didn't use her newfound power to negotiate a solution for future incidents.

Great Guy–Foolish Decisions

When men feel uncomfortable and frightened, instead of letting us know that, they're more likely to decide to cover it up. The more vulnerable they feel, the more likely they are to adopt defenses to cover up their out-of-control feelings. This is true of both men and women. However, because men have more power historically, their defensive "bad" behavior is often more aggressive and harmful. Hard-core feminists have often characterized men as lacking warm feelings and unable to feel or show compassion. This, of course, isn't true. It is true that sometimes men become so shut down emotionally, they appear this way.

It's also true that men feel pressure from society to appear strong at all times, even when they aren't. They are more likely to overreact to their insecurities by overcompensating with extremely controlling behavior. It is important for women to understand this so that they don't mistake men's cold and controlling behavior for true strength, and become intimidated by it. A strong man (or person) doesn't need to hit, scream at, pull away from, or control someone smaller than himself. Only a person who is afraid of losing control overreacts to that extent. You need to realize that his "bad" behavior is his cover for his own insecurities and fear of you seeing through him.

Key in changing a man's behavior is seeing it as his problem.

Men's Bad Behaviors		
controlling	avoids closeness	angry outbursts
know-it-all attitude	withdraws and won't talk	secretive
jealous	blames me for everything	lectures me
takes me for granted	doesn't come home	condescending
not romantic or loving	acts like he doesn't need me	drinks too much
physically attacks me	cheats	overspends
disrespectful	Mama's boy	sexist
puts his friends before me	judges what I do	revengeful
workaholic	critically/verbally abusive	rude to my friends
doesn't help with kids	never helps with housework	selfish
uninvolved with family	always sexually aggressive	avoids conflict

You have the power to change all of the behaviors just listed—not necessarily in his behavior with others, but definitely in how he behaves with you. This is true, of course, only when you have equal power in the relationship. Yet, he may at any time choose to leave you and continue his bad behavior with others, but he will know he cannot continue his bad behavior with you. And you need to know and believe that it's better to lose him than to keep him and be treated badly.

Why He Tries to Act Tough (The "Manly Man" Code)

Some of these behaviors seem childish, others rebellious, and many macho. Why? Where did he learn to behave like this? Little boys may learn to avoid from their mothers—but they learn how to be men from their fathers. They watch how Dad treats Mom. They see Dad act tough and cold even when Mom is crying. (Dad's afraid of losing control and being manipulated by Mom's emotions, so he shuts down.) Men also learn from their fathers that when they don't feel tough or strong, or know what to do, just fake it (by acting like nothing affects them). Not all boys learn this of course. Some boys ignore their dad's teachings and become "nice guys" who are overly emotional and try too hard. Most boys learn the "Manly Man" Code from their fathers and never learn to become the loving, caring men they're capable of becoming. To better understand the Manly Man Code, we must understand how important appearing strong and masculine is to men.

The "Manly Man" Code (What Strong Means to a Man)

- Showing a woman he can't be controlled, i.e., rebelling against her, ignoring what she says, etc.
- Doing whatever he wants, regardless of what she says or feels.
- Having many women sexually to show how virile he is.
- Believing that nothing is worth crying over (especially not a woman).
- Never being so weak as to let pain affect him.
- Never accepting responsibility for his mistakes—always blaming her.
- Choosing not to engage if he thinks he can't win.
- When conflict cannot be avoided, intimidating her to throw her off track.
- Lying to a woman rather than hurting her with the truth.
- Denying his own personal problems (they make him look weak).
- Avoiding negative feelings by drinking, gambling, or working too much.
- Rigidly sticking to his way of doing things—it make him appear sure of himself.
- Avoiding intimacy so women can't get their hooks into him.
- Never letting her see him sweat (not being vulnerable with anyone at any time).
- When in crisis, pulling himself up by his bootstraps and handling it by himself (no whining, counseling, or discussions).

Most men believe that strength is the ability to not let emotions affect them. Avoiding, ignoring, pretending, and enduring become the defenses a man uses to appear strong. In fact, when he endures your nagging, he believes he is being strong. These unemotional behaviors, of course, do not in reality show strength, but instead, help a man build a facade of strength to temporarily cover up his insecurities.

The problem is that many men believe their own tough act and never learn that true strength comes from facing problems, feeling the emotions involved, and allowing those emotions to lead them and their mates to a solution. We wish they understood this; however, they don't have to "get it" for us to change their behavior.

Instead of buying into a man's facade of strength, chuckle to yourself, "Look at the big tough act he's giving me. Whoooh! I know he's just scared and trying to bluff me. I'm still going to hold my stand and tell him, 'Either we work this issue out or I'm not going with you to dinner. Let me know when you want to talk about it.'"

Then, if he doesn't respond and negotiate a solution, you must pull away from him and do whatever will make you feel better. Usually three times is the charm, meaning it will take you at least three times of setting boundaries (and keeping them) for him to believe you will no longer accept that particular "bad" behavior. You don't yell or nag or whine, you simply set a consequence and follow through. Then you avoid him until he comes to you ready to discuss the issue. You then restate what you want, hear him out, and work out an agreeable solution that works for both. That's what Allison and Sid were finally able to do.

After several sessions of talking through their issue, Allison finally realized how she should have changed her own behavior. She should have asked Sid clearly, "Why don't you come over for dinner early? Say, five o'clock?" If he answered yes, she should have asked, "Are you sure you want to? Does five really work for you?" She could have added, "Honey, be honest. If that time doesn't work, just tell me." Then if he commits to 5 P.M. she should set a boundary such as, "If you're not here by 5:15, I'm putting the food away and you have to take me out to the restaurant of my choice when you arrive. Deal?" Of course if he says 5 P.M. won't work, explaining that he intends to work on the boat, she needs to be okay with it or try to negotiate a different deal with him. What's more important is what she shouldn't do—make him feel guilty or disrespect his needs.

How He Thinks Differently from You

Men don't think like us because their values and beliefs are different from ours. Women value connection, cooperation, and feelings. We know men don't think like us when we really listen to them. They say things like, "Never let them see you sweat!" "Go ahead and give him enough rope to hang himself." "Don't ever show your hand." Men say crass things to their friends and no one gets upset. Because of their training to cover emotions, act stronger than they feel, and never show weakness or vulnerability, they value "action," not thinking about an issue or feeling it. They think we're crazy for analyzing issues; we think they're crazy because they don't. The truth lies somewhere in the middle.

Remember that men's values come from sports and business—competition, one-upmanship, and win-lose strategies. Knowing this, we need to give up our unrealistic expectations that men (left on their own) will eventually focus on our feelings and give us what we want. Instead, we must show men "win-win" solutions that will work for both of us.

How Does the Perfect Man Behave?

Sometimes we get confused and think, "But I don't want a wimp. A man who treats me badly is better than a wimp!" Contrary to what some women believe, the perfect man isn't necessarily a guy who will do everything you say; he's not the classic "nice guy" or a wimp. The man we want is an emotionally honest, responsible man who admits he wants a warm, loving, respectful relationship with us even if he's not quite sure what it takes to have one. When he is shown a way to avoid discord, arguments, or tension by facing issues and resolving them, he eagerly works with us, leading us both to pleasant, positive feelings.

He will follow our lead, as long as we're being fair. However, he is his own person, so he will speak up when he disagrees or does not understand something. This man will try to be the best he can be as a person, a lover, and a mate. He won't need to protect himself from us or hide behind defenses. He is true to himself and has integrity in his dealings with us and with others. He communicates his needs and negotiates without giving up his personal power. This perfect man is "present" in his support and availability. He lets us into his private world. He desires the closeness and the intimacy that we desire, and he does whatever is necessary to maintain the bond between us. Instead of shirking responsibility like a lazy teenager, he eagerly takes on half of the day-to-day duties, working as a team player, knowing this is what's necessary to keep our lives running smoothly. And, yes, you alone, by changing your behavior, can get these loving, caring, cooperative behaviors from him and get back that loving man you once knew.

Britney did change her behavior. Although she was skeptical, she made a decision to change herself to try to change Kyle. Britney first had to look at what she was doing to encourage Kyle's bad behavior. She realized she had surrendered her power in the relationship. No matter what Kyle did or said, or how bad his behavior was, he could always count on Britney being there for him (which she had thought was good behavior on her part). At the same time, she whined and complained to her friends. She also pushed Kyle away with her constant nagging, thinking, "What else can I do? He never listens to me anymore."

I explained to her that Kyle had no reason to change his behavior or even listen to her since he was never threatened or afraid of losing her. I showed Britney how to stop being so "understanding" of Kyle's deep-rooted problems, and instead focus on her own needs.

"Concentrate on being more selfish and see whether or not Kyle is capable of meeting your needs," I told her. Britney thought this sounded coldhearted and way too simple. "Besides, Carolyn, you know when I talk to him about this, he's never going to go along with it."

"He doesn't have to agree with it," I said. "You can discuss it with Kyle, if you want. However, you don't have to get his permission and he doesn't even have to agree to cooperate with you for these techniques to work. In fact, it might be better if you don't tell Kyle what you're doing. I guarantee his behavior will change in some way, even if he doesn't know why. For every action, there is a reaction, and we're going to change your actions to get new reactions from him."

We started with simple ground rules. From here on, Britney would no longer enable Kyle's bad behavior by behaving badly herself (waiting for him and whining about it). Instead, she would behave like a healthy, responsible adult woman. For example, Britney would refuse to see Kyle if he didn't plan their dates in advance and would instead make her own plans if she didn't hear from him. At first, Kyle's behavior got worse. He was angry she was acting like this, and wasn't taking Britney seriously. He tried to scare her into backing down—he withdrew, stopped calling, and even acted as if he wanted to end the relationship. Britney had trouble following through because she felt bad that her behavior was upsetting Kyle so much. Instead, with my help, she wrote Kyle a firmly worded letter making it clear that she still loved him, but that his behavior would have to change if they were to continue. She was now threatening abandonment. Finally, after dropping by her house unannounced several times to find her gone, he decided to cooperate and plan dates with her. He eventually felt a spark of renewed respect for Britney. When Kyle finally realized that Britney was not going to surrender her newly reclaimed, rightful half of the power in their relationship, he began to listen for the first time and cooperate with her requests.

Did Kyle capitulate and suddenly become the healthy, respectful, and loving man of Britney's dreams? Not completely, but he was behaving more like the man she fell in love with. But also with her new attitude and new behaviors, Britney was well on her way to becoming the woman she used to be (which made her happier and more confident). And this strong, healthy, "non-nagging" woman is the woman Kyle had fallen in love with. He needed to see Britney's strength to be motivated to change and become warm and loving again. Finally, Kyle relented. "What do I have to do to keep you in my life? I love you."

Together, they negotiated the ground rules for their future relationship. They learned to express their feelings more openly and honestly, and they learned that they could argue without shutting each other out and without jeopardizing their love. Of course, there were some setbacks along the way, but every time Kyle failed to keep a commitment, Britney fought the urge to chase after him and instead pulled back and set a boundary. Now that Britney had effective ways of dealing with Kyle, she stopped talking bad about him to her friends. She began to feel more secure in the relationship, so Kyle began to open up more.

Five months after our first session, Britney called to say, "It's a miracle! Kyle is a totally different man. He's really affectionate; he talks about our future. I can't believe how much he has changed. We're even having sex again!" I had to remind Britney that Kyle would never have changed his behavior if she hadn't had the courage to change hers.

Getting Back the Man of Your Dreams

Men are not bad; they're just scared. Their bad behaviors reflect their own problems and insecurities, not necessarily rejection of us. The truth is men and women want love and respect, but each gender values these qualities differently and goes about achieving them differently. For a relationship to be healthy, it must be equal and these differences must be understood and respected.

Not all men can or will change, and not all relationships can be saved. Your man could be an alcoholic, a cheater, or an abuser. If so, he has a serious problem that probably requires more than simple behavior modification. By using the techniques in this book, however, you can change almost any man's bad behavior, no matter who he is. The techniques I'm teaching you will not change a man's personality or cure his addictions. You can only change the way he treats you.

Ten Clues He's Worth It

1. There are at least some women he respects.
2. He has loving moments with you.
3. He is strong but also able to ask for help in certain areas of his life.
4. He can be vulnerable with children and pets.
5. When you do hold your ground, he responds.
6. He understands the concept of an equal relationship and admits to wanting one.
7. He knows a healthy couple he admires.
8. He has taken some steps to change his behavior.
9. He desires quality time with you.
10. He sometimes admits he's wrong.

Should You Try to Change Him?

Is the "man of your dreams" inside your mate? I don't know. But I do know that if the following three questions are true, I can show you how to find out.

1. **Is he committed to the relationship?** (He must be invested to making it work or it will be hard to gain enough power to change his behavior.)

19

2. **Are you still in love with him?** (You need to be in love with him to stay motivated enough to hold the boundaries.)
3. **Does he have redeeming qualities?** (Is he a good father, have you seen glimpses of his warmth? He needs to have redeeming qualities as a human being to guarantee the likelihood of success.)

If all three answers are "yes," you'll probably be successful at changing him back into the loving man you once knew. If you're not sure, just know that changing your behavior will help you become a better person and behave healthier in all your future relationships with or without him. By changing your behavior, and setting boundaries with your man, you can not only get him to treat you the way he used to, but also develop a better, more deeply bonded, healthy, emotional, and romantic relationship with him.

Men's Secrets

- I'd like to feel closer to you, but I don't know how.
- I'd share my feelings if you wouldn't think of me as weak.
- Each time I give in to you, I hate you a little more!
- Your emotions frustrate me but also entertain me.
- I fear being in love will allow you to control me.
- When you act like my mom, it turns me off!
- My controlling ways are fed by your unwillingness to stand up to me.
- I let you yell at me to relieve my guilt so I can be bad again.
- When you act needy and desperate, I want to get away from you.
- I'd feel like a wimp if I told you each time you hurt me.
- When I press you for sex, I'm really just feeling insecure.
- If I told you how much I really love you, I'd feel like a wuss.
- I believe I'm strong because I am able to endure your bad behavior.

◀ Points to Remember ▶

1. Men will treat you as badly as you will allow.

2. A woman cannot change a man, but she can change the way he treats her.

3. Most of men's bad behavior comes from trying to cover up their insecurities.

4. Men avoid confrontation with women because they believe they can't win.

5. Men use women's nagging to justify continuing their own bad behavior.

6. To men, strength means not letting their emotions affect them.

7. Men believe they lie to us for our own good.

8. It's better to lose him than to keep him and have him treat you badly.

Chapter 2

He's Not the Enemy— It's a Relationship Out of Balance

We want to believe that our mate is the problem and that if he would just change, everything would be better. But he is not the enemy, nor is your mother-in-law, or his friends, or his job. The true enemy is an out-of-balance relationship, usually caused by the surrendering of our power. We surrender our power because of misinformation about relationships that makes us want to be warm and loving, even when our mate is cold and rejecting. That ultimately leads to the joint dysfunction we play out with him, which ends up destroying our relationship.

The Love Myth

The misinformation we hear makes us believe that people who really love each other don't have to negotiate their responsibilities; they always know what the other is thinking, that true love doesn't require work. We're taught that when we're in love, we shouldn't have to worry about who has more control, whether there's equal give and take, who's participating, whether one partner acts like a victim or tries to control the situation. We believe we shouldn't have to worry about whether our mate will lose attraction for us or what to do to keep our romantic bond strong. We don't plan for the possibility that he won't find a job or never will stand up to his meddling mother, which will cause us to lose respect (and then love) for him. We were taught that "being in love" is all we need and the rest will fall into place.

We wake up one day and realize that it's not like that at all. Resentments have built up. Attraction and passion have gone by the wayside. And we've let it happen. We seem surprised. Why didn't we see it coming? The truth is that we did, but we ignored all the signs, and we both adjusted to our dysfunctional relationship. After all, our relationship looked like every other relationship we saw—our parents, our friends.

Instead of looking at our own behavior, we blame him, or his family, or the friends who don't like us, or his career. We want to believe we made a wrong choice and he's just a bad person. We can't believe our relationship was destroyed because of how we handled ourselves in it. And we certainly can't believe we have the power to change our relationships. But we do.

Don't feel guilty that you couldn't save your first marriage or wish you'd held onto that wonderful guy from five years ago. What's important is that you look at your pattern in relationships. What roles do you usually play? What "bad" behaviors of yours helped cause the demise of your past relationships? (For further work on this issue, turn to Appendix A.)

It's not just about your bad behaviors or his—it takes two people to create dysfunction. However, it takes only one person to stop it. He can't behave in an unhealthy way if you aren't there to receive his bad behavior. If one person in the dysfunctional pair stops his or her bad behavior and behaves in a healthy way, the dynamic will change. In fact, the change might even end the relationship, but if it does, the relationship was probably built on addiction (his problems matching your problems, and vice versa, and a need on both parts to play them out). If the relationship doesn't end, it will get better. Guaranteed.

Remember: Relationship problems stem from bad, immature behavior, not bad people. What are the rules of good relationship behavior? Sadly, most of us have never learned them. But if we stop to think, we realize we can change the tenor and quality of our relationships with most of the people in our lives by how we behave. That's because we know that how we behave can alter how others behave toward us. With friends or coworkers, we know that it takes forethought, being careful about what we say and how we say it, and a willingness to negotiate through disagreements. But when it comes to romance, we forget all that because we believe that thinking about love steals its magic.

Once we fall in love, it's as if the rules of human behavior—the gravity of strong, healthy relationships—are suspended. We excuse our failure to deal with problems in our relationship with a plaintive, "But I love him," as if that explains why we choose to encourage him to behave in ways that we know will make us unhappy. We float, drift, and never seem to have our feet on the ground quite the same way again. We are off balance, and so are our relationships. Love may not be blind, but it certainly has the power to distort what we see in our mates, in our relationships, and even in ourselves. In relationships as in physics, for every action, there is an equal and opposite reaction. Men do not act selfish and inconsiderate in a vacuum. His "bad" behavior usually prompts some responding behavior from you, usually equally "bad" and destructive to the relationship. Your two behaviors constitute the relationship dynamic, and it is usually dysfunctional.

Secrets I've Learned As a Therapist—and What Every Woman Needs to Know

What therapists know—and what most people either don't know or refuse to believe—is that concepts governing relationships are almost as immutable as scientific principles, and by not understanding relationship dynamics we blindly play into our mate's "bad" behavior.

Twelve Secrets Only Therapists Know

1. Each partner in a dysfunctional relationship falls into the role of either controller or victim.
2. The gender of the roles doesn't matter; the dysfunction is the same.
3. When we think we're in love, we are more often *seeking* love than *giving* it.
4. Victims believe they're better than controllers.
5. Both men and women feel unappreciated in their traditional roles.
6. Everyone feels "not good enough" in some way.
7. Rejection is the key to power in all relationships.
8. Bad relationships are never just one person's fault.
9. The way your mate treats his family is usually the way he'll treat you in the future.
10. Most women chase their husband's love because they long for more love and attention from their fathers.
11. Most men fear commitment because they felt suffocated or controlled by their mothers.
12. Intimidating people are really insecure and will back down when counter-intimidated.

To really understand relationships, you need to look at them the way therapists do. Pretend for a moment that you're an anthropologist who has just stumbled upon an undiscovered culture, where people behave very different from the way you do. If you're a good observer, you'll find the logic behind the behaviors that at first seem so alien. You'll see that every interaction, every cultural rule and taboo, serves a purpose. It's the same way within the "culture" of our relationships. Although you may often feel frustrated and confused by your partner's behavior or your own, it isn't because the truth is unfathomable and mysterious—it's because you never learned how to really read a relationship.

Your first step is to realize that most of what you learned about relationships is probably wrong, misguided, and sometimes even dangerous. Chances are, what you learned came from watching people in their own unhealthy relationships. It's very likely that the couple you learned the most about how to relate to others and how to expect others to relate to you is your own parents. You cannot have a relationship with your mate that is any healthier than the one you have with your parents.

If you had a very strict father, don't be surprised if you choose dominating men who are like him, since you grew comfortable with your father's bad behavior. We often end up with mates who behave very similarly to one of our parents—especially a parent with whom we have unfinished business. (For more on this, see Appendix A.)

After your parents, your girlfriends probably taught you about relationship behavior. From junior high school on, we women tend to turn to girlfriends for guidance about men. The problem is, few of our girlfriends have the type of relationships we would want for ourselves (and thanks to their venting to us, we may be in a better position to see that than they are). Most important, though, women who have good, healthy relationships usually don't discuss their problems with other people, not even "best friends." Often, discussing problems with our friends becomes a "whine fest" where we complain and justify our own bad behavior. Our girlfriends then enable us to keep our bad behavior and often provide enough relief that we never end up confronting our mate. A good motto is: Don't ever tell a friend anything about your mate you haven't already told him.

The next thing you need to realize about relationships is that all relationships have problems—problems even come with "good" relationships. Rather than avoid or deny problems, or just blame our mate, we need to learn to face them confidently and to approach them with the knowledge that we are part of the problem and we will find a solution. A good relationship is not the result of how well two people agree but how well they can disagree, confront their differences honestly, and resolve them in a fair manner.

We tend to overemphasize the differences between men and women in ways that oversimplify our understanding and demean our partners. Men and women are not predictable, but their relationship dynamics are. When we feel free to express our innermost thoughts, it becomes clear that men and women both want essentially the same things in a relationship: affection, support, respect, and emotional and sexual intimacy. Granted, women and men may differ in how those qualities should be expressed or in what proportion they take priority in their lives. But in an equal, loving relationship, these differences are easy to negotiate. It's healthy to want to be loved, cherished, and adored. The problem is how we learn to obtain those things in a relationship.

Even if you were raised by parents who had a healthy relationship (and very few of us were), much of what our peers and our culture tell us is "normal" is not healthy. The principles and values we apply to healthy relationships with family, friends, coworkers, children—even pets—seem to fly out the window when it comes to love. Many of us believe that a new relationship is bound to be "better" than a long-term one—more exciting, more fulfilling, more magical. We often assume that a partner will eventually lose interest, respect, or attraction for the other. When the relationship starts to sputter, we do nothing to stop it, because we don't believe that we can. So we resort to finger pointing and blaming instead of modifying our own behavior and setting boundaries. We're torn between two untrue, contradictory, and destructive beliefs about men: To be happy in a relationship, we have to change him, and it is impossible to change anyone else's behavior. No wonder we're confused and unhappy in love. We complain that he'll never change, but we never learn how to change our own behavior to change his. We bemoan the lack of respect from our mates when our own behavior seems to demand disrespect.

And, yes, we are each unique; however, the nature of man-woman relationships and the patterns of problems they encounter are not unique. In fact, in most situations, relationship dynamics are more consistent than not. Regardless of the crisis that brings couples into therapy, their problems are almost universal. More often than not, they grow out of: a lack of equal power between partners; poor communication skills; unspoken (and usually unrealistic) expectations; repeating patterns from childhood; and personal insecurities. These problems add up together to create what I call "the dysfunctional fit."

The Dysfunctional Fit

There are two major roles in a dysfunctional relationship—controller and victim—one partner has the power and the other one doesn't. It's not totally black and white because each partner usually has some control in the relationship, i.e., he controls which car they buy and she controls decorating the house. But in most relationships, one partner dominates and exerts most of the control, while the other partner passively allows it. Most commonly and traditionally, the man controls and the woman allows it, becoming a victim. However, when reading the following descriptions, don't be surprised if you've taken on the traditionally male role of controlling and he has taken on the victim role (which is traditionally female). (Although I use "he" when I discuss controllers and "she" when I discuss victims, the gender is completely interchangeable, and the dysfunctional fit is the same.) Couples also sometimes switch roles back and forth, even in the same relationship: You may play victim by sacrificing for him—and then get angry about it and become controlling. What's important is that you try to see what role you're playing and stop playing it—whether it's victim *or* controller.

Characteristics of a Dysfunctional Relationship

- Each partner believes it's the other partner's fault.
- One partner plays controller, the other plays victim.
- Each partner displays "bad" behavior with the other.
- Neither partner is solution-oriented.
- Each person's insecurities are tapped into by the other person.
- Neither partner ever feels as if he or she can win.
- Both partners feel increasingly bad about themselves *and* their mate.
- Each person holds on to his or her irrational beliefs.
- Neither believes he or she should have to compromise.
- Each partner increasingly resents and disrespects the other.

She Chases His Rejection

▶ *Bethany and Nick's Story*

Forty-four-year-old, never-married Bethany had a history of dating men who wouldn't commit to her. Nick, her recent boyfriend, had just left her after three years. Before ending it, he had pushed her away at times with statements like, "We don't have the same interests." When he said this, Bethany took up skiing and scuba diving—Nick's favorite sports. Each time he presented a problem, Bethany tried to fix it, believing that this is what you do when you're working on a relationship. She thought if she tried to please him, he might eventually see her as good enough to marry.

Bethany didn't understand that she was the only one working on the relationship. Nick wasn't as invested as she, and everything she did gave him more power in the relationship, and her less. Nick lost more and more respect for her, as she pleased him and demanded very little back.

Bethany was an attractive, intelligent stockbroker who owned her own house and had a large circle of friends and many interests of her own. So why did she so easily hand the power over to Nick and other men she dated? Why was she so desperate for love?

She had a decent childhood, was not from a broken home, and had a good education. But Bethany was still insecure and deep inside felt "unlovable." In digging into her past, she revealed that her relationship with her father was very distant. Her father was a workaholic when she was growing up, and no matter what she did, she couldn't seem to get his attention. Her father died when she was only fourteen. Now with Nick, as with many other men in the past, she was as desperate for his attention, as she had been with her father. Nick, who had commitment issues, was the perfect "dysfunctional" match for Bethany. His rejection kept Bethany feeling "not good enough" while her desperate behavior justified Nick's choosing not to commit to her.

Victims Are No Better Than Controllers

The difficult part about getting women who act like victims—even those who are unhappy or considering breaking up—to look objectively at their relationship is that victims don't want to accept that they're as much at fault for allowing bad behavior as the person is for doing the bad behavior. Controlling, domineering behavior seems so much worse to us than nagging him or whining to our friends. Inherent in the victim role is the sense that this role is somehow noble and good, as if we were martyrs, while controllers are inherently bad. Remember, without a victim, there can be no controller. Both roles go hand in hand. And if you're a victim and hold onto the myth that the victim role is somehow better than the controller role, you won't be able to change your own dysfunctional relationship dynamic.

Controllers Are Not Strong

Another myth that people often believe is that being controlling is strong. Compared to victims who allow others to control them, controllers look strong. However, dominating others and acting overly aggressive are simply an overcompensation for deep insecurities. Does someone who is really confident and in control need to push others around? Because they don't have control of their own lives, controllers believe they must control others. Neither controllers nor victims take responsibility for their own lives. Neither role is action-oriented or risk-taking. Controllers focus on their mate's behavior instead of their own. Victims assume they can't control their own lives, so they let others control them and then resent it. Being healthy means taking control of your own life (and your actions) without trying to control anyone else.

The Pilot and the Baggage Handler—and Their Addiction

▶ Sue and Ryan's Story

Ryan, an attractive thirty-seven-year-old airline pilot, came into my office complaining about his wife. "She's crazy," he said. "She throws tantrums, curses, yells, screams, and even breaks things. I think she needs some serious help! One minute she loves me, and the next she throws me out of the house. She's constantly on my case and bitching at me. I can't take it anymore!"

"Why have you stayed?" I asked. Ryan answered, "I don't. I move back into my parents' house when she gets this way, but then I always go back." Ryan presented himself as a healthy, intelligent, stable man who just happened to end up with a crazy woman. He told me how he grew up in a near perfect home (which is always a sign of denial) and Sue grew up in an abusive home. He admitted that initially he probably tried to rescue her, but now believes he simply married out of his class.

Enter Sue, a tiny thirty-four-year-old airline baggage handler, divorced with a seventeen-year-old son, and definitely a firecracker! "Ryan is controlling, verbally abusive, and always threatens divorce. He moves back to his parents every time we have a disagreement.

He's a commitment-phobic who doesn't have a clue what it takes to deal with issues in a relationship. He thinks he rescued me because I had bills and was a single mom, when the truth is he had no friends and was incredibly lonely when we met! Who rescued who?"

There are always two sides to every story, and this is especially true in marriage counseling. There's always some truth in what each partner tells me, but each one, of course, tells the story from his or her own point of view.

It all boiled down to this: Ryan and Sue were both deeply addicted to this relationship because their individual problems (insecurities) matched up perfectly to create a very snug dysfunctional fit. Sue grew up with a very controlling, verbally and physically abusive father who made her believe she was not lovable. When Ryan stepped into her life, with his cocky pilot attitude and condescending way of treating her, it felt normal. It became Sue's goal to prove to Ryan that she was good enough, thereby setting herself up to play the victim role with him.

Ryan, on the other hand, claimed his family was perfect, but finally admitted that he was basically a social misfit in school, always focusing on airplanes and flying instead of girls. He never dated much and still has difficulty making friends. Sue was outgoing, emotional, and alive—something Ryan craved to be himself and wanted to be around. Ryan had built a facade of strength and confidence to cover his insecurities about being liked, and Sue bought into it completely. This gave him the upper hand in the relationship and the controlling role.

What Roles Do You Play?

Are you jealous? Sexist? Domineering? Needy? Passive? Is he? Any one of these roles is as destructive to the relationship as the other, and all are built on insecurities. If you're a victim, it doesn't matter what style of victim you play (princess, passive-aggressive, manipulative, needy, avoidant, or addict), you hand over your power in the relationship. If you're a controller, it doesn't matter if you act domineering, obsessive, jealous, like a con artist, sexist, cheating, or abusive, you try to control others. These two roles working together create the dysfunctional fit that is behind the problems in your relationship.

The most fascinating and useful part of discovering you and your mate's personality types is that knowing them makes each of your behaviors understandable and predictable, and gives you the information you need to change your behavior to influence his. Following is a list of dysfunctional personality types (identifying each as a victim or controller) showing the ways in which most of us recognize them by what they do and what they say. Which one are you? Which is he?

Dysfunctional Roles

▶ **Type of Person:** Passive/aggressive (Victim)
May Say: "Don't worry about me; what I think doesn't matter," "You do what you need to do."
Is Thinking/Feeling: It isn't fair that I never get my way. I'm tired of being the one who sacrifices. I'll show him!
May Do: Finds ways to get even that are indirect and nonconfrontational.

▶ **Type of Person:** Domineering (Controller)
May Say: "You can't do that, because I said so!"
Is Thinking/Feeling: If I can't control my partner, I'm not much of a man and will probably lose her.
May Do: Confront and intimidate until you do what he wants.

▶ **Type of Person:** Avoidant (Victim)
May Say: Nothing.
Is Thinking/Feeling: It doesn't matter anyway. He'll never change.
May Do: Nothing—until one day, seeming out of the blue, he or she walks out the door and you never know why.

▶ **Type of Person:** Jealous (Controller)
May Say: "I need to know where you are every minute."
Is Thinking/Feeling: If she loves me, she doesn't need to go out, dress sexy, etc.
May Do: Follow, hound, spy on, accuse, and/or stalk partner.

▶ **Type of Person:** Manipulative (Victim)
May Say: "You know you shouldn't do that."
Is Thinking/Feeling: He'll change his mind once he sees my point.
May Do: Guilt-trip you to try to change your mind.

▶ **Type of Person:** Sexist (Controller)
May Say: "That's what women are supposed to do."
Is Thinking/Feeling: Men and women each have their roles and there are good reasons for that.
May Do: Treat partner like property, use gender to explain/excuse bad behavior, and refuse to change.

▶ **Type of Person:** Passive (Victim)
May Say: "Whatever you want is okay with me."
Is Thinking/Feeling: It doesn't really bother me that much. Besides, if I continue to let him have his way, he'll eventually appreciate me and give me what I want.
May Do: Communicate indirectly by nagging, whining, and complaining.

▶ **Type of Person:** Abusive (Controller)
May Say: "It's your fault I have to punish you."
Is Thinking/Feeling: It's her job to make me happy no matter how it affects her.
May Do: Harm partner physically, verbally, and/or emotionally.

▶ **Type of Person:** Needy (Victim)

May Say: "I need you to be there for me at all times."

Is Thinking/Feeling: If my partner loves me, it means he will help me through any situation I consider a crisis—no matter what. I'd help him if I could, but I'm too weak.

May Do: Love you when they need you, then hate you for being strong. Engage in self-destructive behavior.

▶ **Type of Person:** Princess (Victim)

May Say: "What about me?" (in response to everything)

Is Thinking/Feeling: If my partner loves me, he will do everything he can to please me.

May Do: Seduce you into forgetting the real issue at hand and focus on her feelings instead of your own.

▶ **Type of Person:** Cheater (Controller)

May Say: "What's wrong with you? You're just imagining things."

Is Thinking/Feeling: If she tried harder to please me, I wouldn't be interested in other women.

May Do: Flirt, cheat, accuse partner of cheating to distract her.

▶ **Type of Person:** Obsessive (Controller)

May Say: "But I have to know why."

Is Thinking/Feeling: If my partner loves me, she will know that I constantly need her to explain her behavior.

May Do: Never let up until you explain yourself and eventually agree to do things his way.

▶ **Type of Person:** Addict (Victim)

May Say: "You need to understand that I can't help myself."

Is Thinking/Feeling: He needs to understand that I have a problem I have no control over.

May Do: Harm self and try to take you down with her.

▶ **Type of Person:** Con Artist (Controller)
May Say: "I'm doing this for you."
Is Thinking/Feeling: As long as I say the right things, she will love me and be compelled to forgive or ignore my bad behavior.
May Do: Hurt you emotionally or financially while convincing you he's not doing anything wrong.

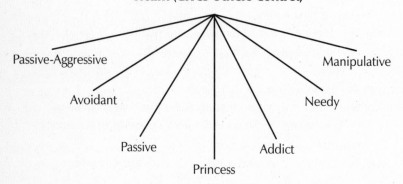

Victim (Gives Others Control)

Passive-Aggressive

Avoidant

Passive

Princess

Addict

Needy

Manipulative

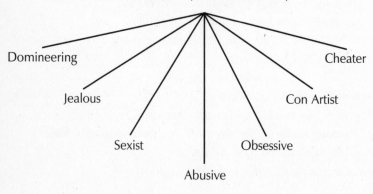

Controller (Controls Others)

Domineering

Jealous

Sexist

Abusive

Obsessive

Con Artist

Cheater

What Is Your Dysfunctional Style?

Many people switch back and forth between victim and controller behaviors. But as you read the dysfunctional roles listed earlier, you probably saw that you and your mate lean toward one or the other most of the time. What's important for you to know is that both roles are unhealthy, both roles come from deep insecurities, and both roles have to be changed to have a healthy relationship. You need to figure out the part you're playing with your mate, take responsibility for it, and try to change it. More specific ways to do this will be shown in future chapters.

Once you know both your styles, you can figure out what type of dysfunction you play out together. Again, each of us is unique, and so is the partnership between two unique individuals. It is a testament to the constancy of human nature that despite how different we and our relationships are, pairings between certain personality types are common and predictable. This is good to know, because often the types of problems couples experience and their style of approaching them are highly predictable.

Certain personality types fit together hand in glove. The two dysfunctional partners depend on each other to behave the way they always have. The fit itself is addictive, because his bad relationship behavior seems to justify her bad relationship behavior, and vice versa. If you ever wonder why you love him one minute, then hate him the next, you probably fit one of these pairings.

Following are the most typical pairings and how they usually work together to maintain the relationship dysfunction.

Dysfunctional Pairings

Her: Passive-aggressive
Him: Domineering
▶ **What Happens:** He exerts his control directly, while she responds by quietly getting even. Both feel controlled and build resentment.

Her: Princess
Him: Abusive
▶ **What Happens:** She likes attention and does anything for it, which gives him the power to be abusive toward her. He spoils her and then punishes her.

Her: Avoidant
Him: Addict
▶ **What Happens:** She enables him to never deal with his problem by avoiding confrontation; neither ever faces problems.

Her: Obsessive
Him: Sexist
▶ **What Happens:** She chases his love, and he exploits her neediness to keep her in her place.

Her: Abusive
Him: Passive
▶ **What Happens:** She sees herself as strong and has no respect for him. He is proud that he's strong enough to handle her abuse without letting it get to him.

Her: Needy
Him: Addict
▶ **What Happens:** Each wants the other to fix their problems and both become self-destructive in different ways.

Her: Abusive
Him: Abusive
▶ **What Happens:** Constant fighting for control; both are verbally and sometimes physically abusive.

Her: Jealous

Him: Cheater

▶ **What Happens:** His behavior intensifies her jealousy and the more jealous she is, the more he justifies his cheating, setting off a vicious cycle.

Her: Passive

Him: Con Artist

▶ **What Happens:** He uses her, and she whines to her friends.

How to Develop an Equal, Healthy Relationship

He stopped acting like the man you fell in love with, and you probably stopped acting like the woman he fell in love with as well. Neither of you is a bad person, but both of you have developed bad behaviors that play off of each other to create a dysfunctional fit. To get your mate to again behave like "the man of your dreams," you must stop participating in the dysfunction you play out together. Once you take the risks necessary to take back your power and relate to him in a healthy way, your relationship will change. Then and only then is it possible to have the healthy, loving, respectful relationship that you want.

Couples who have stayed together for a decade or more usually have a more difficult time turning a dysfunctional relationship into an equal, healthy one, however, because they bring to their relationship the corrosive effects of built-up resentment and past hurts. The good news, though, is that couples who learn to work through their problems at this point stand a very good chance of learning ways to protect their relationship for life.

A healthy, balanced, satisfying, romantic relationship is a result of many things. Ultimately, however, it is the result of two people choosing to be thoughtful, mature, and fair with each other even when—and especially when—circumstances or emotions push them to feel anything but. I believe that most troubled relationships get that way because one or both partners abandon their responsibility to show respect for their mate. They poison the relationship environment with immature, inappropriate relationship behavior that throws the relationship out of balance.

An equal, healthy relationship is far better than what most of us think of as a "perfect" relationship; it is something more compelling than simply sexual attraction, and something more empowering than domination or martyrdom. An equal, healthy relationship is a relationship between two adults of equal power that involves the deepest bonding possible between two people who are not parent and child.

◀ Points to Remember ▶

1. It takes two people to create a dysfunctional relationship, but only one to stop it.

2. Your relationship with your mate can not be any healthier than the one you had with your parents until and unless you clean it up with them.

3. Don't ever tell a friend anything about your mate you haven't already told him.

4. His bad behavior does not justify yours.

Chapter 3

You Have to Change Your Behavior to Change His

I've always found it both perplexing and fascinating to see women in my office who are fully capable, mature, reasonable adults in every aspect of their lives except romance. With everyone but their mates, these women command respect, speak their minds, and use their influence judiciously to get what they want. When it comes to the men they love, however, they don't act like strong women, but like schoolgirls—nagging, bitching, and whining at them, then gossiping with their friends and family members about them. They never ask their partners for what they really want—the people they should be communicating with. Instead, they believe that men should know how to behave without being told what to do.

"Why Can't He Just Change?"

By talking *at* their mates instead of communicating *with* them, women unknowingly send the following message:

I do not respect myself or this relationship. I am intimidated by or fed up with you, or both. I do not believe you are capable of changing, so I therefore must behave the only way I know how—with my nagging, bitching, and whining, I don't see why I should behave with any more maturity, reason, or restraint than you do. I once hoped for more but now I have low expectations for us and for our lives together. While I'm not happy with the way things are between us, the fact that I am still here tells you that I will accept the way things are.

When women engage in bad behaviors such as nagging, bitching, and whining, they're using the same weak, ineffective defenses they used with their parents as adolescents. Those were unequal relationships, in which they had no real power. As adults acting like powerless little girls, they unconsciously foster an emotional environment conducive to their mates behaving badly—either like overbearing, controlling daddies or spoiled, self-centered bad boys.

The world is full of men and women who are adults in most areas of their lives, but wimpy and immature when it comes to love. They cling to outdated, sexist, stereotypical ideas about the nature of men, women, and love that have not changed since high school days. Some of those ideas—that you can never change your mate, that love means never having to say what you really want, that being unhappy with your mate is acceptable and inevitable, that your mate "should know" the right thing to do—undermine not only relationships but a woman's self-esteem.

"Why Doesn't He Just Offer to Help?"

▶ *Rosalind and Rod's Story*

Twenty-eight-year-old client, Rosalind, a lawyer, came in for therapy only two years after she was married to Rod. She was already filled with resentment—especially since they'd had their first child. She felt like she had turned into "Mom"—not just to their little girl, but to Rod, too. "Why doesn't he want to help me around the house? I do things for him because I love him. If he loves me, why doesn't he try to help?" Her fantasy? "I want my husband to say, 'Honey, would you like me to make breakfast this morning?' Why do I have to ask him or beg him to help me? It's not fair."

I told Rosalind that it was just a fantasy to expect her husband to offer to help her. "You have him trained very well in how to be selfish, how to be a taker." Rosalind didn't understand that she was playing the victim role and enabling him to take advantage of her. She was setting herself up to be used by sacrificing for him, then feeling unloved and resentful toward him when he accepted her sacrifices. She nags, pouts, and sends him sarcastic jabs, never realizing for one moment that she is partly to blame for his bad behavior. She's playing the perfect victim to his self-centered, controlling role.

"He Makes Me Act Like That"

Not surprisingly, many women fall into the habit of justifying their own bad behavior on the grounds that their mate has behaved badly ("Of course I nag him, because he never listens."), or excuse their mate's bad behavior because of something they believe they did to provoke it ("Maybe if I had kept my mouth shut when his mother told me she thought our kids watch too much TV, he wouldn't have gotten mad and gone hunting this weekend.").

When we nag or behave negatively toward our mate, we tell ourselves that he makes us act that way, never realizing that we also make him act that way. Yes, he triggers a reaction from us. But then our reaction triggers one in him—and on and on. Each of us believes we would change if the other one did. But we have to stop pointing the finger and try to figure out why we ourselves act this way. Maybe we fantasize how relationships are supposed to be, like Rosalind did. Maybe we're afraid to confront for fear of abandonment. Maybe we believe sacrificing for him and putting up with his bad behavior will make him love us more. Maybe we actually believe that our punishing behaviors will make him feel bad enough that he'll change. Do you believe it's your right to nag? That he makes you do it? That you're powerless to change him? This is victim thinking, and is disempowering. This incorrect thinking keeps you from having the relationship you want.

"I Thought I Was a Strong Woman"

▶ Sharon's Story

My client, Sharon, twenty-eight and single, came into my office in tears. She dated a man for a year and during that time, he gradually pulled away. Eventually, he stopped having sex with her, started spending time with one of her girlfriends, and finally began to date other women. The more he pulled away, the more she clung to him, begging him to never leave her. He finally told her he was in love with someone else and that it was over. She came into my office brokenhearted and humiliated.

Most women are guilty of giving up their power before negotiations ever start, which is what Sharon had done. Women have far greater power to change their relationships than they ever dare to imagine. I helped Sharon understand that the more this man had treated her badly, the more she handed him the power to keep doing that to her—which made him lose all respect for her. She couldn't believe it. "I always saw myself as a strong woman. I thought I was smarter than that! Why didn't I realize all this?"

I explained that intelligence has nothing to do with emotions and that she probably can be strong. However, she gave all her power to this man. Why? Because she loved him so much? No, but that's why she thought she did it. What we call, "loving too much" is really our desire to prove that we are lovable enough.

We dug deeper into her own problems, to the dysfunction she learned as a child from her parents. Her parents fought constantly without ever resolving issues. She watched her mother allow her father's inconsiderate, inattentive, verbally abusive behavior. This taught Sharon that a man's bad behavior is normal, and putting up with it is what every woman has to do to keep her man. How could she know to stand up to a man when she had no role model? How was she to know how a man should treat her when her own father behaved badly toward her mother? Sharon learned to accept men's controlling behavior from her dad, and to respond like a victim from her mom.

Not only did Sharon's parents model these dysfunctional behaviors for her, but in their relationship with her, they also damaged her self-esteem by making her believe this is what she deserved. Sharon's mother made her believe she was powerless. Her father shared very little of himself with Sharon, leaving her feeling emotionally abandoned and rejected by him. This set her up to crave men's attention to the point of behaving in humiliating ways to win a man over. She, like many women, believes she's in love with a man when he rejects her. That "in love" feeling is really her desperate desire to prove to him that she's "good enough."

How Women Squander Their Power

Generally speaking, women have the capacity to be more careful listeners, more effective communicators, and more cooperative negotiators than men. Yet for various reasons we women misuse these skills and squander our power. We become justifiably angry, and then misdirect it. We identify the behaviors that upset us, then make excuses for our partners to continue engaging in them. We also fail to take advantage of the propensity to act, to *do* rather than *talk*. When faced with an adverse situation outside of relationships, most men are adept at dealing, responding, and negotiating to solve the problem. Women often complain that when they discuss their problems with their mates, he will assume she is looking for a solution, when in fact all she needs at that point is to be heard. Men complain that women seem to just "talk and talk." Men are baffled at their mates' reluctance to "do something," to fix the problem and change the situation. A successful relationship depends on finding a middle ground between the two different ways you and your mate approach relationship problems. It's healthy to discuss and analyze problematic situations as long as the ultimate goal is to find a solution.

One of the biggest mistakes we women make is that we confuse talking (and talking and talking) with communicating. We honestly believe that a man will welcome being confronted about his flaws (according to us, of course). Worse, we also believe that after we put him down enough, he will make amends, change his ways, and be that perfect man, or at least promise to try. By now, you probably know that this doesn't produce lasting change in either your man or your relationship. In fact, talking about the problem, with no actions, solutions, or ultimatums on your part, makes him stop listening (why bother, he'll hear it again). When we talk about a problem, it takes away the intensity of our feelings and makes us feel better without ever actually having to take action to solve the problem. But talking without action makes a man not only disrespect us, but never take us seriously when we're upset.

Four "Good" Behaviors That Really Are "Bad"

- **Forgiving:** "That's okay, I know you didn't really mean to hurt my feelings (even though you do it again and again)."
- **Excusing:** "I'll tell the kids you have to work late and that you'll see them tomorrow (even though they never see you anymore)."
- **Pleasing:** "I want to do that for you just because I love you (hoping you'll do the same for me)!"
- **Sacrificing:** "I'll do whatever it takes to make this marriage work (whether you do or not)."

Women's "Bad" Behaviors

Women usually don't see their own behavior as bad because it often starts out as "nice," or sacrificing—which we consider "good." We believe we're giving out of the goodness of our hearts. Or we're just "trying to get along" by not holding him accountable. It's not until we don't get back what we expected (love, gratitude, etc.) that our behavior turns "bad." However, it's our "good" behavior that causes our resentment and eventual punishing behavior.

How Men See Our "Good" Behavior

- *Forgiving* as Allowing Abuse: Forgiving and forgetting what he did to you yesterday. *You hope* maybe he'll model your good behavior. *He sees* that you'll put up with anything.
- *Excusing* as Enabling: Saying he's mean or inconsiderate because he's tired. *You hope* that since you're being nice he'll get over it. He thinks you must be stupid to keep letting him off the hook.
- *Pleasing* as Desperation: Trying to make him happy. *You hope* he'll reciprocate. *He believes* you try so hard you're pathetic.
- *Sacrificing* as Weakness: Concerning yourself with his needs instead of your own. *You hope* your sacrifices will make him feel more loved. *He believes* you're too weak to take care of yourself.

When we don't get the response we want from him—his love, attention, or change in behavior—we become hurt and angry. Then our punishing behaviors kick in and we push him further away from us.

Four Victim Behaviors Men Hate Most

- **Neediness:** "Why don't you love me?"
- **Dependency:** "You're my whole life!"
- **Smothering:** "You won't be gone long, will you? I'll miss you."
- **Whining:** "Why does everything always happen to me?"

She Nags—He Avoids

Couples commonly play out their dysfunctional relationship in the "Nagging/Avoiding Cycle." It's natural to avoid people who nag, scold, or criticize us; we want positive reactions from people, not negative ones. We ourselves don't like to be nagged, so why would we think a man will respond positively to us when we display this behavior?

Six Punishing Behaviors Men Fear

- **Nagging:** "Why won't you ever pick up after yourself?"
- **Scolding:** "I can't believe you did that! What were you thinking?"
- **Guilt-tripping:** "You're so selfish!"
- **Badmouthing:** "My husband doesn't ever buy me presents."
- **Criticizing:** "You're a lazy, inconsiderate jerk!"
- **Sarcasm:** "That's right, honey, you always help around the house—and when did you clean the bathroom last?"

When two people meet and begin to fall in love, they are usually on their best behavior. A woman looks her best all the time, laughs at his jokes, and is generally pleasant to be around. The man is more attentive and considerate. They're both paying attention.

Then, when things begin to go wrong in the relationship, we

often ignore it at first, not wanting to rock the boat and hoping he will change. Eventually we tire of the behavior and begin to nag and scold him, thinking this will prevent future occurrences. As we nag and scold, he begins to tune us out, ignoring everything we say. Then he begins to avoid us altogether since we're no longer fun to be with. You nag because of his bad behavior. He avoids you because of yours. He begins to believe his friends who have been telling him: "She's trying to control you, why do you put up with her?" Finally, he's justified in pulling away from you and never having that close loving relationship that you both wanted. Once this process is set in motion, only you can stop this downward spiral. It doesn't matter whether his bad behavior or your nagging comes first, the cycle feeds itself, snowballs, and someone has to stop it. That someone is you.

Ten Excuses Women Use to Keep Nagging

1. "I have to nag at him or nothing will get done."
2. "He knows my nagging is out of love."
3. "If he would just change, I wouldn't have to nag him."
4. "If I don't point out what he's doing wrong, who will?"
5. "I don't nag any more than any other woman."
6. "My mother taught me not to ever give a man an ultimatum."
7. "I can't change at this stage of the game; this is just the way I am."
8. "It's too much work to change how I communicate with him at this stage in life."
9. "If I actually tried to make him change, he'd leave me."
10. "I'll stop nagging him as soon as he grows up and takes some responsibility around here."

Why Women Must Initiate the Change

You must accept that to have what you want, you will probably have to initiate the change. Remember, I'm not asking you to sacrifice anything "for him." Quite the opposite. I am asking you to stop sacrificing, stop giving too much, and stop handing over your power. The person who most desperately wants to keep a relationship usually tries the hardest. That person is probably you. However, instead of "trying hard" by catering to him, I'm asking you to hold him accountable and equalize the relationship to get what you want. This is healthy behavior you need to learn whether you stay with this man or move on to someone else.

Most women are better at relationships than men and, therefore, have the most power to make something happen. The fastest, surest way to change your relationship begins with changing yourself into an equal partner who does not evoke or condone his bad behavior. You must become a strong person, a savvy negotiator, and a woman he'll want to respect, admire, and pursue. Yes, he needs to change, too, and he probably will change as he adjusts to your new behavior. The relationship will improve or one of you will leave, and that, you'll begin to learn, is a positive outcome, too.

Why Women Resist Changing Their Own Behavior

Are you the kind of woman who believes that complaining, nagging, and withholding affection are the best cards you can play? "That will show him," you think. But it never does, does it? Remember: If you are unhappy in your relationship, if nothing you've done to change how he treats you has worked, you're obviously pursuing a losing strategy. It may be the approach your mother, your sisters, and all of your friends endorse, but take a good look at their relationships. Don't take their advice unless you want a relationship like theirs.

Inherent in the victim role is a feeling of self-righteousness and a belief that "I shouldn't have to be the one to change." In a perfect world, maybe your mate would change his bad behavior first. But it's not a perfect world and in reality, you're the one who wants the relationship to improve. If he's the controller in the relationship, he's probably happy with things the way they are, but you're not. So you can either feel smug in your self-righteous fantasy of how things should be, or you can change yourself first, which will change the dynamic in the relationship and ultimately change the way he treats you. It's up to you!

Five Ways to Stop Nagging

1. Admit to yourself and to him that you do nag—and make a commitment to stop.
2. Decide which issues are most important, work those through, and let go of the rest.
3. Give him a code word or subtle gesture to use with you when he believes you are nagging.
4. Instead of nagging, state your feelings and wants and give him an ultimatum.
5. Instead of trying to force him to see or do it your way, develop a backup plan that meets your needs.

Rosalind came to realize that her nagging, scolding, and pressuring Rod was no healthier than his selfish behavior. She realized she was acting like a victim and letting him have the control, so she decided it was time things changed. She started by confronting him about one chore she resented—cooking dinner. She told Rod she wanted him to make dinner three nights a week. But he said he couldn't do it on a regular basis because he never knew when he'd get home. Rosalind came back to my office and said, "Now what?" I suggested that she ask him to clean up the kitchen every night if he has an excuse as to why he can't cook. It doesn't matter how the chores are split up, only that they're are divided equally. Rod had to realize that dinnertime, as well as other household chores, are as much his responsibility as hers. Until now, Rosalind didn't even realize this. Once her attitude changed, so did Rod's. Rod finally agreed that dinnertime was his responsibility as well, and he agreed to kitchen cleanup. Rosalind was on her way. She brought up one issue at a time, and began to negotiate with Rod. She no longer sacrificed, or nagged, or whined. She was determined to create an equal relationship with Rod—in every area.

◀ Points to Remember ▶

1. Don't take advice from friends or family unless you want a life like theirs.

2. Sacrificing always causes resentment.

3. Victims believe they shouldn't have to change.

4. Women who sacrifice always finish last.

5. Nagging is a powerless behavior.

6. When a woman nags, the man always avoids.

7. The quality of a relationship is determined by the quality of each individual behavior that occurs within it.

8. Your behavior toward your mate won't change who he is, but will change how he behaves toward you.

9. When a woman chooses to behave badly, she sets the stage for her man to behave badly.

10. Mature, healthy people attract mature, healthy mates, and vice versa.

Chapter 4

How to Get Back Your Power—and His Respect

If your partner has most of the power, living with him is probably like living with a parent. And if he's acting like a parent, you're probably acting like a child. So, the first thing you must do to get him to listen to you is to stop all childish and victim behaviors.

Part of the problem here is the way men and women communicate differently. Women like to talk and commiserate while men like to hide in their caves. However, if we want to negotiate and resolve issues with men we need them to come out of their caves and talk to us, and we need to be able to talk to them in a way that makes them want to listen.

Getting Him to Hear You

Men's ears are tuned to hear "action" words, not explanations of problems. They want solutions, not criticisms. They need to hear "command" and "confidence" in the delivery, not confusion and begging. If you don't sound sure of what you're saying, and don't mean it when you threaten, you might as well not talk. Besides, men don't listen to women who don't have equal power in the relationship, i.e., if he has all the power, it doesn't really matter what you say.

I know you think that if he really loves you, it *should* matter—and it should, but the reality is that it doesn't. Remember, people will get away with whatever they can. And if you don't have equal power, he can do whatever he wants. What are you going to do about it? Complain? That's okay. He'll let you complain and then go ahead and do what he wants.

Seven Ways to Get Him to Listen

1. Stop talking so much. Don't repeat yourself and/or talk about unimportant issues.
2. Talk to him only when there are no competing distractions.
3. Ask, "Can you hear me?" or "Can we talk for a minute?" before you talk to him about anything important.
4. If you believe he's not listening, say, "Tell me what I just said," then wait and see if he heard you.
5. When he stops listening, stop talking. Then say, "Let me know when you're ready to listen," and walk away until he's ready.
6. Change your tone of voice from irritated or whiny to clear, direct, and confident.
7. Make a deal with him: "I'll do this for you if I can have your attention for the next ten minutes."

"He Won't Let Me"

▶ Nancy and Mark's Story

Twenty-one-year-old Nancy kept telling me that I need to get her husband Mark to stop treating her like a child. "*He won't let me* work more hours," "*He won't let me* take the baby out of town to visit my grandma," "*He makes me* do all the cooking and housework, even when I'm in school and working." I asked her how he "makes" her do all these things. Does he threaten her? Beat her? "No, he just gets mad," Nancy told me. "So what?" I replied. "Let him get mad. You can get mad too."

Women like Nancy come into my office wanting me to "make" their men treat them better. "You tell him he's wrong to do that," they beg. And certainly, I can help these men understand that their behavior is bad, and that they need to change. But these women believe that all it will take for him to change is for him to be reprimanded by a professional like me. And often these men do "get it"—that they've behaved badly. However, whether they get it or not matters very little if these women go back into their powerless positions in the relationship. Without knowing it, these women who are acting like victims, indirectly beg their men to control them. For instance, my sister once accused me of controlling her and I agreed to stop. In her next breath she brought up a problem and asked in a whiny voice, "So Carolyn, what do you think I should do?" Then she got mad at me when I refused to tell her what to do (since I'd promised to stop controlling her). She didn't realize how often she was setting me up to control her.

I explained to Nancy that Mark would never stop treating her like a child as long as she lets him—no matter what I say to him. She has to stand up to him herself. She has to tell him she's going to work more hours unless he wants to negotiate with her over finances. She has to plan her trip to her grandma's and let him know she's going with or without him. She has to stop doing all the cooking and housework. And if he won't cooperate and work out a schedule with her, she needs to divide up the chores (on a chart) and let him know which ones are his. When he doesn't make dinner Tuesday night like he's supposed to, she not only doesn't do it herself, she feeds her baby and herself (dining out, if possible), without nagging or bitching at him, and certainly without giving in. She lets him know that if he doesn't keep up his end of the deal, she won't either. It shouldn't be too long before he's ready to negotiate.

Remember Rosalind in Chapter 3 who fantasized that her husband Rod would offer to make breakfast? Well, she did just what I asked Nancy to do (with the rest of the chores), and to her surprise, Rod not only began picking up half of the chores, but last week, he did offer to make breakfast. And—Rosalind let him.

Trying to prove to me how controlling Mark is, Nancy actually brought in a list of "Rules for the Relationship" Mark had drawn up. Of course the rules all favored him. Nancy was distraught over this list until I pointed out that this is simply his side of the negotiation. As an equal partner, she now needed to present hers. She and I then presented her side of each rule and prepared her to negotiate with him.

Men Don't Want an Equal Partner, Do They?

Women have been fighting for equality with men since the beginning of the feminist movement. Women have made great strides in the workplace as well as dispelling sexist myths in society as a whole. However, very little has been done on the home front. Men do now know that it's politically incorrect for women to do all of the housework. However, even though ideas about equality have changed, the action part of the equation leaves a lot to be desired. Most men still expect women to take on the responsibility of the home. And many women themselves put the ring on their finger and immediately take on the old-fashioned beliefs regarding the "wife" role. The problem continues because men expect it—and women do it. Why do we do it? It's all we know. It feels natural. But most important, we believe we're showing him love. We aren't. We're setting ourselves up to be victims.

Women fear that men don't really want a strong woman. It's true that men don't want dominating, bitchy women, but that's not what a strong woman is. A strong woman is what he really wants, but can't even verbalize what that is. Though most men believe they want an accommodating woman who will cater to them, when they have a woman like that, they quickly tire of her, and want to move on. Remember, men like a challenge. How challenging is it to be with a woman who will do everything you want?

So do men want an equal relationship? The answer is yes. In this kind of relationship, they're happier, more respectful of you, and feel better about themselves. But do they know this? Probably not.

"She's Not the Woman I Married"
▶ *Darlene and Bob's Story*

Bob is in the middle of a divorce that his wife, Darlene, doesn't want. He wishes he was still in love with her, but he's not. Bob says he was originally attracted to his wife because she was beautiful—and full of life. When he met her, she was heavily involved with her nursing career, had a lot of friends, and was very sexual. Over the years, she lost her pizzazz. She quit working to raise their son, Jon. Since then, she's worked at several different jobs but has had no real career path. She's decorated and redecorated their house. She's not happy, and she's extremely insecure. Their divorce is imminent and she still doesn't know why he's leaving. He says he can't believe she's asking him that—they haven't had an emotional or sexual relationship for years. What does Bob feel for her? Pity, but no attraction, even though she's still physically beautiful. Darlene blames Bob for taking her life away. And their traditional marriage roles did help do that. But Darlene needs to take responsibility for choosing to become a victim by giving up her own identity for the sake of Bob and the marriage. Then, and only then, can Darlene change her life and become a strong woman again—with or without Bob.

Men Want a Challenge

People in general don't want things that come too easily, and this is especially true of men. When something is easily attainable, it loses its value. The diamond market is an example of this. Only so many diamonds are allowed into circulation at once so that diamonds will hold their value, keeping diamond prices high. Whether we're dating a man or married to him, if we are too available, he will devalue us. The single woman who waits by the phone usually doesn't get the call. The married woman who works, manages the household, handles childcare, and never goes out with her friends has no better luck: Her husband not only doesn't have to work hard to get her time or attention, he takes both for granted. Does it mean he doesn't love her? No. But he doesn't respect her, probably won't negotiate with her, and will eventually fall out of love with her. Overly available women are not only *not* a challenge, but they're boring. People (especially men) appreciate and value things they have to work hard for. To keep his love and respect and your power, keep him challenged by not being too available, not giving too much, and staying vital with your own identity intact.

"I Still Want the One I Can't Have"
▶ *Ian's Story*

I was chatting in a bar one night with an attractive man who came on to me and I rejected him because I said he was too much of a "player"—he had a different woman with him every time I saw him. We began talking about relationships and he said he dated around so much because he couldn't have "the love of his life." He had dated this woman four years ago and she broke up with him, sending him the message indirectly that he wasn't good enough for her. He had never let go. From time to time he would contact her to see how she was doing or send her a card. He usually got a cool response, but this just fueled the fire for him. His greatest fantasy? To someday have sex with her and marry her. Meanwhile, he dated and had sex with tons of women who all believed they had a chance with him. But they didn't. He was "in love" with the only woman who rejected him. She was a challenge—a woman he couldn't have.

It Takes a Strong Woman to Bring Out the Healthy Man in Your Mate

For any of the techniques in this book to work, you must become a strong woman—a woman he respects, but doesn't fear or despise; a woman with equal power, but not one who tries to control him. A strong woman is a woman who respects and loves herself. She is tough but vulnerable (when safe), honest but wisely reserved. She is fair and not self-serving *or* sacrificing in a relationship, and—most important, and perhaps most surprising—she is fair to herself.

If these qualities do not come to you naturally, don't worry. The truth is, in the world of relationships, strong women are self-made, not born. Being a strong woman requires knowledge, self-control, courage, and selfishness (yes, selfishness) plus a change in attitude, thinking, and behavior. A truly powerful woman knows that she can influence her man's behavior and change her relationship—and not by giving in or catering to his needs, but by holding her ground, being true to herself, and requiring others to negotiate with her.

How to Up Your Value: Become a Strong Woman

A strong woman doesn't stay in a one-sided relationship. She doesn't allow a man to control her, and she doesn't become the controller herself. As someone once said, "The only thing worse than a man you can't control is one you can."

A strong woman will insist that her mate negotiate all issues with her. And she knows that her partner must always believe there is a chance he can lose the deal altogether if he doesn't negotiate fairly. Seldom do we have to actually walk away from the negotiating table and completely end the deal. However, the other side must know that it's a possibility.

A strong woman will make a choice to walk away rather than participate in an out-of-balance, dysfunctional relationship. Sure, she may be afraid to be alone and worry about the children or finances, but these are all things she knows she can find solutions to on her own. She knows that problems are easier to solve on her own than they are with a partner who won't cooperate.

A strong woman is not an angry woman, although many women believe they must hold on to their anger to stay strong. It's true that you must be able to call on your anger quickly to be able to defend your stance if and when your partner is unfair or attacks you in any way. However, if you don't show your soft, warm side, there can be no intimate relationship, and no reason for him to want to negotiate. Women who are stuck in anger either become the controllers in the relationship or are unable to have any relationship with a man at all. When women say they can't find any man who can handle a strong woman like them, the truth is that they can't find a man who wants to handle an angry woman like them. (For more on what to do to get past the anger, see Appendix A.)

A strong woman is someone he can depend on (without being dependent) in times of trouble, someone who will stand behind him even as she stands up for herself, and vice versa. A strong woman is not afraid of being vulnerable, because she knows she will not give up her power. Moreover, she is not afraid to confront him, because she knows that she is lovable. She knows that in her strength, her man will find a safe place to let down his guard and become more emotionally vulnerable and involved with her.

A strong woman is a woman her mate will view as a mirror image of himself—someone he can understand, respect, and trust. We often think of relationships as being compensatory, as opposites attracting, as a place where we find the parts we need to make ourselves complete. When we seek out partners to make us whole, it's usually in an unhealthy way. That's why the victim invariably finds the controller. Then neither partner has to grow. They hook together, completing each other in an unbalanced, dysfunctional way. Both partners then feel stuck, can't find solutions to their problems, and begin a downward spiral of their own self-esteem in the relationship. There is no way to win in a dysfunctional relationship. When the relationship is out of balance, the respect for each other deteriorates until the love is gone.

On the other hand, mates who are mirror images of each other have mutual respect. This does not mean they are exactly alike, nor do they necessarily agree on everything. The aspects of themselves that they mirror in the other are their strengths and qualities necessary for a balanced relationship. You might almost see it as the relationship equivalent of "If you build it, he will come." If you are strong, forthright, and independent, not only will you attract a mate with those qualities, but he will also admire and treasure those same qualities in you. When you stop looking to your mate to make up for the qualities that you lack, you will stop being dependent, and stop putting yourself in a victim (or controlling) role. That will set the stage for a sound, equal, loving relationship.

"Do I Have to Work Outside the Home to Be Equal?"

Yes, to be truly equal, you need to have your own income source. A woman without financial power seldom has enough respect from her mate to have an equal relationship. And I say career, not job, because a career implies something you've chosen to do, something you hopefully have passion for. There are two parts to the "working" equation for women. First, equal power in a relationship means that you must have enough money to take care of yourself if he's not in the picture. Not equal money to him, but enough money that you are not dependent upon him and that he knows you have the power to leave if he doesn't treat you right. Second, you must work at something you care about. Why? Do you really respect a man who has only a "job" and no career goals? Probably not. Then why do you think a man will respect you if you don't have career goals?

But you say, "What about staying home with the kids and the value in that?" Most women who stay home with the children never make a clear deal with their husbands before they do that. They instead assume he agrees, and assume he values their choice. Ideally, the deal with your mate needs to be made before you get pregnant. The deal needs to look something like this:

> I'd like to take off the first year after the baby is born. Do you think we can afford it? If so, are you willing to have your salary cover all household expenses, as well as personal spending money for me? I don't want to be put in the position of having to ask or beg for personal things, so we need to figure this out in advance, as well as how much I can expect you to help with the baby.

Then you hear his side. (Remember, there are two sides to every negotiation.) He may say:

> I'm not comfortable covering everything for a whole year. How about six months and I'll continue with half of the housework during that time, as well as some childcare? Your personal expenses will be limited, however, because there will only be so much money to work with. And it's important to me that you not be gone from the workplace for so long that you have difficulty going back.

You then say, "Okay, but . . ." and you will continue until you've worked the deal out. Then write it out and sign it. With personal money allotted in advance and a signed agreement, you will have protected your power in the relationship and kept the relationship equal and healthy.

You may think, "But I like things the way they are. I want to stay home and manage the household, and have him provide the income. Can't that be equal? We're both doing our part." It's not impossible to have equality in a traditional relationship like that, but it's not likely. Because each role is so opposite from the other, feelings that neither is appreciated run rampant and resentments on both sides usually skyrocket. If you choose to do it, the best way to protect the relationship, again, is with a very specific contract that both agree to. We'll discuss this in further detail in Chapter 9.

The Downside of Relationships Built on Need, Not Love

If you're fighting the idea of an equal relationship, you need to ask yourself if you might be in your present relationship for the wrong reasons. If your goal in life was to find a man to take care of you so you wouldn't have to work or grow and change as a person, then you probably don't want an equal relationship, and that's your choice. However, realize that the trade-off for being taken care of is giving him control. Without knowing it, that's probably a deal you've both subconsciously made already. Remember that if you aren't willing to change your role, you have nothing to negotiate with to change his.

Relationships built on need are addictive relationships. If you feel you can't live without him, you probably can't, but this is not a good thing. You've probably become dependent on him to make you feel good, because you don't know how to make yourself happy. Or maybe you're dependent on him financially because you're insecure about your ability to support yourself. If you continue to lean on him for these things, you will only get weaker and weaker, needing him more and more, and fooling yourself that this desperate need for him is actually love.

Dependency is, of course, caused by insecurity and does not have anything to do with love. Imagine yourself without him and decide how you would make yourself happy and/or support yourself. Do these things, even if you stay with him, and see how you feel about him when you become strong and are no longer weak in these areas. Then and only then will you know if you truly love him.

Another reason you may be staying in an unbalanced relationship could be because you're afraid to be alone. If so, you're probably also afraid to take the risks necessary to equalize the relationship. Again, it's your choice. Just remember, change needs to come from both of you. You'll need to overcome your fears of being alone to be strong enough to use the techniques in this book to change him.

Equalize Power, Don't Control Him

Controller and victim roles don't always follow gender lines. Out-of-balance relationships aren't always caused by a man who is controlling and a woman who is a victim. Often it is the reverse. I know, because I became a controller after I ended my marriage to my husband John.

It took me a while to figure out why I had chosen the controller role. When I married at twenty-one, I played victim to John, who was just like my father, and we acted out my parents' relationship perfectly. When I finally got the courage to leave him and his controlling, abusive ways, I changed completely. It's common for the pendulum to swing all the way to the other side—especially for victims to turn into controllers when they've had enough. I became my father, not realizing it of course. But what were my choices? My two role models were Mom and Dad, and I didn't know anybody in a healthy relationship. It wasn't until my relationship with Alan that I became completely aware that I had turned into my dad. Luckily, I had shared quite a bit of information with Alan about my dad. One day when we were arguing, Alan asked me, "You said you always hated your dad for the vicious way he talked to your mom—aren't you acting just like him right now with me?" I had to take a time-out and think about what he said. I knew he was right. I always said that when mad, my dad went for the jugular, and I was now doing that with everyone, including Alan. Alan's confrontation turned my life around—and our relationship.

"You Have to Do More—I'm Still Not Happy"
▶ *Jo-Ann and Michael's Story*

Jo-Ann, a thirty-two-year-old proud woman, who didn't work outside the home, was a perfect example of a female controller. It was difficult to see how she got the control in the first place, and why her husband Michael had let her keep it.

Jo-Ann came into my office complaining about how Michael was so passive that he didn't stand up to his parents when they were rude to her. She said she also felt emotionally abandoned by him, since he never shared his thoughts with her. This hurt her badly because abandonment had been the story of her life. Her father abandoned the family when she was ten. Because of that her mother left the kids home alone and began working three jobs to support the children. Then, Social Services took the children and placed them in a home. Jo-Ann was now in a deep depression and had put on fifty pounds in the last year. She didn't know what to do.

We worked on some of Jo-Ann's personal issues and a few months later she brought Michael in for marriage counseling. It was immediately obvious who "wore the pants" in the family, and it wasn't Michael.

"I just try to do what I'm supposed to do—and now she's nagging me about being more emotional too? I work three jobs because she wants to have a tummy tuck and then move back to Boston next year to be near her family. When I come home between jobs, she says it's my duty to spend time with our son, and I know she's right. She stays at home all day with him, but I'm exhausted. On weekends, she has a list of things for me to do the minute I wake up, and gets mad at me if I want to sit and read or watch TV for even ten minutes. Now I'm hearing that all this is still not enough to make her happy. Now I need to become more 'emotionally available'? Okay, then sign me up for therapy every week and I'll see what I can do!"

I explained to both Michael and Jo-Ann how the relationship was out of balance, that Michael could not "make" Jo-Ann happy, and what role each was playing in the dysfunction. In future sessions, I helped them make better, more equal deals with each other; helped Jo-Ann back off on the pressure and control; and showed Michael how to stand up to her.

Whether it's a man or woman in the controller role, controllers keep their control by not admitting their own faults and insecurities. I helped Jo-Ann admit to Michael that she's never been happy—she says she's been depressed since she was ten, when her father left and she never heard from him again. Knowing this, Michael understood better that it wasn't him that made her unhappy, and no matter what he did, he couldn't fix her abandonment issues. Once she acted more vulnerable with Michael and explained these issues, Jo-Ann realized that these were issues she needed to deal with on her own and that taking them out on Michael was not only unfair, but also nonproductive.

"How Did My Relationship Get So Out of Balance?"

In those moments when you feel your relationship sliding downhill, you may ask yourself how it all came to this. When the relationship is new or working at a healthy level, it's easy to understand what draws us and holds us to our partner. But confusion reigns when the relationship begins to flounder. The attraction between two people is often a mystery to others, especially when it's clear that the relationship is troubled. Each of us has probably thought to ourselves, or said aloud to our friends, "What on earth does she see in him?" And yet it's a question very few of us ever ask ourselves about our own relationship.

66

For centuries, philosophers and poets, women's magazine editors, and self-appointed sex gurus have pondered the question of attraction. What is it that makes one person so irresistible to us? Sometimes the answers are obvious: good looks, pleasing personality, status, shared interests, concern for us, similar values, outlook on life, and so on.

Other times, however, it's certainly a mystery why we choose to stay with the partners we do, even when they make us unhappy or treat us in ways that we don't like. Often, without knowing it, our attraction is based on the "dysfunctional fit" we discussed in Chapter 2. When Bob "rescued' Darlene from her family, who treated her badly, the relationship was out of balance from the beginning. Then, as she stayed home with the children, she lost the little self-esteem she had. In Bob's eyes, she lost her vitality, and he lost respect for her.

Because she had been so abandoned by her family, Jo-Ann needed Michael to prove his love for her (by doing things for her) every moment. More puzzling, of course, is why Michael did these things. The answer: He came from a military home where he was used to following orders. Jo-Ann found the perfect fit for her dysfunction.

Many times a relationship based on the dysfunctional fit disintegrates, as each person gets healthier. Sometimes, when the relationship is no longer built on need and addiction, the draw to be together disappears. The longer the relationship has been dysfunctional, the less likelihood there is of repairing it. The years of toil in trying to make it work tire couples out and often kill the spark, especially when that spark was never built on a strong foundation of true love to begin with.

Sometimes couples panic when one begins to get healthier. They feel the change happening, and quickly try to draw the other person back in to keep the relationship together the way it was, even though both people are unhappy. As you begin to change, watch for this and fight the desire to keep the addiction alive. Women come into my office asking, "How do I know whether I really love him or not? Am I just with him because he's like my father (and I need his approval), or is it true love?" I tell them that there's only one way to know for sure: change your behavior and become healthier. If he responds, see how you feel about him when the roles, neediness, and roller-coaster ride of emotions are gone. When the dust settles and he's treating you like an equal partner, is there love left? Only you will know that.

Ten Steps to Becoming a "Functional" Partner

Although it has taken both of you to throw this relationship out of balance and keep it there, you can change the dysfunctional fit by changing your part.

1. Identify and Admit Your Part

If you play the controller role, you need to be vulnerable and admit it to your mate, as well as share other information to help equalize the relationship. If you play the victim role, to get the power back, you need to explain to your mate that you realize you haven't been standing up for yourself, but intend to do so in the future. However, don't say it until you mean it and are ready to follow through.

When you don't admit the role you play to yourself and your mate, it's easier to fall back into the role and play it out. I find that people seem to have much more difficulty admitting that they're playing victim than controller, because once they do, they can no longer blame their mate. Admitting your role is admitting that you are allowing your mate to treat you this way. Until you do that, you can never change your behavior to change his.

2. Don't Be Intimidated by Him

If you believe that he is "above" you, or better than you in any way, you can't have an equal relationship with him. Every person has strengths and weaknesses—he may have come from money, you may have been more popular in school; he may be smarter in politics, you may be smarter in understanding people. Don't let him hold on to the position that he is better than you as a person. You may need to make a list of his weaknesses. If he is prone to criticizing you, ask him to stop, and if he doesn't, say, "Okay, if this is how we're playing the game, here are all the things I think are wrong with you." If you can't say this to his face, write it out and give it to him. Whether you have put him there or he himself fights to stay on the pedestal, take him off, at least in your eyes, or you'll continue to behave like a victim.

Ten Ways to Change the Way You Perceive Your Man

1. *Know* that dominating behavior is just a cover for insecurities.
2. *Realize* that his lack of friends speaks loudly about his inability to have healthy relationships.
3. *Know* that his tough act and aggressive explosions come from his inability to deal with his anger.
4. *Understand* that his rigidity and self-righteousness come from a fear that you'll find out he's wrong.
5. When you are feeling intimidated by him, *think about* someone who intimidates him to remind yourself it's just an act.
6. When he is not sharing his feelings with you, instead of taking it personally, *remember* that he is afraid to appear weak.
7. *Realize* that his withdrawn, secretive ways stem from his fear that you will find out that he's not as strong as he appears.
8. *Know* that his need to control you comes directly from his fear of being controlled by you.
9. *When* he tells you that everything is your fault, remember that he always blames others for his problems.
10. *Know* that his possessiveness comes directly from his insecurity and fear of losing you.

3. Work on Your Own Personal Strength

Look at your own bad behaviors. Promise yourself that you'll never again make excuses for him or complain about anything he's doing that you are allowing. Focus on your own self-empowerment, not on him.

Vow to get back your identity and keep it intact by being a vital, attractive woman who men want to be with. What have you given up since you've been with your mate? Friends, interests, goals? Begin to put them all back into your life. What issues keep you weak? Are you intimidated by your mate because your father was dominating? If so, deal with your father issues to make yourself stronger. (See Appendix A.) Gain his respect and your strength by making yourself as happy and healthy as you can be.

Any area of your life, whether it's financial, career, or just your own happiness in general, that you aren't in charge of, puts you in a position to be dependent upon a man and in an unequal relationship. Make sure you have a realistic plan for solving any problems you have in any of these areas—on your own. That doesn't mean you can't ask for and have his support. But always think, "How would I handle this situation if he were not in my life?"

Developing your personal strength requires that you learn to focus on yourself—that you become more selfish. "Selfish" isn't necessarily a negative word. It can be a self-nurturing word. You can't be strong if you don't nurture and feed yourself emotionally. When your mate asks you to do something, ask yourself these questions as you decide whether or not to do it: "What's best for me? Under the same circumstances, would he do this for me? Will I resent him if I do it?" Never do something you'll resent unless you make a deal where you will clearly get something back that you want. And certainly don't help someone out who wouldn't help you out in the same way. In other words, if you're thinking about cleaning his apartment, be realistic—would he clean yours? It doesn't matter that he'll buy dinner (unless that deal is truly okay with you), you know he probably wouldn't clean your apartment—even if you were sick. Then don't do it—it will throw the relationship out of balance!

4. Pull Away When He Doesn't Participate

As I said before, men like a challenge; they like to work at things. If he stops participating with you, and you keep participating with him, you're condoning and enabling his "avoiding" behavior, teaching him that he doesn't have to work at the relationship.

Women also have a tendency to overexpose themselves by giving a man too much information—and then wondering why he takes advantage of it. We usually tell all, indirectly asking a man, "So, you do still love me with all my flaws, don't you?" Men tend to be secretive about their flaws and then send us the message, "You've got a lot of problems—unlike me, who is really strong." It's another way we give men our power. The rule: Open up only as much as he does. When he opens up more, you can too.

Women also instinctually chase after a man who pulls away, when what works is to reject him more than he's rejecting you. He's more likely to react, and come toward you when you send him the message, "Maybe you're not good enough for me!"

I did this with Alan when he became cold and critical with me and wouldn't tell me what was wrong—I said, "Fine, then I don't want to be around you." I got my things out of his house and went home. When he called a day or so later, I told him he needed to explain to me why he'd been acting that way. He wouldn't acknowledge his bad behavior or admit any problem. I stayed away and didn't call him for over five days. He kept calling and asking what was going on. "I'm busy getting over you by doing the exercises I tell my clients to do," I replied. And I was—making lists of his negative traits—to keep myself strong. Eventually he admitted his bad behavior, told me what was wrong, and we sat down and worked it out. Instead of reacting to his criticisms of me, I had rejected him.

71

When a man rejects you, you need to learn to reverse the rejection. The following chart demonstrates what I mean.

Reversing the Rejection

IF YOU CHASE HIS REJECTION BY . . .	YOU CAN REVERSE HIS REJECTION BY . . .
telling him how much you love him, hoping he'll tell you the same.	stopping all talk of love, and when he says loving things, don't always reciprocate.
giving him cards and gifts he doesn't acknowledge or reciprocate	sending no more cards, letters, or gifts and not acknowledging his.
feeling compelled to call him at work every day	not calling him and being too busy to talk when he calls you.
accusing him of ignoring you when you're together in the evenings.	ignoring him by doing projects, reading, or even leaving for the evening.
letting him get away with bad behavior toward you.	telling him his behavior is unacceptable and leaving his presence each time it happens.

5. Control Your Own Behavior

Control your own behavior, and stop trying to control his. Don't allow his bad behavior to "make" you behave badly. Take the higher road and don't nag, yell, scream, mother him, or anything else. He *doesn't* make you do it. When he behaves badly and you don't respond with bad behavior, he will be the one who looks immature and ridiculous, not you. Instead, state how you feel about what happened, tell him what you want, ask him to change his behavior, and let him know you'll remove yourself from his presence if he doesn't stop. Then follow through.

6. Practice "What's Good for the Goose Is Good for the Gander!"

All rules for this relationship apply to both of you. If he has a night out, so do you. If he monitors how you dress, you monitor his clothes. All household and childcare duties are negotiated equally. Whatever one does, the other is also allowed to do. If he spends $100 foolishly, don't bitch at him; just tell him you will take your $100 and spend it as foolishly as you want.

7. Communicate with Power

Set good boundaries with specific consequences. This will be discussed in detail in Chapter 5.

8. Keep Access to Money

By making sure you always have access to money, you have the option to leave at all times. We talk more about this important point in Chapter 8.

9. Always Have a Backup Plan

When you are negotiating it's important to have a backup plan in case your man doesn't accept your ultimatum. This is covered in more detail in Chapter 5.

10. Learn to Take Risks and Counter-Intimidate

Victims don't believe they should have to fight. You must have "fighting" skills even if you never have to use them. If you were attacked in an alley, you would hope you could fight off your attacker. The same is true when you are psychologically attacked. There are times you need to be able to be aggressive to get someone to back down. We talk more about risk-taking and intimidation in Chapter 5.

When You Get Your Power Back, You Are His Equal

In order to get back the "man of your dreams," you must become the woman of his. To do this, you must have your power to have his respect. You must become a "functional" partner, whether he does or not. How are healthy men and women in an equal, functional relationship different from everyone else? They:

- Control themselves and do not try to control or accept being controlled by others
- Face their problems for what they are; they don't blame their mate or other people and circumstances
- Give their mate and their relationship their very best, but not their all
- Give without resentment, because they give only when they know they will not resent it later

We may be victims of our pasts, but we are not prisoners. Regardless of what you went through with your family, with other men, or with your current mate, you do have the power to change it all. Once you realize how important it is to keep equal power and you learn behavior modification and negotiation techniques, you can work wonders. All you need is a clear understanding of the difference between the dynamics of a dysfunctional relationship and those of the romantic, committed, exciting, equal, healthy, "functional" relationship you deserve. It's just a matter of taking the actions necessary to change.

◀ Points to Remember ▶

1. Mature, responsible behavior is empowering for both men and women.

2. Chasing his approval is the major way you lose your power.

3. When something is easily attainable, it loses its value.

4. A woman with no financial power cannot be truly equal.

5. Unless you have equal power, he has no reason to listen to you.

6. No one wins in a dysfunctional relationship.

7. Healthy relationships don't just happen; they are created by equal balance of power.

8. A man must have respect for you as an equal to want to negotiate changes with you.

9. Keep him thinking he could lose you.

Chapter 5

Finding the Man You Fell in Love with

Imagine your relationship just the way you want it—maybe the way it used to be. He's romantic, helps around the house, treats you with utmost respect, makes dinner several nights a week, and gets the sitter for your "date night." When he comes home from work, he gives you a long kiss (on the lips) and an emotional account of his day. You know he's attracted to you, but he doesn't pressure you for sex. He's loving, caring, and focused on you. The two of you work as a team. He adores you and shows it. He's the man of your dreams, and you know you're the woman of his.

Is this man too good to be true? Maybe this is the way your husband treated you at the beginning—before you married him? Maybe he was never this wonderful. Either way, don't you deserve to be treated this well? You can be.

Change the Integrity of the Relationship

To have this fantasy (with your own personal variations, of course), you must show him the way to be this man. To start the change and undo the dysfunctional fit you two have become so comfortable with, you must know what needs to change and then hold your mate accountable for those behaviors that are unacceptable. Retraining him will require some risk-taking behaviors you may not be accustomed to, but remember, you have to change your behavior to change his. You'll need to change your *attitude* from "that's just the way he is," to "that's not okay with me," and change your *behavior* from tolerant to confrontational.

She Found a Different Man of Her Dreams

▶ *Alexis, Carlos, and Raymond's Story*

Thirty-four-year-old teacher Alexis thought it was impossible to ever have a man treat her well. Her father was very disrespectful and abusive to both her and her mom. Carlos, the man Alexis was living with for two years, basically ignored her. Every night he came home from work and went straight to the computer. She begged him to go out with her or just spend time talking to her, but Carlos never would, even though he agreed he should. Alexis later realized in therapy that she had given up her power to get what she wanted from him by moving in with him. After Alexis and I reviewed all the ways she had let Carlos have power over her, she confronted him and tried to get some of the power back, but it was too late. He responded somewhat, but not enough for Alexis to want to stay. She moved out and vowed never to set herself up like that again.

Then Alexis met Raymond. She immediately came in again for more therapy, because she was scared to death. She was very attracted to Raymond, but something was too familiar—he seemed just like all the other controlling, emotionally unavailable men she'd known.

Raymond was an attractive forty-five-year-old bachelor who had been quite successful in his own real estate business, had his pilot's license, and owned a home in Denver and a condo in Aspen. He was used to calling the shots with the women he dated. After their first date, he called her from the airport the next morning to say, "My plane was delayed so I thought you might drive out to the airport [one hour away] and have breakfast with me and entertain me while I wait for my plane." Alexis said, "Excuse me? You want me to do what? You are joking, right? I have a busy day at work. Just give me a call when you get back in town."

Though she was proud that she handled the situation so well, Raymond's selfish attitude concerned her to the point that she wasn't sure she should even go out with him again. I told her to think of him as an experiment—that she needed to practice handling a man like this. As they continued to date, she felt constant conflict with him on almost every issue, but Alexis stood her ground, forcing him to continually negotiate with her. "This is a lot of work," she told me, "and at times I feel like I'm becoming the controller in the relationship." Sometimes it did seem as if she was overcompensating for her lack of power in her past relationship with Carlos. But whatever she was doing, it was working.

Within eight months, Raymond backed off on his controlling attitude, and became loving, respectful, and very focused on Alexis. Unlike Carlos, Raymond began to talk about their future and discuss marriage plans. Alexis finally got what she wanted.

He Doesn't Have to Agree for This to Work

When negotiating, you must alter your communication style to be more powerful, direct, and healthy in order to dramatically change what goes on in your relationship—with or without his cooperation. Alexis never asked Raymond to cooperate with her—she just stood her ground and made it impossible for him to have the control. You don't need to explain yourself or ask for his permission to change your relationship. Of course you can ask for suggestions for solving certain problems, and if he doesn't respond, just set a boundary or "leave the ball in his court" and walk away.

"It's His Fault!" "No, It's Hers"

▶ Gretchen and Art's Story

Gretchen believes her husband Art will never change. She cites his sexist upbringing and ongoing depression as reasons why he won't improve no matter what she does. "Then what are your options," I asked, "to leave him, or put up with his bad behaviors?"

I knew what Gretchen was really saying—what every man or woman says to me at the beginning of couples counseling: "My mate is impossible to live with and the problems in our relationship are all his fault. I hope you're smart enough to see what I've had to endure. Most of all, I hope you can fix him." Gretchen believed that she was right and Art was wrong—and she never let him forget it. She was the controller in the relationship.

Her controlling behavior with Art included:

- Arguing her point over and over, to try to prove that she's right
- Criticizing him with personal attacks when he doesn't see things her way
- Dominating the conversation by talking over him until he shuts down and gives in, *or* finally giving in herself, sacrificing her own needs, and never letting him forget it

Gretchen believes that fighting with Art in this way is being strong. "At least I'm not being a doormat like my mother was." And it's true. She's not a doormat; she's a steamroller.

Stop Fighting Dirty

Gretchen and Art both truly believe they're right about each issue. Each one puts his or her self-esteem at stake and fights it out (in their own dysfunctional way) until someone gives in. This is dirty fighting and leads only to the disintegration of the relationship. In their case, it's usually Art who gives in and eventually plays victim because he hates conflict the most.

I explained to both of them that it takes two people to have a bad relationship, and that no one person is at fault. I emphasized that their mate's bad behavior does not justify each of their bad behaviors. Intellectually, they understood this but, like most couples in this situation, they still tried to convince me how "right" their own positions were. Once they realized I wasn't buying into this line of thinking, they let go of trying to prove their mate wrong—and this is when the real therapy began.

Dirty Fighting

1. Using intimidation to force your point.
2. Arguing right and wrong, instead of looking for solutions.
3. Attacking your mate's integrity.
4. Pretending nothing is wrong, then blowing up.
5. Making false threats.
6. Passive/aggressive behaviors.

Creating Your Own Justice

It's possible, and more probable, to get what you want from your mate if you learn the concept of creating your own justice. When we practice creating our own justice, we no longer assume that life is fair or that our mate will act a certain way if he loves us. Instead, we accept the responsibility that our action creates a reaction from him. We also accept the reality that he will try to get away with whatever he can, and we accept the responsibility of setting boundaries to keep him from treating us badly. By creating your own justice, you show you have power—then and only then will he pay attention and work with you.

Whether we want to believe it or not, a relationship is a game full of power struggles, and negotiation is the way we play the game. Men and women who play the victim role have the most difficulty with the concept of negotiation because they usually believe they shouldn't have to negotiate. Why? Because life should be fair. He should automatically treat me that way if he really cares about me. And it's true, he should . . . but he doesn't. This is the difference between idealistic thinking and realistic thinking. Idealistic thinkers believe that eventually (without having to take control of a situation), justice will prevail. Realistic thinkers know that you must create your own justice. To create justice for yourself, you must learn to communicate with power. To do that, you need to express yourself in a clear, direct, and powerful way. Following is the formula for powerful communication that can be your model for future communication with your mate (and anyone else).

Four Steps to Powerful Communication

1. *"I feel _____ when you _____ ."*
   Tell him what you feel about his behavior.
2. *"I want _____ ."*
   Tell him clearly what you want.
3. *"Will you _____ ?"*
   Ask him to make a commitment to give you what you want.
4. *"If not, I will _____ ."*
   Give him an ultimatum, letting him know that, if he chooses not to participate, you have an alternate plan.

By following these steps, you force yourself to look at ways to solve the problem if he doesn't cooperate, removing all your dependency on him.

Most of us never learned to communicate with power or set boundaries. Boundaries are psychological fences that we place around ourselves for protection from harm from other people. Few of our mothers understood the concept of personal boundaries, and in fact, neither did our fathers. Our parents just put up with each other's bad behavior and complained and/or exploded every so often. Maybe there was an "understood" agreement that Dad would provide for the family while Mom stayed home with the kids, but neither one ever discussed it clearly or agreed to the deal. How was Mom to get her spending money? And did she agree to pick up after Dad all the time? If thought through and discussed, very few women would ever agree to the deals they find themselves in now. But remember—everything can be renegotiated.

We not only have the right, but also the responsibility, to tell other people what we will and won't put up with. In fact, a good empowering statement to use regularly when setting a boundary is, "That's not okay with me!"

"If You're Not Doing It, I'm Not Doing It"

▶ Jane and Gary's Story

After complaining that her mate Gary always forgot her birthday, my client Jane told me she was taking him out to dinner and buying him a gift for his upcoming birthday. When I asked her why, she replied, "Because it's the right thing to do, and maybe he'll learn from it." I pointed out, "All he'll learn is that he gets something for nothing. You're teaching him that he can ignore your birthday and your feelings and still be treated wonderfully when it's his turn. Is this really what you want to teach him?"

Jane then asked, "Isn't withdrawing my love on his birthday a punishment?" I said, "You could call it that, but I call it a consequence. He did nothing for your birthday. Surely you don't want to continue this inequality in the relationship? You need to be considerate enough to let him know that you aren't going to do anything for his birthday. Because of his behavior, you're assuming that the new guidelines in the relationship are, 'Neither of us goes out of our way for the other's birthday!' You and Gary can change the guidelines, but whatever the rule is, it must be for both of you."

We came up with a plan of action for Jane, and I coached her through it. A few days later, in an even tone of voice, Jane told Gary, "Since we did nothing on my birthday, I guess that's the game plan for this year. So I'm just letting you know that I have nothing planned for yours."

"That's fine," Gary replied calmly, because he knew from past experience that there was no way Jane would not do the "right" thing and at least get him a card and present—even if she said it was from the kids. You can imagine his surprise when his birthday arrived and there were no gifts, no special dinner, and no birthday card. After Gary spent his birthday sulking and playing the martyr (the perfect time for Jane not to relent and continue to stick to her promise), she said, "Shall we change the game plan for next year? You seem noticeably upset, and I understand because that's how I felt on my birthday. Let's change the deal." No whining, no blaming, no argument.

Jane's old behavior was to whine and sacrifice; her new behavior is to create her own justice.

Did Gary change his behavior? We don't know. But Jane took her first step in no longer accepting his bad behavior. As she continues, Gary will either begin to change or the relationship will end.

Negotiating Fair Deals

A healthy relationship is not based on one person winning and the other losing, but instead on compromise; that is, both people win something in the deal. And how do you know if a deal is fair? One simple test is to look at the terms of the deal you and your partner have negotiated and honestly ask yourself if you would consider it fair even if you didn't know which side you would be on. Granted, when you negotiate a fair deal, you'll lose the adrenaline rush of having gotten your own way. But if you remember that you will eventually lose the relationship when only one person wins, it might make compromise more interesting, if not more exciting. If you're the partner who most often loses, think about why you have accepted what you didn't want. And if you usually win, you probably hate the idea of compromise. But remember, if you're always the winner, your mate resents you more and more each day, and that means your relationship will keep eroding.

Mutual respect is necessary for compromise, because it's difficult to compromise if you don't have respect for your mate's right to a different point of view. Differences are part of what attracts us to our mates. Differences create sparks. It seems that we are initially attracted to a man being different and then ultimately try to change him to be more like us. Why isn't it okay that he thinks romantic movies are silly and you hate action flicks? He doesn't have to see it your way or you see it his. For an example, you can negotiate and resolve this issue in several different ways:

- You can take turns deciding what movie you'll see.
- You can see the type of movies you like with your friends.
- You can rent the movies you like and watch them on your own while he does something else.
- You can trade something else to get your mate to go with you—"I'll make your favorite dinner tomorrow night if you'll go see that movie with me."

When I explained this type of negotiation to one female client, she said, "That all sounds like bribery. I'm not bribing him to do something he doesn't want to do!" Why not? It works, and what you're doing now doesn't. "But he should just want to go with me without any bribes!" Yes, and you should just want to watch violent movies or football for him. I don't think so.

I realize that fights over movies are probably the least of your problems and that most couples' issues go much deeper. However, the point of this chapter is to show you as simply as possible the skills necessary to get resolution through negotiation. Then, in the next few chapters, we'll tackle specific, major issues most couples fight about on a regular basis.

When There Is No Solution or Compromise

There are times you may want to agree to disagree. With simple issues such as he loves football and you think it's stupid, you can decide to agree to disagree, because it's a waste of time to argue. Neither of you is going to change your mind—and shouldn't. When you agree to disagree, you make a pact not to let this difference upset your relationship. Simply state, "I know you love football, and you know I hate it. Let's just agree to disagree. You go ahead and enjoy your games, just don't expect me to participate in any way [no making snacks or sitting on the couch with him]. In fact, when you're watching games, I'll be at the mall or out with my friends until the game is over. Deal?" "Deal."

There are other times when one of you should simply give in, letting your mate know it will be his turn to give in next time. Say, "You know, it doesn't really matter that much to me this time. I'll agree to Mexican food tonight. However, you owe me one." This allows you to give in while maintaining your power and making a deal for the future.

Because couples are so used to fighting for their own point of view, they seldom remember to look for a compromise, a deal that's fair, or a true solution. Once you get into the habit of compromising to find a solution, you have a model for all future problem solving. The two of you can become so adept at negotiating that when facing an issue, you both automatically think, "Let's handle this the way we handled that last problem. Okay?"

Looking for Solutions

To find solutions, couples must move out of their win/lose thinking, and commit to a truly give-and-take relationship that involves win/win negotiations. Both people need to communicate, have a willingness to compromise, and respect the negotiating process, as well as each other. Negotiation does more than resolve problems—it gives you and your partner a chance to better understand one another; it lays the groundwork for resolving future issues together; and it helps protect the bond between the two of you.

When He Won't Negotiate

As I've said before, your man doesn't have to agree to work with you for you to find solutions to problems. You can suggest he negotiate with you because it would really be in his best interest—he'll get to ask you to change in some way—but if he doesn't want to, that's fine. If he won't cooperate, then don't try to use the negotiation strategies in the next few pages; instead, refer to the Four Steps to Powerful Communication I showed you earlier in this chapter, and focus only on what you want. If he is unwilling to negotiate, you need to set consequences, boundaries, and ultimatums that will change your life significantly and most likely change his behavior in the process.

Creating Consequences, Setting Boundaries, and Giving Ultimatums

If we want power in a relationship, we need to understand how to work with consequences, boundaries, and ultimatums. We're not talking about revenge, punishment, or doling out severe paybacks. On the contrary, creating consequences, setting boundaries, and giving ultimatums take the place of these more severe reactions.

"You're Out until You Help"

▶ Mary and Patrick's Story

Mary (a long-distance phone client) was in a ten-year relationship with Patrick when she decided she was tired of giving more than 80 percent in the relationship, while he did most of the taking. She asked him to start helping with the housework and kids, but he flat-out refused, even though she helps run their business, does all of the household chores, and does 100 percent of the child care. So Mary walked out of their business and gave Patrick an ultimatum: Help with chores or move out of their house. Patrick moved out, but it took him four months before he took her seriously enough to agree to go to a marriage counselor with her. That night she was so excited, she let him spend the night (giving up some power again). Guess what? No surprise that Patrick missed the first three therapy appointments. (More about how they worked out these issues in later chapters.)

Remember, controllers do not give up their power easily. However, by using the following guidelines, you will be able to change your behavior enough that he can't control you.

Guidelines for Consequences, Boundaries, and Ultimatums

- You can set boundaries only on behaviors that affect you directly: "I feel upset when you ___, and want you to stop." Not, "You need to stand up to your mom" (that's none of your business).
- Consequences should be based on ways to protect yourself and/or what you can do to be okay with the situation. It's best, but not necessary, to relate the consequence to the problem: "If you aren't here by seven o'clock to take me to dinner, I'll leave and go to dinner with my girlfriends."

(continued)

Guidelines for Consequences, Boundaries, and Ultimatums
(continued)

- Consequences must be spelled out in advance (or they aren't consequences, they're punishments): "If you don't stand up to your mother about this, I won't go with you to her house for dinner on Sunday."
- Never give him a consequence that you'll have trouble following through with.
- For you to modify his behavior, you must follow through with your consequences a minimum of three times consecutively.
- Make sure the consequences match the crime, i.e., "If you aren't home in time for dinner, I'll throw it out," not, "I'll divorce you."
- Always distinguish between who he is and his bad behavior, i.e., "Your behavior is upsetting me"—not, "you're upsetting me."
- When you think someone may do something you don't like, setting a boundary (with a consequence) in advance can often keep the situation from happening, and it definitely sets a precedence for how future incidents will be handled.

Examples of consequences appropriate for adults are: making him promise to do a chore, leaving his presence, refusing to participate, refusing to do something you usually do for him. Remember that consequences are fair only if you've warned him—"If you do that, I will . . .", or "The next time you do that, I will . . ."

Win/Win Negotiations

To negotiate a win/win deal, you need to understand the four elements that go into achieving a workable solution. You must *gain equal power* in the relationship, *know your own needs and wants*, *listen to the other's point of view*, and *understand the trade-offs* needed to achieve a fair compromise.

Gain Equal Power

If you try to negotiate with your mate from a powerless position, he will probably laugh at you. The minimum you must do if you feel you don't have equal power is let him know, "I will not continue to live like this. Either you'll work with me to save our relationship, or I will do whatever is necessary to make myself happy, and not worry about what that does to our relationship. It's up to you." To keep your power, you then proceed, whether or not he agrees or even responds. This is what Mary did when she left the family business and told Patrick to change his behavior or leave.

Ten Ways to Gain Power in Your Relationships

1. **Keep him wondering:** Let your mate know you will not continue the relationship the way it is. Never say, "I'd never leave you."

2. **Competition:** If you're single, insinuate that there are lots of other "potentials" who will give you what you want. If you're married, let your mate know that if he continues his bad behavior, your friends are a better option to spend time with than him.

3. **Un-investing:** Never get more invested in the relationship than your mate is. And if you already are, do whatever is necessary to start un-investing, i.e. find new friends, financial avenues, etc.

4. **Gain expertise:** Gather information and documentation to back you up on whatever subject you are negotiating.

5. **Overload him or her with junk:** Find several minor issues you can offer up in a negotiation to get something more important back.

6. **Broken record:** Without nagging, repeat your request over and over, let your mate know that this issue will never go away until it's resolved.

7. **Put on your game face:** Don't let your mate see you sweat. Try not to take negotiations personally, and if you do, never let him know how emotionally upset you are about the situation.

(continued)

8. **Identification:** Make your mate identify with your pain. If he won't negotiate helping with dinner or the dishes, help him identify with how you feel by no longer washing his clothes.
9. **Equalize the rules:** Identify his bad behavior, telling him that what's good for the gander is good for the goose. As long as he chooses that bad behavior, you will too.
10. **Leaving the ball in his court:** If your mate refuses to negotiate, let him know what you intend to do to take care of yourself, and that if and when he wants that to change, he needs to come to you because "the ball is in his court."

Know Your Needs and Wants

One reason women often have difficulty with the concept of negotiating is because they're unclear about what they really want. Before you begin any negotiation, take time to fantasize about how the relationship would look if it were perfect. Then break down the fantasy into a list of "wants."

Listen to the Other's Point of View

Listen to what he's saying. Knowing what he really wants helps you make a better deal. Try to see if there's a deeper need he's not revealing to you, so you get down to the real issue. This is hard, because we usually try to get him to listen and understand our point of view, not vice versa.

Understanding his point of view is not the same as giving into it—it's a way of gaining power to make changes. If your mate yearned for his mother's love, he may make deals with you if you agree to simply behave in a more loving way toward him. If he felt controlled by his dad, using intimidation techniques may work or they may make him rebel. Knowing how he has reacted before in similar situations helps you predict how he will react to your requests. (See Appendix A.)

Remember, never put your mate on the defensive by attacking, nagging, criticizing, or doing anything else that will alienate him. Always allow him to save face. Be ready to offer him a way out, a possible solution that doesn't make him feel like he's lost the deal.

Understand the Trade-offs

Negotiations—even those that work in your favor—demand trade-offs. Neither partner should walk away from a negotiation feeling as if he or she has won it all or lost it all. Always winning breeds guilt, and always losing breeds resentment—two killers of love. Fair compromises create good feelings.

Of course, it may not always be possible to achieve a perfect, fifty-fifty balance of power in every negotiation. However, it's important that ultimately the balance be maintained in the relationship as a whole. So, for example, if the deal on housework seems to give you more of what you want (help with the shopping) and less of what he wants (freedom from household chores), you both must ensure that somewhere else in the relationship, you strike a deal that works more in his favor. In exchange for extra help around the house, you might offer to curtail or reschedule one of your outside activities so that you both can have a night out without the kids every week. Be sure the trade-offs are clear when the deal is made, otherwise resentments might creep back in. If he doesn't hold up his side of the bargain, then threaten to withdraw your trade-off, too.

For example, Gretchen and Art discussed household duties and Art agreed to pick up the kids more often so Gretchen could get her business off the ground, but he started to renege on his bargain. When Gretchen complained, I asked, "What consequences did you set up to ensure he wouldn't fail to keep his agreements with you?" Gretchen replied, "We forgot to do that. Besides, Art is a grown man, and should know better."

I asked, "Do you want to do something that will work, or

prove that he's immature? Is there something else you're willing to trade to get what you want?" She replied, "No, I just want him to do what he says!" I said, "I know, but think. What else will he never do that you want him to do?" "Mop the kitchen floor!" I told her it wasn't too late to tell him that's what she wants since he broke his agreement with her. However, since the consequence is now after the fact, he didn't have to agree, so was there anything she could trade back at this point? How about, "I promise to let go of my anger at you about this issue if you will mop the kitchen floor tonight."

Art gladly agreed. Gretchen had given him a way to save face and still have a good evening with her after all. Instead of playing victim or controller, she set up a win/win situation for both of them.

Successful Negotiations

The steps to successful negotiations are similar to the steps for powerful communication, with just one added step: Let's make a deal. If you're pretty sure he will not negotiate with you, just use the Four Steps to Powerful Communication, and set your boundary. If a negotiation seems possible, use the "let's make a deal" step before you give him the ultimatum; and if he'll make a deal, the ultimatum may not be necessary.

Five Steps to Successful Negotiations

1. *"I feel _____ when you _____."*
   Tell him what you're feeling about his behavior.
2. *"I want _____."*
   Tell him clearly what you want.
3. *"Will you negotiate this with me?"*
   Get a commitment from him to agree to negotiate with you.
4. *"Let's make a deal: you do _____ and I'll do _____."*

Begin to negotiate, offering up solutions with trade-offs you're both happy with.

5. "If not, I will _____ ."

Give him an ultimatum: If you won't work this out with me, I'll handle it in a way that doesn't include you.

Preparing to Negotiate

It's often helpful to prepare for your negotiation by writing the steps out so you can be very clear. Follow your script if necessary, so he can't pull you off track. Think ahead of time about how far you will and won't go in your bargaining, and what your bottom-line stance is. What do you fear his might be? Prepare for his worst response, and hope you don't get it. Once you've reached a deal, it's good to write down your agreement, signing and dating it. People have a way of forgetting what they've agreed to, and you really don't want to have to renegotiate the issue all over again.

Three Things You Never Do When Negotiating

1. Keep talking (explaining your point) once he's agreed.
2. Make a stupid threat—one he knows you won't follow through with.
3. Give in for the wrong reasons, i.e., "I'm tired of fighting," or "It's not worth it."

Work Your Way Up to the Big Issues

Unless you're at the point where big changes must be made or you're filing for divorce tomorrow (which is the point where many clients are when they come into my office), start small to get some practice on how setting boundaries works. For instance, if he leaves beer cans on the coffee table, tell him (in a lighthearted way), "I'm going to start charging you a dollar for every can I end up having to throw away. Is that a deal?" If he agrees, follow through and be sure to collect. If he won't agree, then ask him what he believes his consequence should be. Don't be surprised if he comes back at you with, "Okay, and you owe me a dollar every time I have to move a pair of panty hose before I get in the shower." Call his bluff by agreeing. And then you'll have your first negotiated deal!

Take the behaviors he needs to change one at a time and think about what you can change in return (or ask him to tell you). Using the Five Steps to Successful Negotiations, try to make win/win deals: "If you'll stop criticizing me, I'll be warm and loving to you when you come home." If he refuses to make a deal, go on to the ultimatum, setting a consequence that will happen each time he does the behavior you don't like: "Every time you criticize me, I will leave your presence for at least a half hour."

Negotiating Statements You May Find Helpful

- "Here's how I feel and what I want. What do you feel and want?"
- "This part is not negotiable, but I can negotiate this part."
- "I'll sacrafice this time, but the trade-off is that you owe me one."
- "I'm not hearing what you really want. Please tell me."
- "Instead of criticizing *what I want*, just tell me *what you want*."
- "I think you may be confused. What is it you think I'm asking for?"
- "Let's just agree to disagree on this one."
- "Since you're not saying, I'm guessing that what you really want is _____. Is that right?"
- "If you don't tell me what you want as a trade-off, I'll have to assume that you're okay with it the way it is. Let me know if that changes."

Using the Five Steps to Successful Negotiations, you can change almost anyone's behavior toward you—boss, child, parent, or lover. Besides practice in using these five steps, all you need is the courage—courage to take a stand, to believe you deserve what you're asking for, to decide you'd rather be alone than treated badly, and to hold your mate accountable for his behavior!

Handling His Intimidation, Retaliation, and Other Aggressive Behaviors

When Alexis started dating Raymond, she said, "I can tell that he's the type of person that you don't cross. He's made it clear to me that when people don't see it his way, he just writes them off!" I told her, "That's just a method of intimidation. Don't fall for it! And besides, if it is true, it simply means that Raymond is the type of person who will never negotiate with anyone. He'd rather be alone and in control than work through issues and have intimacy. If that's true, you don't want this man in your life anyway."

I also reminded her that people who use intimidation, like Raymond did, or retaliation, like Kyle did with Britney in Chapter 1 (when he stopped calling after she stood up for herself), are all just insecure and frightened. If they can intimidate you into never confronting them and scare you with their tactics, then they never have to deal with their own issues or ever negotiate or have intimate relationships. Don't let intimidation techniques work on you.

Fighting Fire with Fire

Most women hate to fight because we were never taught how, we believe it's not ladylike, we think it's mean, and we believe we shouldn't have to. I can talk most women into standing up for themselves and setting boundaries. But if their mate becomes intimidating, they often stop asserting themselves at this point and think, "See, it just doesn't work." These same women, if attacked in an alley, might not fight back for fear their attacker will get angrier. Many women end up dying physically or psychologically, because they refuse to fight aggressively. They've never learned that it's sometimes necessary to hurt the other person when you are being harmed physically or psychologically. It is often the only way to stop an aggressor. It's true that we seldom need extremely aggressive behavior, but if you never develop that "don't mess with me" fighting instinct, your mate will be able to intimidate you and put you back into the victim role.

Of course, if he ever hits you or you're afraid of being hurt physically, I don't recommend that you get into a physical brawl. Instead, call 911 and press charges. But what do you do if he goes over the line psychologically when arguing with you? I want you to outsmart him, not out-argue him. Don't scream at him or yell, or name-call, or say things you wish you hadn't—that's seldom successful in stopping him. In fact, it usually escalates the war. The goal instead is to behave in a way that will cause him to back down.

Counter-Intimidation

There is a fine line between fighting dirty and fighting aggressively enough to counter-intimidate someone. You need to make him realize that he needs to back down and not go down that particular road with you ever again.

For instance, if he says, "You're so insecure, you're pathetic," you don't respond with dirty fighting to make him feel more insecure than you by saying, "Who was it that failed first grade? You're the pathetic one!" Instead, to counter-intimidate him, you might just say, "Don't even go there!" And then, finish what you were saying. Or you might need to threaten to fight like him by saying, "If we're going to talk insecurities, I know a list of yours a mile long we can discuss. Is that what you want? I don't think so—so back to the topic at hand." Counter-intimidation has more to do with a "don't mess with me!" attitude, than direct criticisms or put-downs.

Counter-Intimidation Techniques

Calling his bluff	If he threatens divorce, say, "Okay," then leave the names of divorce attorneys or circled apartment rental ads lying around.
Using his own techniques against him	If he says, "I'm leaving," say, "No, I'm leaving."
Leveling the playing field	If he intimidates with, "But I bring in most of the money, so I will decide," say, "Then I'll cash in my IRA so I can decide instead."

The goal of counter-intimidation is to not let him take you off track, while also not escalating the war. What would Alexis say back to Raymond today if he said, "When people don't see it my way, I just write them off"? She would say, "You don't want to hear what I've done when people have crossed me!" Then she would go on with the conversation as if he hadn't said anything. By the way, the times she's "crossed" him, he not only didn't leave, he often folded like a rubber duck.

Does It Have to Be about Fighting?

Yes, it's true that you may have to "fight" to get back the man of your dreams, and I am sorry, but that's what happens when you've let issues slide for years and resentments compound. When your mate behaves pretty much however he wants, you have to fight to get enough power back for him to agree to negotiate with you. For him to treat you the way you want, you'll have to negotiate every area of your relationship that is out of balance. Whether or not you play the victim or have the control, you will improve your relationship as a whole with each issue you and your mate are able to work through.

◀ Points to Remember ▶

1. Boundaries are psychological fences that we place around ourselves for protection from harm from other people.

2. If a deal is fair, either side of it will look good to you.

3. You must respect your mate's differences to be able to negotiate fairly.

4. We often want to change in him the very things that attracted us from the start.

5. We have the right—and responsibility—to tell people how we want to be treated.

6. The longer he's had his way, the longer it will take for him to agree to negotiate.

7. To stop playing the victim, you must create your own justice.

8. Key to changing his behavior is changing your attitude from tolerant to confrontational.

Chapter 6

Achieving Emotional Intimacy with Him

Do you play the victim or controller role emotionally? If you play the victim, you may:

- Put up with his coldness or avoidance
- Whine and complain that he's not loving enough
- Open up to him emotionally even when he doesn't open up to you
- Chase his love, trying to win his approval
- Send him the double message he needs to stay "strong," while asking him to be vulnerable
- Think that's just the way he is

If you play the controller, you may:

- Bitch at or criticize him
- Blame him for your unhappiness
- Withhold loving feelings
- Refuse to discuss issues with him

What Women Want

Most men we know are either macho (the controllers), or wimpy (the victims). They either show no vulnerability, sharing very little with us, or share so much that we can't respect them. They either act as if they don't care about us at all, or drive us nuts with flowers and phone calls. If given the choice between the macho guy or the wimp, we'll always choose macho. We wish we wouldn't, but we can't stand men who are too nice to us. Is it because we have low self-esteem? Partly, but it's more about the wimpy guy having no self-esteem. If the macho guy is faking it (and he is), at least he has the good sense not to look as pathetic as he may feel—and we do respect him for that.

What we really want, however, is a man that's in between macho and wimpy. He shows us love, but respects himself. He's strong, but doesn't have to always be right. He shares emotions when it's appropriate, and closes up when it's not. The healthy man and the healthy woman are mirrors of each other—emotionally, they look exactly alike.

Men Have Emotions, but They're Afraid to Show Them

When I accuse male clients of being unemotional, they always say to me, "But I do have emotions!" And of course, it's true. Men have and feel emotions just like we do. But they, of course, have difficulty expressing them because of their childhood training. As I said before, fathers teach men that it's weak and unmanly to show any emotion but anger. Then mothers teach them that it's wrong to show anger. Then we—their wives and girlfriends—teach them that if they are emotional with us, we'll lose respect for them. Society has programmed us to expect men to "handle" their emotions, and often by "handle," we mean not have any weak or insecure feelings. So they pretend that they don't—because we want them to.

Are You Ready to Hear What He Has to Say?

Often our own secret dependencies keep us wanting a man to be stronger and more fearless than we are so we can lean on him if we need to. To have him be emotionally open with you, you have to be ready to let him off the pedestal. You have to honestly want an equal relationship—want him to be your best friend. Usually, when we say we want him to be more emotional than he is, we mean just in a loving way. And of course, that's not possible. If your mate becomes more emotionally available, he will need to share all of his emotions—even the ones you don't want to hear. That's what happened with Tricia.

"Is My Wagon Really Attached to You?"

▶ Tricia and Kevin's Story

Tricia brought Kevin into my office because he was unemotional and she believed that was the cause of numerous problems in their relationship. She said she wanted him to do several sessions with me alone and learn to open up and share his feelings with her so they could be closer. He agreed to individual therapy with me and began to work on his emotional issues. After four or five sessions, I suggested Kevin bring Tricia back in with him to start opening up to her in my office. She came in and he began to reveal some of his frustrations to her about how controlling he thought she had been in the relationship, as well as his fierce unhappiness and deep insecurities in his career. Tricia was noticeably upset. She looked at Kevin with complete disgust, ignoring the comments about her own controlling behavior, and said, "I can't believe this! I wanted you to become more loving, not pathetic. You're sure not the man I thought I married! I can't believe I've had my wagon attached to you! I thought you were a strong, successful man, but I guess I was wrong! I think we should separate!"

Kevin was shocked—and so was I. What emotions did Tricia

want to hear from Kevin? How much he loves her? How wonderful she is? Only "good" emotions? Kevin's greatest fears came true. When he opened up and shared with Tricia, she saw him as pathetic and weak, and divorced him.

What should Tricia have done? First, she needed to understand that men have all of the same emotions that women do—and that includes insecurities. Also, Kevin is weak only if he does nothing to deal with his insecurities. She should have said something like, "I'm surprised. I had no idea you had so many things you were unhappy about. I hope we can work them out and I hope you'll keep sharing with me, because I love you."

Men Need to Feel Safe to Share

If you want your mate to be more loving and emotionally intimate with you, you have to provide an environment that is safe for him to open up:

- One where he won't be ridiculed or labeled a wimp
- One where he won't be worried about hurting you
- One where he feels listened to
- One where he won't feel he's letting you down by being himself

Teach Him What You Know Emotionally—but Don't Shove It at Him

Most women have more basic information about the emotional part of a relationship than men do. We learned this from self-help books, talking to friends, and discussing our emotions as we were growing up. Because we "know" more, we are usually the person who has to take the lead emotionally. However, when we try to help our mates understand our need for emotional intimacy, we often push them too hard. We nag them about it, and try to make them "get it," whether they're interested or not. Then they resent us, clam up more, and the cycle repeats—we want it, they won't give it; we try harder, they resist us more. This is lose/lose.

If you give you mate advice when he doesn't ask for it, or try to change him by forcing him to "get it," you are simply being controlling. Yes, even when you're "right" in the sense that he needs to grow in this area. This is overstepping his boundary, and you're not respecting his belief system. And furthermore, he probably never asked for your advice or help on this subject. You'd be livid with him if he tried to tell you (when you hadn't asked) what to do with your job review at work. When you think about it, where do you get off? Remember that whenever you try to control, you put him in a victim role and he will either pull away or get defensive.

For your mate to ever change and become more emotionally intimate, you have to change your behavior in a way that makes him want to come toward you. Pressuring, judging, lecturing, or acting self-righteous never makes anyone want to get closer to you. What works is: not spending time with him when he's unemotional; his seeing you happy because you're emotional with others (modeling); showing him that it's not only safe to share with you, but it turns you on; and being emotionally honest with him about the effect his unemotional behavior has on you.

"But Will He Ever Get It?"

We want our men to deal with their pasts, analyze past loves, recognize their patterns, and stand up to their moms. Will it ever happen? I don't know. But I do know this—the harder you try to make it happen, the more likely it won't. It's true he has a lot to learn, but no one learns anything until he or she is ready. You probably didn't know how controlling you've been on this subject, but let's hope *you're* ready to "get it" now.

How I Got Alan to Open Up

Alan was a typical, unemotional man when we met, although it took me a while to see it. When he was married, he didn't share his emotions with his wife. When they had a conflict, he either left or just shut down and avoided. If it was not an important issue, he just let her have her way. When it was important to him, he usually just did what he wanted regardless of what she thought. When I tell this to people who don't know him, they say, "What a jerk!" Alan isn't a jerk, but he certainly behaved like one in his marriage. Even he admits that. He lost respect for his wife early on in their seventeen-year marriage. She never had or took the power to change his bad behavior.

When we began dating, I said to him in the first month or so, "I feel like I've told you more about myself than you've told me about you, and that makes me uncomfortable, so I need you to share more with me." His reply concerned me greatly: "Sure, go ahead and ask me any questions and I'll answer them." I explained that I wanted to know every important thing about his life, not just answers to questions. He laughed. We struggled with these two opposing concepts for a while, but he eventually began to share because I was persistent. My boundary? When he didn't share, I also stopped sharing. There were several times I shut down and withdrew from the relationship until he opened up to me again.

In case you are with a man like Alan, who will answer questions, but doesn't know how to share freely, be sure the questions you ask him are open-ended questions about himself, not questions that can be answered with "yes" or "no." Share information about yourself gradually, asking him for similar information, never sharing more than he does. Listen carefully to what he's telling you, repeating the feeling words so he will know he was heard. And when you ask him a question, remember to stop talking—give him a chance to answer. Don't be afraid of the quiet moments while you wait for his response.

Stop Enabling His Unemotional Behavior

How often have you asked your mate to share with you what's wrong, and when he doesn't, you still go to dinner with him or sit next to him on the couch and watch TV? This is "enabling," or putting up with his bad behavior. Even if you act mad at him while you're with him or nag him, you're still accepting his emotional unavailability.

It's okay to allow a man to "withdraw into his cave" if he needs to think about an issue before he talks it over with you. He doesn't have to share with you on demand, as long as he doesn't take his bad mood out on you. But he does have to promise to talk about it, so be sure you get a commitment from him for a set time in the future—"I'll get off your case about this if you promise me we'll have a long talk about it tomorrow night. Is that a deal?" If he doesn't agree (or if he agrees but doesn't follow through), withdraw from him and tell him why: "If you won't talk to me about why you're acting this way, I'm going upstairs to bed [or out with my girlfriend, or whatever]." The point that you make is that his behavior is not acceptable to you. If he doesn't share what's going on, you won't spend time with him.

Don't Excuse His Bad Behavior with Others

Do you excuse his bad behavior with his family or coworkers with, "You know how he is, he never remembers birthdays [or returns phone calls, etc.]"? How often do you cater to his moods, put up with his little explosions, and lose friends because he holds a grudge against someone he won't work it out with? You're enabling his bad behaviors and that will ensure that's just the way he'll stay. You shouldn't tell him how to handle his relationships with others, but you shouldn't accept his bad behavior either—"I know you're still upset at George, but Cynthia and I have nothing to do with that, so she and I are having dinner Friday night. It's up to you guys if you want to join us or not."

Share Your Feelings with Him

We may "understand" our emotions better than men—we're certainly more likely to analyze our problems, admit our feelings, cry when we're upset, and act moody and whine about problems in our lives. But those behaviors have nothing to do with emotional intimacy. As far as sharing our feelings about a man directly to that man—which is what emotional intimacy is all about—we're seldom any better at it than men are, especially when those feelings are anger. Few women communicate to their mate in a direct, clear, confrontational way that lets him know what they want and what they'll do if they don't get it. Unless you do this, you're not behaving in an emotionally intimate way yourself, so why would you expect him to?

An early episode of HBO's *Sex and the City* left me frustrated about this very issue. Carrie, played by Sarah Jessica Parker, is having a conversation with Big, her ex, after finding out that he's engaged to someone else. She's trying to keep her cool, but is asking questions to find out why Big is engaged to this new woman and didn't choose her, when a confused Big says, "I don't get it." Carrie says, "You never did," and walks away smugly—with probably every female viewer at home going, "Yeah, you tell him!" Several of my female clients brought it up in their therapy sessions, because they saw this scene as very empowering for women.

Women feel empowered and believe they are "right" about how emotionally stupid men are. "See," we say, "I told you he was too stupid to get it, too emotionally out of it to realize he's really in love with me." And in some ways, it's true that Big wasn't always emotionally available and really didn't "get it." But then neither did Carrie, although she thought she did. Actually, Carrie never realized that because she feared losing Big, she began mirroring his unemotional behavior. Each time he was disrespectful or implied they didn't have a future together, Carrie didn't respond. She was hurt (and should have been angry), yet she ignored his comments, and didn't hold him accountable for his cold and disrespectful behavior.

She was building a case against him (to protect her ego) that he was, "just that way—he just didn't get it!" In their on-again, off-again relationship, every time Big asked Carrie out, she always went—no matter how badly he had insulted or treated her the time before. Each time she was cheerful (which wasn't emotionally honest), and she even continued to sleep with him, never mentioning how hurt or angry she was about the way he treated her on their previous date. Carrie hid her real feelings and real personality from Big because she was afraid of losing him. She stopped being herself with him, and was her "real" emotional self only with her friends. Yet she was upset he didn't fall in love with her, when how could he? He didn't even know the "real" her. In fact, a few times her anger came out in bizarre ways, and Big just thought she was crazy.

Don't Share More Than He Does

Our mates need to know our feelings about their behavior, but if and when they do not share with us or negotiate with us, we need to stop sharing. We often seem to think it's our obligation to share everything about ourselves. But when we open up and our mate doesn't, it puts us in a vulnerable position (the victim role), giving him the power, and throwing the relationship out of balance.

Usually when we open up with our female friends, we become closer, because they automatically reciprocate by sharing with us. We mistakenly believe the same is true when we open up with men. We forget that men's values are different from ours, and that winning is usually their goal. If we are the only ones opening up, men are more likely to use information we give them against us, rather than to bring us closer.

When he's not sharing, and we share too much about ourselves, a man devalues us in his eyes, often seeing us as weak or even crazy. That allows him to take control since he knows how insecure we feel. He can even pretend (often to himself) that he is stronger than we are because his weaknesses are not exposed.

Seldom does it occur to us that to get the emotional intimacy we want, we may need to change our behavior by not opening up so much. In fact, we often end up carrying the emotional part of the relationship, enabling him to stay unemotional. To create equality in the relationship emotionally, we must require our mate to meet us halfway. If you've already opened up more than your mate, stop giving him information about you and tell him he must share information with you before you will continue.

Men Want to Figure It Out Before They Share

I remember feeling frustrated with Alan one particular time when he seemed upset, and I asked him what was on his mind. He was moody, yet evasive for several days, finally giving me a quick summary of a problem he had at work and how it had now been resolved. I asked him why he wouldn't talk to me about it over the last few days when it was happening, and he replied, "Because I didn't have it figured out yet."

"I want you to share with me *while* you're figuring out a problem so I can be there for you when you're upset. I feel like you won't let me in so we can share and be closer," I responded. The concept of sharing vulnerable emotions while he's working through them was foreign to him. He often used the quote, "Don't let them see you sweat!" He talked about his Marine Corps training where he learned not to let things get to him. He explained how he believed he needed to stay strong and solve his own problems—without support. He assured me that he wasn't avoiding being close to me. He agreed that he would try to share more when he's upset, but reminded me, "It won't feel natural."

Like most men, Alan thought that sharing emotions showed weakness. He was still going through divorce proceedings, and was obviously hurting badly one night when I asked him to please share with me what was going on. He finally did. He began to cry and share details of his divorce and how awful it all was—as I held him. To me, this was one of our most touching and emotionally intimate moments—an emotional breakthrough. The next morning, Alan was very uncomfortable. He told me he regretted sharing with me and apologized for being so weak the night before. I told him that the experience made me feel closer to him than ever—and it even turned me on. He looked quite surprised. He assumed that I would now think less of him, and maybe even question my love for him. He was relieved. He now felt safe to share. After that, he began to trust my response to his emotions, and began sharing more and more. And no, he didn't turn into a wimp—instead, he became my very best friend.

I remember what finally made me know that Alan is my emotional equal. Whenever we had an issue, I was usually the one to say, "We need to talk." One night I was upset about something but was tired and didn't say anything. Alan came into the bathroom when I was taking my makeup off and said, "Are you okay honey? If something's wrong, let's talk about it." Instead of avoiding, he was emotionally tuned in to me, probably more than I was to myself at the time. It made me feel incredibly loved.

Withdraw When He's Cold and Rejecting

Carrie did what most women do when they feel rejected—chase after him trying to win his approval. When a woman does this, she's behaving as if she has no pride, she gives up any power she had in the relationship, she loses value in her mate's eyes, and she puts the final nail in the coffin of their relationship.

This is the key mistake women make in dealing with commitment-phobic men—which Big was. This type of man always rushes a relationship at the beginning, loving the romance and instant (and false) intimacy. Then he gets scared of the closeness and pulls away, looking for reasons to devalue this woman. A woman who chases plays right into his fear of commitment, because she seems to be acting obsessive or "crazy," justifying his reasons for leaving her. However, if a woman withdraws when he begins to pull away, she sends him the message that he's the one that's not good enough. This makes him question his own behavior instead of hers. This taps into his own insecurities and puts the power back in her court.

How should Carrie have handled Big? Certainly not by criticizing and begging him not to leave her. And certainly not by asking why she wasn't good enough for him, and the other woman was. Those are victim behaviors. In fact, Carrie acted like a victim throughout the relationship and lowered her value in his eyes early on by being too available. The first time Big suggested that they had no future, Carrie should have pulled away, which would have given her some power and self-respect back. If he came after her, she would have had enough power to get him to negotiate, or she could have set some boundaries—"If you treat me disrespectfully again, I'll leave the party and not see or talk to you for a week. And if you really see no future for us, I see no reason to go out again. There are plenty of other men who are interested in me that I'd rather spend my time with" (using competition to gain power). Would this behavior have gotten Carrie her man? We don't know for sure, but we do know that she would have at least left with her self-respect intact, and her smugness would have been more appropriate. If he didn't come back, a relationship that would have ultimately ended anyway, would have just ended sooner.

How to Get Him to Share Emotionally

1. Make it safe for him to share by listening and accepting his feelings.
2. Teach him what you know about sharing emotionally, but don't shove it at him.
3. Stop enabling his unemotional behavior.
4. Don't excuse his bad behavior with others.
5. Share your feelings with him.
6. Don't share more than he does.
7. Withdraw when he is cold and rejecting.

The Perfect Little Wife

▶ *Lynn and Peter's Story*

Attractive, thirty-six-year-old Lynn said that Peter had always been cold, unemotional, angry, and controlling for the full sixteen years they'd been married. In fact, Lynn believed all men were that way. Her father certainly had been that way, Peter was, and most of the men she knew were, and she had adjusted very well to that behavior. She played a "perfect little wife" role, catering to his moods and explosions, but secretly hating him a little more every day. She stayed busy with her children, charities, friends, and workouts at the club, where she began developing some flirtatious "friendships" with men who exercised there too. When one man called the house and hung up when Peter answered, Peter lost it, and insisted that he and Lynn see a therapist.

At their first session, Peter accused Lynn of having a secret life. Eventually she admitted that she was being flirtatious and even fantasizing about other men. With my help, Lynn finally got angry and told Peter what an emotionally unavailable "ogre" she thought he was and always had been. Peter had no clue that Lynn felt this way because she always acted as though everything was fine between the two of them. Lynn admitted she stayed with Peter for two major reasons: the children and the lifestyle. His $400,000 a year income, the house on the golf course, the club memberships, and the fact that she would never have to work, were, to her, viable trade-offs.

Peter was shocked and wanted to know how long she's felt this way. "Ten years at least," she told him. He couldn't believe it. He felt shocked, cheated, and hurt. "Why didn't you tell me before?" he pleaded. "Because I didn't think it would make any difference— I know that's just the way you are," she replied.

Peter was appalled both at Lynn's behavior and his own now that he was forced to look at it. He'd never been held accountable for the bad behaviors Lynn described to him—his dominating ways, angry outbursts, and unfair sexual demands (which Lynn had begrudgingly complied with). He didn't like the picture he was seeing of himself—but he didn't back away and avoid this time. Peter was a good businessman and faced problems at work, so he threw himself into the therapeutic process the same way he threw himself into his career. "Let's solve this. I want to change. I want a wife who wants to be with me and wants to make love to me," he said.

Lynn was reluctant, telling Peter, "You'll never change." But it was really Lynn who had more trouble changing. Peter asked her to give up her flirtatious ways and stand up to him when she's upset. He agreed that in exchange he would try to monitor his own behavior and become more loving and emotionally available. He also agreed to work in therapy with me figuring out why he had this angry, controlling behavior—and what to do about it.

Peter looked back into his past to find his deep-seated anger. He remembered constant battles with his mom growing up. She was a self-proclaimed man hater, and his father was emotionally passive. He realized he took the worst from both parents and had become emotionally passive like his dad (which made him "oblivious" to Lynn's secret life), and angry and combative (like he was with his mother). Peter eagerly worked in therapy, eventually confronting both parents about their behavior—which he understood would help change his own behavior. (For more on this, see Appendix B: Update on Characters.)

Then, I helped Lynn learn to stand up to Peter. The first boundary she set dealt with the condescending tone in his voice: She decided to say the code word "bonsai" each time she heard it, and that meant he was to stop his aggressive behavior. She was to warn him that she would leave his presence if he didn't stop, and then leave if he continued. When he acted irritable and frustrated, she was to ask him what he was really upset about. He was to try to figure it out, then tell her and work it through. If it was not about her, he was to tell her that and not take it out on her or the children.

Lynn was surprised that Peter wanted to change his behavior, that he actually didn't want to act dominating and cold. With her help, he began to change. Lynn started changing too, and began to stop flirting. But what Peter wanted the most? For her to stop playing the "good little wife" role and be "real" with him so they could finally get close emotionally.

Lynn had trouble understanding that when you love someone, you owe it to that person to let him know when he's doing something that may potentially harm the relationship. It's less important to confront people you don't care about because they are expendable. However, out of fear of losing someone we care about, we're more likely to confront a store clerk than our own husband—because we love him.

What to Do When He . . .

Here are eight scenarios based on the Five Steps to Successful Negotiations, which we covered in Chapter 5. These represent eight common situations and the five things you can say to gain a positive outcome in each case.

When He Withdraws and Sulks . . .

1. *I feel* upset when you withdraw from me.
2. *I want* you to talk to me and tell me if something is wrong.
3. *Will you* talk to me and try to work this through together?
4. I think you want me to stop certain behaviors, and I will if you'll discuss them with me. *Is that a deal?*
5. *If not* (and you're going to continue to sulk), *I'm* going over to a friend's house until you're ready to talk.

When He Tries to Punish Me . . .

1. *I feel* punished by your refusal to go to my office party.
2. *I want* you to stop acting this way and go with me to this party.
3. *Will you* get ready now so we can leave at six o'clock?
4. I'll agree not to stay late if you'll get dressed now and go

with me. *Is that a deal?*

5. *If not, I'm* going to call Suzy and take her. Or, I'll see you later then, and I'm not sure when I'll be home. (Whatever you do, don't beg him to go, or come home early, or stay home and coddle him.)

When He Has Angry Outbursts . . .

1. *I feel* scared when you get out of control with your anger.
2. *I want* you to stop screaming and throwing things and take a time-out until you calm down.
3. *Will you* leave my presence until you can talk to me calmly?
4. When our arguments start to escalate, either of us can say "red pepper," and that means we stop and agree to come back in one hour and try to finish the discussion. *Is that a deal?*
5. *If not, I will* leave your presence. And if you try to stop me from leaving, I'll call the police.

When He Won't Participate . . .

1. *I feel* upset when you won't participate with me and the children.
2. *I want* you to schedule two evenings a week and one weekend day to do activities with the family.
3. *Will you* come home at six o'clock every Tuesday and Thursday for dinner and clear your schedule this Saturday so we can all go to the zoo at one o'clock?
4. I think you want a night out with the guys. If you'll agree to this, you can have every other Wednesday with the guys. *Is that a deal?*
5. *If not, I will* stop making dinner for you and take Sundays for myself, leaving the kids with you that day. (And if he doesn't take the kids, you'll get a sitter.)

When He Lets His Issues Affect Our Relationship . . .

1. *I feel* upset when you're in a bad mood every time you drop the kids off at your ex's.
2. *I want* you to stop taking it out on me when she screams at you. I also want you to do whatever is necessary to get in a better mood before our time together.
3. *Will you* stand up to her, or arrange another way to get the kids to her, or talk it out with me to get in a better mood before we go out?
4. I think you want me to be more polite when I see her. I'll promise to do that if you'll do this. *Is that a deal?*
5. *If not, I will* not go out with you while you're still upset about what has happened with her.

When He Talks Down to Me or Criticizes Me . . .

1. *I feel* hurt and angry when you talk to me like that.
2. *I want* you to stop it and talk more respectfully to me.
3. *Will you* stop talking to me like that right now?
4. I'll stop nagging you about helping around the house if you'll stop talking to me that way. *Is that a deal?*
5. *If not, I will* leave your presence until you're ready to speak to me in a respectful manner.

When He Breaks Promises . . .

1. *I feel* disappointed when you tell me you'll do something and don't follow through.
2. *I want* you to think things through before you make a promise to me so you can be sure you can keep it. I also want you to agree to a consequence for every promise you break.
3. *Will you* stop telling me things you don't mean, keep the promises you do make, and pay me fifty dollars for every

promise you don't keep?

4. Tell me something you want me to change and I'll pay you fifty dollars for each time I still do it. *Is that a deal?*

5. *If not, I will* stop making plans or agreements with you.

When He Wants to Talk to Me and Be with Me Constantly . . .

1. *I feel* suffocated when you call all the time and constantly demand my attention.

2. *I want* you to back off and give me my space. *I also want* you to get other friends and interests to take this pressure off me.

3. *Will you* agree to stop calling every day? Give me two nights a week to myself without trying to make me feel guilty? Get some outside interests?

4. I know you want me to take a long weekend trip with you. I'll do that in one month if you'll back off as I've asked. *Is that a deal?*

5. *If not, I will* stop taking your calls every day and begin to back away from this relationship by spending more time with my friends.

If you're sure your mate won't negotiate with you, you don't always have to offer the "let's make a deal" step. Without that step, you need to simply set a boundary, using the Four Steps to Powerful Communication that we discussed in Chapter 5.

Improving the Emotional Climate

When Peter called Lynn from his cell phone and said, "I'm here to pick up Ian [their son] and I can't find him—where the hell is he?" Lynn said, "Bonsai," the code word for "I don't like the way you're talking to me." Peter quickly realized what he was doing, apologized, and began to speak to her more respectfully. Lynn couldn't believe how little stress there was around the house when Peter no longer had permission to behave like a spoiled child, throwing his tantrums. Peter now realized that being the provider and making big bucks did not entitle him to take his frustrations out on Lynn or the kids.

What Unemotional Men (and Women) Need to Know About Emotions

- It takes more courage to face a problem and resolve it than to hide from it.
- The better you know yourself, the more we can share, and the closer we can become.
- Getting in touch with feelings and wants is a necessary step that leads to finding solutions and taking action.
- Anger not expressed is stored and ends up being taken out on yourself or others.
- Both men and women have insecurities and emotional pain, and both have the strength to work through them.
- For a relationship to grow and deepen, both partners have to continue to grow personally.
- Emotional communication with a man is what turns us on and makes us feel close enough to want to be sexual with them.
- The more you understand your past, the better you can control your own future.
- The more emotionally honest you are, the more authentic you are, and the higher your self-esteem truly is.
- Becoming emotionally involved with someone does not mean you can never leave.

Peter wasn't the only one improving the emotional climate, however. Although Lynn never had nagged like many other women, Peter had always felt her resentment through her coldness. However, with Peter's new improved behavior, Lynn began to trust Peter and warm back up to him. She started feeling stronger and more confident and began to change her opinion about how men really are. With their new agreements in place, both felt freer to be themselves at home—and both felt more loved.

◀ Points to Remember ▶

1. Emotional intimacy requires sharing your feelings toward your mate, openly, honestly, and directly *to* your mate.

2. Anger and confrontation are a part of love.

3. Men have to feel safe with you to share their emotions.

4. Once he opens up, it may be difficult for you to hear what he has to say.

5. Don't share more about yourself than he does.

6. Withdraw when he's unavailable emotionally.

Chapter 7

Handling Sexual Differences

Do you play the victim or controller role in bed? If you play the victim, you may:

- Feel hurt that he won't have sex with you
- Feel turned off to him because you resent the way he treats you
- Blame him or make him feel guilty that you don't have orgasms
- Assume he's no longer attracted to you
- Not know what turns you on
- Be shut down sexually
- When he doesn't have sex with you, you may feel unloved

If you play the controller, you may:

- Pressure him for sex, reminding him that you have needs too
- Get angry when he won't make love your way
- Use sex to manipulate him

- Criticize him about his lack of skill in bed
- Withhold sex to punish him.

Why You Are Attracted to Him and Why It Goes Away

Even though you've enjoyed great sexual passion with your mate, you woke up one day and no longer wanted him to touch you. You stopped getting that rush when he comes home. Kisses go from lingering to quick pecks, usually on the cheek. You often avoid all sexual contact, sometimes without even being aware that's what you're doing. You often look back and think of how attracted you were, and wish you could have kept some of that passion. Most couples don't deal with the slow death of their sexual passion until there is a crisis. And that crisis is often an affair.

From a Suit to Shorts and Half T-Shirt, with His Belly Hanging Out

▶ *Margaret and Donald's Story*

Thirty-three-year-old Margaret and thirty-one-year-old Donald are in a mixed marriage—she's black and he's white—but their racial differences actually cause very few problems for them. The real problem is that over the last couple of years, Margaret has lost interest in having sex with Donald.

Donald is an investment banker who works from home in shorts and a T-shirt and, on weekends he dresses in a half T-shirt with his belly hanging out (he has gained weight) and torn shorts, and sits on the couch drinking beer and watching sports. It was a muscular, attractive, well-kept man in a suit that Margaret fell in love with, but now she no longer remembers what Donald even looks like dressed up. She finds herself working on the computer later and later each night to avoid having sex with him. Donald suspects she's having an affair because she now travels in her new job as a sales representative, and never has sex with him anymore. But Margaret swears she's not cheating, and Donald doesn't have a clue why she's turned off.

Even though Margaret has control in this relationship, both sexually and financially, she never wanted either one, and actually feels victimized because of it. She never wanted to be the primary breadwinner (she makes twice as much money as he does), and she truly wishes she was still attracted to Donald. Margaret needs to let Donald know that she's losing attraction for him, which of course is an extremely touchy issue—one that's very difficult to discuss.

Using the Five Steps to Successful Negotiations, here's what Margaret needs to say:

1. *I feel* less attracted to you because I never get to see you looking good anymore, especially since you don't dress up for work and dress even worse on the weekend.

2. *I want* you to try to look good when you're around me. When we dated, you looked so hot all the time and I was really turned on. Let's dress up and go out once a week, and some nights let's just clean up and have a glass of wine together before we go to bed.

3. *Will you* try to pay more attention to how you look when you're around me?

4. I know you want me to be sexual with you again and I will try to make that happen if you will do what I'm asking. *Is that a deal?*

5. *If not, I'm* going to continue to avoid going to bed with you, and you need to know that I'm gradually losing my attraction for you.

Donald agreed to the deal, but added: "You never even try to come to bed with me at night, so I need you to promise to stop working on the computer every night and go to bed with me at least three or four nights a week. Will you?" She agreed.

Here is Margaret and Donald's deal: He agreed to pay more attention to how he looks when he's with her. She agreed to go to bed with him three or four nights a week. Margaret's old behavior was avoiding. *Her new behavior* is confronting the issue and asking for what she wants. *Donald's new behavior* is trying to look good around his wife so she will be turned on.

Passion Killers: What Turns Women Off?

- When he acts like my parent and gives me advice.
- When he seems disinterested in my life.
- When he has to be with me every minute.
- When he never has time for me.
- When I think he is lying or cheating.
- When he wants sex more than he wants me.
- When he is critical.
- When he acts disrespectfully.
- When he looks at other women.
- When he lets his appearance go.
- When he talks down to me.
- When he doesn't let me be me.
- When he makes others more of a priority than me.
- When I feel fat and ugly and think he sees me that way.
- When he acts wimpy.
- When he does things I consider gross.
- When he doesn't know what to do in bed.
- When he is selfish in bed.
- When I'm not happy with myself.

What You Loved, You Now Hate

We're often attracted to someone initially because of how

different he is from us. We loved many things about him that we considered "masculine." We admired him for putting in long hours at work, helping out a friend, having lots of buddies, working out at the club, spending money on a hot new car. Similarly, he was turned on to many really feminine things about you. He thought it was cute that you spent two hours getting ready for him and he loved it that you wore short skirts and low-cut blouses. He thought it was sweet that you visited your mom every Sunday and listened to your girlfriends' problems. Each of you had a very distinct personality, your own personal friends, special interests, and weird idiosyncrasies.

As the relationship progresses, often the same qualities that attracted you become bones of contention. He works so much that he's never home; the friend he helps just uses him; several of his buddies cheat on their wives; he works out when he should be picking up the kids; and he's still spending money on hot cars that should be spent on the family. When you mention these things, he wonders why you're upset, and says, "You knew who I was when you met me." These issues don't get resolved and your resentment begins to build. And so does his, because he thinks you're trying to change him. And he, of course, has his own resentments toward you because you still take two hours to get ready, and when you leave the house in your sexy outfit, he wants to know who at work you're trying to impress. And he'll never understand what the bond is between you and your mom or girlfriends that keeps you on the phone all the time instead of watching television with him.

Every issue left unresolved cuts a deep crevice into the core of your love for each other—and makes you want to be touched less and less by this man. And sometimes it affects his sexual desire for you as well, although men can usually separate love and sex and still want sex. That in itself often makes you even angrier. "How can you expect me to make love to you after you just talked to me like that!"

You Give Up Your Identities

Maybe you're dressing more conservatively now and have given up those long calls to girlfriends. He may have pulled away from his buddies because you don't like them, and now picks up the kids in that station wagon you talked him into. Not only do you both resent it when you make these changes or sacrifices, but you and your mate become boring. The parts you "gave up" when you sacrificed for your mate have dulled your personalities and now both of you are less interesting to the other. Couples who believe that couples in love "sacrifice" for each other (rather than compromise) end up giving up major parts of their personalities and resenting it.

As I've said before, to keep the sexual attraction in a relationship, couples need to *compromise*, not *sacrifice*. Certainly, a family car is necessary, but if he loves sports cars, how about an older, cheaper one as a second car? Instead of each of you giving up your friends, how about you negotiate how often you see them?

"I'd Rather Punish Him Than Make Love to Him"

▶ *Marilyn and Larry's Story*

When twenty-nine-year-old Marilyn came into my office, she was depressed. Although she knew she had problems with her boyfriend Larry, she thought it was her depression that was causing her low libido. Marilyn had broken up with Larry, but *he* was having trouble letting go, so she continued to see him.

Back when Marilyn and Larry began dating, Larry was still in love with his last girlfriend, which he told Marilyn about, and she opted to stay in the relationship anyway. Larry spent most of his time back then hanging out with his buddies, while Marilyn acted like a victim, waiting for his calls. Lately Larry has been pressuring Marilyn sexually, but she's not turned on. She said, "It's not just about Larry—I've lost all sexual feelings altogether! I have no desire to have sex whatsoever. I admit that I'm confused about Larry. I still see him, but am not interested in doing things with him. Yet I don't want to lose him. He wants to get back together and says he'll do anything. And, of course, sex is always about him, not me."

I asked Marilyn if she had ever told him all the things she's upset about—essentially why she won't take him back. She said she hadn't told him because it would hurt him. I reminded her, "Your coldness hurts him more and doesn't allow the two of you to move on in the relationship. In fact, I think you're enjoying punishing him for the way he used to treat you. That's not helping either one of you." She admitted that she was enjoying having the power and watching Larry squirm, trying to figure out how to win her back. Then she agreed she would tell him why she has been so cold.

Marilyn eventually talked to Larry about most of the issues. A few weeks later, she came in with a smile on her face. Even though all the issues weren't resolved with Larry, she said to me, "The strangest thing has happened. I'm feeling sexual again. And I'm really enjoying it!"

Attraction Based on Dysfunction

Marilyn's original attraction to Larry was based on her need for approval from a man who wouldn't make her a priority—the same thing she felt from her dad. If your attraction was based on dysfunctional roles the two of you played out together, the attraction sometimes dissapates once you clean up the issues between you. However, you will only know if there is true love and passion between you (not just addiction) by resolving the issues causing the dysfunction, and then see if the draw is still there. Sexual problems are often simply just a reflection of what else is going on in the relationship. So, the good news is that often by cleaning up the problems in a relationship, your attraction and desire to make love to him will return even stronger.

125

Everyday Turnoffs

There are many reasons why we lose attraction for our mate. Some go unnoticed because they have to do with our everyday lives. Once you had children, did you become his mom too? Has sex just become routine? Do his habits or lack of cleanliness turn you off? Does he pressure you for sex, so you have sex with him when you don't want to, and then resent him? If any of these points are true with you, they can be worked out by using the Five Steps to Successful Negotiations. Veronica, however, waited until it was too late.

She Gave in Sexually, but Learned to Hate Him

▶ Veronica's Story

Twenty-four-year-old Veronica came into my office and had already decided to leave her husband of three years. Their marriage had been going along pretty well until the night Veronica was raped and almost murdered two years ago. She had accepted a ride home by a man she later learned was a serial rapist and murderer. After being raped and beaten, she pushed open the car door at a stoplight and escaped while her rapist thought she was unconscious in the backseat. She assumes he was driving her to a place to kill and dispose of her as she later learned he had done with the others. This trauma obviously changed Veronica's life. She did not receive therapy at the time, but tried as hard as she knew how to get back to a normal life once her injuries healed and the trial ended (he *was* caught and put in prison).

Veronica's husband seemed helpful and supportive at the time, but soon began to pressure her to have sex with him. She tried to explain to him that sex felt like being raped all over again each time she tried it, and that it would take her some time to heal. He didn't understand, and kept pressuring her, so she eventually gave in. When she came into my office, two years later, she'd been having sex with her husband and resenting it ever since she was raped. At this point, her love for her husband was completely gone. In fact, she hated him.

Many women continue to have sex with their mates when they don't want to, not just women who've been traumatized. This will always cause resentment, and lead to the demise of the relationship.

I helped Veronica see that she had allowed her husband to victimize her sexually, and that she should have said no. She also should have gotten therapy sooner to deal with the rape issues, and insisted that her husband join her in therapy. The first time Veronica's husband pressured her, she should have said:

1. *I feel* pressured and angry at you when you keep trying to have sex with me, after knowing what happened to me and how traumatized I still am. You make me feel like a sex object, just like my attacker did.

2. *I want* you to back off and stop demanding sex. I want you to show me love, caring, and compassion—those things will make me feel closer to you and will eventually make me want to have sex with you again.

3. *Will you* stop treating me like a sex object and stop being demanding? And will you try a softer, warmer, more loving approach with me?

4. I understand that you want to have sex with me, and I'll get some therapy to try to get past these issues so we can have sex again, if you will stop pressuring me and try to be more compassionate. *Is that a deal?*

5. *If not, I will* withdraw from you more each time you pressure me—until I've had enough, and then I'll leave.

Her husband may have replied, "I'm not sure I know how to do what you're asking." Then Veronica could have answered, "If you're not sure you can do it, come to therapy with me or read some books about sexual issues of women who've been raped. Okay? If not . . ." and restated her ultimatum.

Women Want Emotional Intimacy, Men Want Sexual Intimacy

Interestingly, most couples begin their relationship on the same sexual wavelength—they both want more. But that commonly changes because men and women do think differently about sex. Men usually use the words "sex" and "intimacy" interchangeably because they see no difference between the two. Women, however, see a big difference, and require emotional intimacy in order to desire physical intimacy. For most women in a committed relationship, sex without emotional intimacy is a turnoff, and this baffles most men. So it's your job to make him understand that to feel passionate toward him, you need to believe that he loves and cares about you, and you need to respect him and admire him. If we don't feel emotional intimacy, we lose our attraction for him, and no longer desire sex with him. The longer we feel unloved by him, the harder it is to get the passion and "in love" feelings back.

We believe men should know all this, but they don't because most men don't need to have emotional closeness to enjoy sex. Since this is *our* need, it's *our* job to create *our* own justice and make sure *our* need is met. Besides, once led down the path of emotional intimacy connected to sex, most men eventually prefer emotional closeness with sex—even though they seldom find it necessary. Using the Five Steps to Successful Negotiations, you need to tell him:

1. *I feel* insulted when you expect me to just jump in bed and have sex with you when we haven't had any time to talk or share or be romantic.

2. *I want* some quality time with you each and every time you want to be sexual with me. Why don't we get ready for bed a half hour earlier on those nights, turn off the TV, get in bed, and talk and cuddle to get me in the mood?

3. *Will you* do that? I'm also open to any romantic or "quality time" ideas you may have.

4. I'll be more eager to have sex with you if you'll give me the emotional part I need from you. *Is it a deal?*
5. *If not, I won't* have sex with you on those nights I feel you haven't been warm and loving.

The deal: He gets sex more often and you get more communication and romance.

When the Sexual Power is Out of Balance

Who has the sexual power in your relationship? In reality, the person who wants sex the least actually has the sexual power in the relationship because that person controls the frequency. The imbalance of power in the relationship often shows up with one person controlling the frequency of sex, and the other one playing victim to it. Ironically, when it comes to sexual power, the sexual controller (the person who wants sex the least) doesn't feel powerful when pressured to have sex, and instead feels like a victim for having to say, "no" again and again. This is just another lose/lose situation.

Pleasing Him Sexually Does Not Empower You

There are women who believe that sexual power is the ability to turn a man on to such a degree that he can't bear to stay away from her. But, in the big picture, simply being able to keep a man desiring sex with you doesn't empower you—unless sex is truly all you want. Being too sexually available actually puts a woman in the victim role because, although she is able to get her sexual needs met easily, her emotional ones usually are not.

Remember that men separate love and sex, so pleasing a man sexually doesn't make him love you—it only makes him want to have sex with you again. Since women want emotional intimacy and men want sexual intimacy, women have to use their sexual power to gain emotional intimacy by withholding sex until a man is emotionally invested in them. When women do not demand the trade-off in advance, they never end up getting it.

"My Exes Never Go Away"

▶ Cynthia's Story

Cynthia, who is twenty-seven, attractive, single, and has plenty of money, is a classic "giver." When Cynthia meets a man she likes, she calls him, spends money on him, and goes home with him to give him the sexual experience of his life. She prides herself in being able to give the "best blow job in town." Old boyfriends and ex-lovers never break up with her completely—they always stay in touch with her and often show up unexpectedly for a late-night "booty call." Cynthia's flattered that they all want her in bed and denies to herself that she is being used sexually.

Cynthia wants a long-term relationship with a man and doesn't understand why men never stay with her. I explained to Cynthia that men need a challenge and don't value or respect anything that comes too easily. To have a man hang in for a long-term relationship, she needs to withhold sex until the man has gotten to know her and has invested his time, emotions, and money in her. When a man can have sex with a woman without any commitment or involvement, he puts that woman in the "throwaway" category instead of the long-term "keeper" one.

Cynthia balked at this concept and called it game playing—something she doesn't believe in doing. I told her I understood—*it shouldn't* work that way, but the reality is that it does. Women learned to withhold sex as a power play years ago. Our mothers taught us, "Why would he buy the cow when the milk is free?" Mom wasn't all wrong. With feminism came more sexual freedom and enjoyment for women—and if sex was all we wanted, that concept would work. However, feminism didn't change the sexual dynamic between men and women—Men want it, and women have it. Women want long-term love and romance. And men will usually only trade commitment to get the sex.

What to Do When He's Turned Off

Remember Britney and Kyle from Chapter 1? After seven years together, Kyle was withdrawing from her, even sexually. Here's how Britney dealt with his lack of sexual interest.

She Wants It, He Doesn't

▶ *Britney and Kyle's Story*

Kyle would often tell Britney, "I'm not spending the night because I have to get up early." Then on Saturday mornings when he could sleep in, he'd say, "I have a lot on my mind," as his excuse for not having sex.

Britney, like most women, worried that Kyle had lost his attraction to her. She, at first, whined, "Don't you find me attractive anymore?" He assured her that he did. "What's wrong then?" she asked. "I'm just tired a lot and have a lower sex drive than you," he'd reply. What Britney had to say:

- *I feel* frustrated and unloved when you don't want to make love to me. Having sex once every three months is not just a lower sex drive. It's not normal.
- *I want* you to go to the doctor and find out if something is wrong and get Viagra if that's the answer. I don't want you to spend the night with me when you know we're not going to have sex, and I want you to open your mind to allowing me to try to turn you on, even when you're tired.
- *Will you* do what I've asked?

Kyle replied:

- *I'll* go to the doctor and check into Viagra, although I don't think anything is wrong. But I don't want you to try to turn me on when I'm tired, because it just makes me feel more pressured.

131

I will agree not to spend the night when I'm not feeling sexual. But you have to promise not to get angry when I do that.

Britney's reply:

- Okay, as long as that's not every night. But I also need to tell you that *if you don't* deal with this sexual issue by June (two months from now), I will start dating other people because I won't stay in a long-term committed relationship without sex!

She gave Kyle an ultimatum and tried to set up "compensation" to motivate him to change.

This is Britney and Kyle's deal: Kyle will go to the doctor and see if there's a physical problem, and possibly get Viagra. He also won't spend the night when he doesn't feel sexual. Britney won't get angry when he doesn't spend the night, and if their sex life doesn't improve in the next two months, she'll date others. Britney now needs to assume that the deal will work, and should back off, not constantly bringing up the issue. *Britney's old behavior* was to nag Kyle and take it personally. *Her new behavior* is to set boundaries and follow through.

What to Do When You Don't Feel Sexual

As we discussed in Chapter 3, Rosalind confronted Rod about doing housework, and he's now helping. She no longer resents him, and isn't as exhausted as she was. But she's still not turned on, so she's decided to work on her own sexual issues.

"I'm Just Not a Sexual Person"
▶ *Rosalind and Rod's Story*

Rosalind says she's never been much of a sexual person. She was a nerd in high school, always focused on grades, and never experimented with makeup and clothes like the other girls. In college, she dated infrequently, remained a virgin until she was twenty-seven, and has had only one other sexual experience with someone besides Rod. She and Rod were quite sexual early in their relationship, but when sex began to taper off, that was okay with her—especially since she already resented him about the housework by then.

Rosalind realized that her role as "mom" to her daughter and her husband had taken away all the sexual feelings, so she needed to get past seeing herself as "mom." We talked about how the way she dresses covers up her sexuality and she agreed to experiment a little with sexier clothes. Rod always wanted her to grow her hair long and she thought she might try that, too. She decided to talk to Rod about having a "dress-up date" once a week, when she could try dressing sexy for him. But most important, Rosalind realized that she doesn't really know what turns her on, so she agreed to give some thought to that as well. Though she was somewhat embarrassed, we talked next about masturbation, sex toys, and learning to take control of her own orgasms.

How to Become Sexual Again

1. Experiment with your own sexuality. What turns you on? What used to? Romantic novels, sexy movies, candlelit bubble baths?
2. Do whatever is necessary to stop feeling like just a "mom."
3. If you are too exhausted, ask him to help with something that will free your time and energy for sex.
4. Clean up your own personal sexual baggage.
5. Tell him that pressuring you only makes the situation worse.

What to Do When He Pressures for Sex

Giving in or constantly saying "no" are not your only options to his sexual pressure. You need to clue him in to what you need from him.

"It's Your Fault I Use Porn"

▶ *Kristi and Gavin's Story*

Like many men, Gavin is pressuring and controlling when it comes to sex, while Kristi plays the victim by not setting clear boundaries with Gavin.

Gavin says that Kristi never cared much for sex, even when they were first married. Since they often don't have sex for months, Gavin turned to masturbating while he watches porn. When Kristi caught him masturbating the other night, she told him he was disgusting, and Gavin suggested he wouldn't have to masturbate if they had sex more often. He tried to get her to watch porn with him, but she refused because it grosses her out and makes her want to never have sex again. She knows she was brought up very prudishly, but Gavin's sexual behavior certainly doesn't increase her desire. In fact, it's just one more way she thinks Gavin tries to control her. "Maybe if he were more loving and affectionate with me, I'd be more interested."

Kristi needs to change her behavior by using the Five Steps to Successful Negotiations to clearly tell Gavin:

- *I feel* pressured by you for sex and that turns me off. I also feel disgusted by the raw sex in the porn you watch. I already feel like I'm just a sex object to you and that makes me feel even worse.
- *I want* you to stop pressuring me, and instead show me love and romance. *I want* emotional sharing and talking with you.
- *Will you* give me that? *Will you* be warm and loving with me when you want sex? *Will you* spend time talking to me and sharing with me before you try to have sex with me?
- I'll start having sex with you again if you'll stop all the porn and stop pressuring me for sex. *Is that a deal?*

Gavin replies:

- Sure, I can do that, but I want you to be warmer with me and for you to be the aggressor sometimes. But I know I'll always want to have sex more than you. And when you don't want to have sex with me, it's okay and I'll stop pressuring you as long as you stop getting upset when I masturbate. I won't pressure you to watch the porn or masturbate in front of you, but I plan to continue it and don't want to make it a big secret where I pretend I don't do it either. Okay?

Kristi replies:

- I'm not okay with the porn, but can tolerate the masturbation, as long as it's not in front of me and that when I say no to sex, you don't get mad or pout, or blame me because you have to masturbate.

Gavin replies:

- I'll try to stop the porn, if that will make you feel less like a sex object, as long as I don't have to pretend I don't masturbate.

This is Gavin and Kristi's deal: Gavin will try to be more loving and romantic, and will respect Kristi's no's. Kristi will understand that when she says no (and probably at some other times as well), Gavin will masturbate and she isn't allowed to make him feel bad about it. *Kristi's old behavior* was to avoid the issues or feel victimized by Gavin because he pressured her and made her feel like a sex object. *Kristi's new behavior* is to clearly tell him how she feels and what she wants, and what she'll do if she doesn't get it. *Gavin's new behavior* is to be more warm and loving, stop blaming, stop pressuring Kristi, stop watching porn, and to masturbate in private.

But Kristi hadn't done the final step:

- *If you don't* behave in a loving, respectful way with me sexually, I not only won't have sex with you, but I'll also go sleep in the guest bedroom (the consequence).

Gavin gave his own ultimatum:

- Okay, but if I've been loving and respectful with you, and you still say no—and then you get mad that I masturbate, I'll sleep in the guest bedroom myself.

What to Do When the Sex Is Good and He's Bad

When sex is really good, some women often mistake the great sex for love. When women can't separate love and sex, it puts them in a vulnerable position.

I'll Sleep with You—and Whoever Else I Want
▶ *Jill and Glen's Story*

Jill, a gorgeous, blonde, thirty-four-year-old, successful realtor who owns her own house, has been dating Glen for three years. Sex was fabulous with him from the very beginning, and it still is—which is why Jill won't leave. The only problem is that Jill isn't the only person Glen is having sex with.

About six months into the relationship, Jill found a note from another woman, laying on Glen's nightstand, thanking him for the great sex. She confronted him about cheating on her, and he said, "I never told you I wasn't sleeping with other women. I care about you Jill, but I will always have sex with other women. I've always had more than one sex partner, and always will."

Jill has been putting up with Glen's sleeping around ever since. When things seem to be going well, Jill pretends that Glen isn't really having sex with anyone else, hoping that her fantasy is true, but knowing it probably isn't. Then later, when she finds some proof that he's sleeping around again, she confronts him, and he reminds her that he never agreed to be monogamous.

Jill needs to set and hold a boundary with Glen regarding her need for monogamy, such as:

- *I feel* hurt and humiliated that you say you love me, but refuse to stop having sex with other women.
- *I want* a commitment from you about our future together that includes monogamy.
- Since I know you won't give it to me, *I will* stop seeing you, even as a friend [that's how he has pulled her back in the past] until I've moved on and fallen in love with somebody else.

Jill's old behavior was to act like a victim and allow bad treatment because part of her thought she deserved it. *Her new behavior* is to set a boundary and keep it, knowing that she deserves better. Jill is hoping that if she holds her boundary, Glen will realize that to have her in his life, he has to compromise, and that he'll come back into her life and give her what she wants. But if he doesn't, so be it. Her staying with him and letting him victimize her (and lose more and more respect for her) is no longer an option.

What to Do When He Wants Kinky Sex

Sexual experimentation is fine as long as both partners agree. When one partner is turned off, boundaries need to be established.

"I May Have Done It Then, but I'm Not Doing It Now"

▶ *Charlotte and George's Story*

Charlotte and her husband, George, were wild when they started dating. Both used drugs recreationally and at times brought other women into their bed. Back then, Charlotte enjoyed the sexual experimentation. However, many years and two children later, Charlotte has no desire for other sexual partners—and certainly not other women—but George still does. He says that their sex life has gotten boring and wants Charlotte to agree to spice it up by taking Ecstasy and having one of their female friends join them in a ménage à trois like they used to do. He reminds her that she sure used to like it. She tells him no and he lets it go for a while, only to bring it up again a few months later. What Charlotte needs to say to George is:

- *I feel* angry and put off when you try to push me into doing something I've told you I don't want to do!
- *I want* you to back off on this issue and never bring it up again.
- *Will you* stop pressuring me to do things sexually that I don't want to do?
- I know you want more sexual experimentation from me, and I will agree to that as long as it's nothing I consider over the line. Here are the things I consider over the line [she tells him all of them]. I don't want you to bring those topics up again, but we can look at other ways to spice up our sex life. *Is that a deal?*
- *If not, I will* pull away and not have sex with you for one week each time you bring that topic up.

What to Do When He Doesn't Know How to Turn You On

When a man doesn't know how to turn you on in bed, he needs to gain that knowledge from you.

Show Him, Then Tell Him

▶ *Jennifer and Matt's Story*

My client Jennifer has been on antidepressants for the last four years of her eight-year marriage to Matt. During that time, their sex life went straight downhill. However, she didn't really care since her medication negatively affected her sex drive anyway. After four months in therapy, her depression was subsiding, so she decided to go off the medication. It wasn't long before her sex drive came back. There was only one problem—she remembered that Matt wasn't really that good at pleasing her in bed. He was a selfish lover.

I told Jennifer that this is one of the few areas in which I believe it's okay not to be direct at first, since you don't want to be critical of him or embarrass him. You might move his hands to where you want them, saying, "I like it when you do that." I suggested she might also discuss how a man touches a woman in a movie or porno, asking, "Could we try that?" I suggested that she herself might also buy a sex toy as a gag gift and then suggest they actually try it. If he doesn't get the hint she needs a more direct, confrontational approach:

- *I feel* frustrated sexually when we have sex and you don't pay attention to what I need or want.
- *I want* you to take time touching me more, and learning what turns me on.
- *Will you* spend at least ten to fifteen minutes in foreplay with me as I show you what I need, before you try to get inside me?
- *If not, I will* stop you and say, "I'm not ready yet," to remind you that we made this deal. If you still don't try to turn me on I'll stop having sex with you right then.

Other Sexual Issues That Might Need to Be Negotiated

Here are three more scenarios that you might run into and my suggestions on how to handle them.

When He Likes Sex in the Morning and You Like It at Night

Maybe he feels less sexual at night because he eats big meals late at night. Maybe you feel less sexual in the mornings because of bad breath. Possible compromise: Try having dinner earlier and having sex in the evenings during the week, and/or having sex in the mornings on the weekend and keeping breath mints by the bed or both of you brushing your teeth first.

When You Don't Have Sex Because You Don't Want to Lock the Toddlers out of the Bedroom

Possible compromise: Make a deal with the children where they get a reward (candy or a toy) if they can stay in their room until the hands on the clock are "here and here." Close the door and teach them that they have to knock before coming in. But even if they knock, they lose the reward.

When He Is Turned Off to Sex Because He Was Sexually Abused as a Child

(Note: This is more often a problem for women than men.) You need to be compassionate and considerate of his feelings if he's been abused. However, sex is a normal part of a romantic relationship, so you need to let him know that the problem has to be fixed. Tell him the following.

- *I feel* frustrated that you don't try to do something about your sexual problem.
- *I want* you to see a therapist, or get books on the subject, or confront your abuser, or whatever you need to do to resolve this.
- *Will you* do one of these things? Which one?
- *If not,* you need to know that *I will* not continue to stay in a sexless relationship indefinitely. If I don't see some progress in the next two months, I'm going to look at other options.

How to Handle Your Sexual Differences

1. Communicate and validate that there is a difference in what you both want, and that it is okay (no right and wrong).
2. Show him how to sexually give you what you want, and ask him what he wants.
3. Each listen carefully to what the other wants.
4. Check in with yourself to see if there's anything you would trade off that would make you want to give him what he wants, and vice versa.
5. Don't do anything sexually that you don't want to do, and don't ask him to either.
6. Whatever agreement you make, the sex has to be enjoyable for both of you to keep negotiating.
7. Pull away from him when he pressures you for sex, and tell him why.
8. Don't chase him when he pulls away sexually.
9. Keep looking for win/win solutions for every issue. If one isn't possible, do it one person's way and let him (or her) know he owes you a marker.
10. Make trade-offs, such as, I'll trade you more sex for more quality time from you.

A Healthy Sexual Relationship

A healthy sexual relationship involves much more than sex. It requires an equal balance of power and mutual respect. It provides an atmosphere where both partners' needs are met and respected, and both needs are satisfied. A healthy sexual relationship also often requires compromises.

A healthy sexual relationship looks different as it matures and grows. Sometimes touching and cuddling becomes more important to a couple than intercourse. Maybe talking about your love and gazing into each other's eyes becomes 50 percent of the sex act for you and your mate. Whatever you and your mate deem to be a good sex life is just that.

It's important that the two of you do continue to have sexual intercourse, however, because this is what makes your relationship different from just a friendship. If and when the sexual bond is broken, others can enter and break up your partnership. Sex is the glue that holds the bond together between two lovers.

◀ Points to Remember ▶

1. Don't agree to sex acts that you will resent.

2. Sex between you and your mate changes and matures as you grow together.

3. Giving more than you get sexually makes a man lose respect for you.

4. Sexual problems are often a reflection of other problems in the relationship.

5. As long as no one is harmed, whether a certain sexual act is appropriate or not is just between the two of you.

Chapter 8

Resolving Work and Money Resentments

Do you play the victim or controller role financially? If you play the victim, you may:

- Beg him for money or complain that there's never enough.
- Wish you had a better job, but do nothing about it.
- Let your mate make most of the financial decisions and resent him because he does.

If you play the controller, you may:

- Get angry when your mate spends money.
- Withhold money or financial information from your mate.
- Criticize your mate about his job or low income.
- Want more time from your mate, but also want him to continue making the same amount of money.

Couples Often Have Major Resentments Around Money and Work

When both mates work, women usually feel as if they have two jobs—one at home and one at work. When the man is the sole provider, he usually resents his wife's free time. When it comes to spending money, couples often fight about who makes it, who spends it, who spends more, and what it's spent on. With work issues, couples also fight about whose schedule can be disrupted, whether both work or not, disrespect for a mate's job, number of hours worked versus family time, and salary differences.

Lynn Didn't Know She'd Given Up Her Power until Peter Said, "Get in the Boat and Pick Up an Oar!"

▶ *Lynn and Peter's Story*

When Peter and Lynn (from Chapter 6) first met, she was a graduate student in law, and a self-proclaimed career woman, which was part of Peter's attraction to her then. In the first five years of their marriage, Lynn worked at several law firms, quitting each job in less than one year, and never taking, much less passing, the bar exam. Peter's career in technology, however, advanced rapidly. Once their children were born, Lynn didn't want to go back to work, and Peter agreed that Lynn could wait to go back to work until the kids were both in school. But it never happened. Now, fifteen years later, Peter realizes that he enabled Lynn's secret life (in charities and the health club) by not insisting she go back to work. He resents that he's financed her as she's flirted with other men.

Peter told her, "I feel like we had a deal and you didn't keep it. When I married you, you were a strong, independent woman who swore you would stay that way—and then you never went back to work. I feel like we're in a rowboat and I'm paddling as fast as I can and you're just laying in the back with your sunglasses and big hat going along for the ride. It's not fair! I want you to get in the boat with me, pick up an oar, and help me paddle! I'm tired of being the cash machine. I want you to be my partner and help provide for the family."

Lynn asked, "Isn't there some other way I can help besides getting a job?" Peter said, "We tried that, and that's how you had time to develop your secret world of flirting. If you were busy, it would help your self-esteem and give you a sense of power you don't have now. I need you to get a job. And money isn't the issue, it's your financial participation that I need!" She reluctantly agreed to get a part-time job. But I reminded both of them that since Lynn will be working, she gets to hand over some of the household and childcare duties to Peter. Peter said, "No problem. I look forward to it."

After only a couple of weeks working part-time as a legal assistant, Lynn seemed resentful at me, telling me that her life had gotten worse since therapy, not better. I reminded Lynn that she has to make trade-offs if she wants Peter to be less resentful and volatile, more loving, and more respectful; she has to give him what he wants—financial participation. To get changes from him, she has to make changes herself.

Six weeks after Lynn went back to work, she admitted that everything had gotten much better. Peter was treating her more respectfully, she was actually enjoying her new job and the new friends she was making, and she was feeling a sense of accomplishment she hadn't felt in a long time.

What Do We Want from Him?

We women are often guilty of wanting to have our cake and eat it too. We admire men who work hard and make good money until it seems that's all they do. We want them to make the money, yet have lots of time for us *and* feel no resentment toward us when we want to spend their money. When men accuse us of wanting it both ways, they're right. The truth is, men usually have deep unspoken resentment toward women on the issue of supporting the family, similar to the resentment women feel about doing all the household chores—because ultimately the responsibility is assumed to be theirs.

Once we marry our man, we want more of his time, never thinking that could mean a decrease in income. Seldom will a successful man ever volunteer to cut back on work, especially if you made it clear to him in the past how much the lifestyle he creates means to you. So if you want to negotiate for more of his time, you have to be prepared to make a trade-off like cutting back on spending or working more hours yourself to make up the difference. On the other hand, maybe he has problems with your work schedule. It doesn't matter whether it's you or him, whoever puts in too many hours at work will need the other to negotiate trade-offs to be able to give more time to their mate.

"We're Too Busy for the Relationship"

▶ Deanna and Daryl's Story

Deanna and Daryl are both too busy. Daryl is a workaholic and Deanna is overbooked with school, her family, and friends. When Daryl complains about how busy Deanna is, she says, "Why do you care, you're never around anyway!" Daryl and Deanna have been married just three years, and both have agreed to postpone starting a family for about another five years, until Daryl gets his small accounting firm off the ground and Deanna completes an advanced degree in computer science. Between the demands of his job and her studies, they're often lucky to both be home together on weeknights before eight.

What's interesting about Deanna and Daryl is that they've already negotiated some very important matters. They both want a secure future, and they're both willing to make sacrifices—school, work, postponing parenthood—to make their dreams come true. So far, so good. But even while they have agreed to the schedule they have now, they are each beginning to miss the other, but both are reluctant to express that. Deanna worries that if she tells Daryl how she feels, he may ask her to consider going to school only part-time, and thus pushing back the baby date several more years. Daryl worries that if he tells Deanna how he feels, she will respond by asking him to cut his hours, something he believes would be detrimental to his business in the long run.

Both need to share how they're feeling and find a way to have at least one evening a week together with no interruptions. (Find out how they resolved this issue in Chapter 10.)

She Wants More Time from Him, but Not Less Money
▶ *Gretchen and Art's Story*

Gretchen (of Gretchen and Art in Chapter 5) was upset with Art about his lack of participation with family. She felt that the burden of the home and family was all on her because Art was such a workaholic. Besides putting in his forty hours a week as an engineer, Art brought work home every night and hid out in his home office working on the computer. Gretchen felt he was doing more than he had to—that he let his boss push him around. "Stand up to them!" she kept telling him, "I need your help at home, and your kids need you!" Although she felt victimized, she was acting controlling. In many ways, she was a controlling victim. I asked Gretchen to clearly state what she wanted from Art, and she told him:

- *I feel* frustrated when you come home and go straight into your office to continue working because your boss is asking you for overtime.
- *I want* you to spend time with the boys and me when you get home from work. I also want you to help more with the chores so I can have time to get my antique business off the ground.

- *Will you* confront your boss about the overtime and start spending more time with the family?
- *If not, I will* get sitters and go out with my friends more like I have before, and I know you hate that.

Art was working with me in therapy on his passivity and the victim role he knows he plays with everyone, including Gretchen. He agreed with Gretchen that he should take a stronger stand with his boss, but not just to be more available to the family, but also because he was incredibly stressed and never had time for himself. He admitted that he was getting more and more resentful of Gretchen's free time. Gretchen was taking classes, having lunch with friends, and going rock climbing one to two times a week. He admitted that she was the primary one raising their two boys and taking care of the house, of course. But he was jealous that she is able to find free time—and he never does! But he realized that Gretchen really wasn't the one holding him back—he was. Art agreed to back off on work but only if he could start taking time for himself as well.

Art finally stood up to his boss, and stopped the overtime, gaining more free time for himself and his family. He began standing up to Gretchen as well. Shortly after that, his company made some job and salary cuts, and Art's salary was cut back by 25 percent. Since they managed their money well, Art wasn't overly concerned, and so he stuck to his plan. He scheduled a motorcycle trip with his buddy, began picking the kids up from school, and agreed to help with some of the household chores—especially since Gretchen did need time to try to get her business off the ground. It looked as though Art and Gretchen had struck a great deal—until one month later when the revised paycheck appeared. When the difference in Art's salary showed up on the paycheck, Gretchen was very upset and began to nag and pressure Art again, this time about asking the boss for a raise. "I'm lucky to have a job—this is not the time to ask for a raise," he told her. He also said, "I feel like I can never win no matter what I do."

I confronted Gretchen, "He's helping with the housework, now has more time for the family, is enjoying free time for himself, and is no longer resenting you. Why isn't that good enough? And by the way, what trade-off are you making besides allowing him one night a week out with his friends when you already have one or two nights out with yours? What are you giving back in this deal? If you feel the family needs more income, it needs to come from your business now, or you need to get a job." Art had taken a $40,000 pay cut, and Gretchen knew it wasn't possible for her to make up the difference from her new business. Even Art agreed with her and said he didn't want her to feel pressured to bring in income right now.

"Then," I said to Gretchen, "Art has kept his part of the deal. You must either make more money yourself or back off from pressuring Art about the money and learn to live within the new salary range. Can you do that?" She reluctantly agreed. "And Art, you have to promise not to resent Gretchen for not making up the difference in income yet." He agreed. We put it in writing, agreeing that either one could ask that the deal be renegotiated at any time.

Gretchen has a right to bring up the fact that she is upset about the family having less income, and she and Art could look for a solution that would involve further negotiations and trade-offs on both parts. However, Gretchen does not have the right to pressure or intimidate Art into solving their financial problems after she's the one who asked him to back off from work. She can, however, state how she feels, what she wants, and try to work out a new deal (involving trade-offs) at any time.

Gretchen's old behaviors were controlling, nagging, and pressuring. *Her new behaviors* are understanding and negotiating trade-offs. *Art's new behaviors* are standing up for himself, working less, helping with chores and childcare, and taking time for himself.

It's Not Really His Fault (or Yours) That the "Deal" Is Bad

In out-of-balance relationships, both men and women feel as if they're victims. Lynn felt that Peter didn't understand her role and contribution to the family. Peter felt that Lynn had no clue how hard he worked to bring in the big bucks—especially with the economy slowing down and their investments declining. Each felt unappreciated and resentful. However, by discussing the situation, and putting their resentments out on the table, they could state what they wanted and create a new agreement so that good feelings could come back. If couples can realize that neither they nor their mates are bad, but the agreement between them is, they can enter into negotiations with solutions as the focus.

Mistakes Couples Make

In our desire to make things work we sometimes walk into a deal without really thinking about all the components that make a good deal successful. We might not clarify the terms of the agreement, or we might not get the other person to actually agree to participate, even though we assume he will. We might give up too much or fail to set a time by which something needs to happen. And finally, we often don't realize that a deal can always be changed if both sides agree to renegotiate a new one.

Not Clarifying "Understood" Deals

Most couples make assumptions about work and money without ever discussing the arrangement with each other. Peter resented Lynn for not working when Lynn assumed she would not have to work once they had children. Each had different expectations, yet they never really discussed them. Gretchen resented Art's lack of participation with her and the family, while Art felt that his job as a provider was enough. Each person's feelings are valid, but the deal isn't valid when it's not clarified and both parties haven't agreed to the terms.

Enabling Your Mate Not to Have to Participate

We've all heard this story: A woman puts her husband through medical school and he leaves her once he graduates. Helping a mate financially sounds like a noble and supportive thing to do—and it can be—but more often than not, it teaches your mate that he will never have to participate regularly on an equal basis. It throws the relationship out of balance, creating resentment on both sides. If your mate at any time wants a deal where he won't have to work or will produce less money, be sure you negotiate a good deal for yourself by agreeing to only a certain length of time, and be sure and ask for something back—anything.

What to Do When He Gambles the Money Away

▶ *Katherine and Graeme's Story*

When Graeme married Katherine fifteen years ago, she knew he had been a gambler most of his life. She confronted him about the problem and he promised he would never let his gambling habit interfere with their lives, but he never promised to quit gambling altogether. For the first twelve years or so, he managed to limit his wagers to what he earned from a weekend stint—playing guitar in a wedding band. Katherine never liked the fact that he was still gambling, but as long as it didn't affect the household finances or their ability to meet their expenses, she felt there was nothing she could say. In the past three years, however, Katherine has caught Graeme using his ATM card to take $20, $40, even $100 a week out of their checking account that he couldn't account for. She gave him an ultimatum: "Stop the gambling or get out." Graeme believes she's being unfair because she knew he was a gambler when she met him. Did she really think he'd change?

Katherine has had enough and it's easy to see why she feels the way she does, but she's also to blame for the situation. What smart person mixes her money with a known gambler's? Her ultimatum is too strong for the situation, because she's a part of his problem. They may have had a deal for the last twelve years, but there were no consequences built into the deal. People don't change their bad behaviors when they never have to face consequences. Before abandoning her marriage, Katherine needs to work out a deal that includes consequences that match the crime. She could say (and should have said earlier), "Any time you take out unexplained money from our joint account, you owe me a week's worth of cleaning the house." Right now, however, Katherine wants changes that are more drastic than that.

Using the Five Steps to Successful Negotiations, here's what Katherine can say:

- *I feel* angry and distrustful of you because you've used household money for your gambling habit when you promised you wouldn't. You know I hate the gambling anyway, but I thought that at least we had a deal about you spending your own money on it.
- *I want* you to never spend household money on your gambling habit again. To be sure you don't, I want to change the way we handle our bank accounts.
- *Will you* agree to take your name off as a signer on the joint account and put it all in my name until you get your gambling under control?
- I know you haven't agreed to stop gambling, so I need assurance you will never blow the family money on gambling again. Let me have the control of the family account, but let's each open separate personal accounts where we deposit a certain amount of spending money for each of us

each month. How each of us spends our personal money is our own business. Then, if you want to gamble away the money you've have set aside for your personal entertainment, that's up to you. *Is that a deal?*

- *If not, I will* stop putting my money in the household account and just pay my part of the bills out of an account that is only in my name.

Katherine's old behavior was to enable Graeme and then be angry at him. *Her new behavior* is to set a boundary that will no longer allow his bad behavior to affect her.

Merging Unequal Assets

An old realtor boyfriend once said to me, "I make large chunks of money several times a year, and you make smaller amounts on a daily basis. Why don't we put our money together and help each other out? Let's open a joint bank account." My reply was, "Okay, as soon as you're able to put one of those large chunks of money into my account, let me know and we'll start doing that." Of course I never heard another word about it.

Alan and I don't fight about money because we keep our money separate, each pay our own bills, and split all joint bills equally. Not all couples can do this of course, because not all couples make equal income as we do. However, all couples can lessen their fights about money by setting up better plans and deals than the one that they have now.

Somehow, we seem to believe that we're supposed to join our money with the men we love and they with us, or we don't really love each other enough. Joining money together gives couples the right to start complaining about and restricting their mate's spending, immediately putting one or both mates into a parental (controlling) position in regard to money issues.

Their Equality Soon Unraveled

▶ *Misty and Gordon's Story*

Misty and Gordon had serious resentments about work and finances by the time the two of them came into my office. They had met at a sales conference and were immediately attracted to and respectful of one another. Both had high profile, high salary jobs. As the relationship progressed, they decided that they would marry and Misty would quit her job in California and move to Denver with Gordon because his two daughters lived there with their mother.

When Misty got to Denver, she was unable to find a job making anywhere near the amount of money she made before, and finally just took a lower paying job. Everything seemed fine at first, until Gordon started making sarcastic comments to her about her not carrying her weight financially. "But I do," Misty would reply. "I put my entire paycheck in the joint account, and it gets gobbled up when you pay the bills. I barely keep enough for my lunches. Yet you're on the road traveling and throwing money around all the time." Misty was so angry, she opened up her own bank account and began putting less and less of her check into the joint account (passive-aggressive behavior). And the more Gordon complained, the more she began to label him a cheap SOB. "If you had any class, you'd want to support me totally!" she kept reminding him.

"What happened to the independent, hotshot career woman I thought I married?" Gordon replied. "How come I'm paying all the rent and household expenses?" Gordon began to wonder if she would ever carry her half financially again, and was building deep resentment toward her because she wasn't. Misty felt herself losing power and she herself began to wonder what happened to the hotshot career woman she was. It wasn't fair. After all, she had given up her career with the big money to be with Gordon. Didn't he understand that? Every time she put her paycheck in the joint account, she resented him. When she didn't deposit her check, he resented her. She saw no way to win.

I explained to Misty that she should have made a clear deal with

Gordon when she gave up her job, letting him know that he would be expected to carry more of the weight financially for a while. She thought he should "know" that. She thought that was "understood," but obviously, it wasn't.

Using the Five Steps to Successful Negotiations, I helped Misty create her own justice, and get her power back with Gordon:

- *I feel* ripped-off and angry that you expect me to pay for half of the expenses when you're the one who asked me to quit my high-paying job and move here so you could be close to your children.
- *I want* some leeway, as well as financial compensation for being the one who sacrificed my career, family, friends, and home for this marriage.
- *Will you* back off of your expectations of me financially until I'm able to find a better job—and stop the sarcastic comments?
- Each month I want you to put in two-thirds of the money for the household expenses, and I'll put in a guaranteed amount equaling approximately one-third—for the next year or so. The difference will be my compensation for the sacrifices I made for this marriage. We get to spend the rest of our money on ourselves in whatever way we choose. In the meantime, I'll be looking for a better job with the plan of paying my half in a year or so. But you have to agree to stop making nasty comments about how much I do or don't contribute. *Is that a deal?*
- *If not, I'll* continue to keep my money and give you what I can. And every time you make a nasty comment about the money, I'll give you ten dollars less than I had planned.

Misty's old behavior was passive-aggressive behavior (she cooperated, but rebelled) which came from feeling cheated, unappreciated, and victimized by Gordon. *Misty's new behavior* is asking for the appreciation she felt she deserved in the form of a financial trade-off.

Gordon's new behavior is to stop the sarcastic comments and pay two-thirds of the expenses without resentment, realizing that Misty does deserve some compensation for moving to Denver for him.

Not Setting Timelines on Temporary Deals

When Lynn got pregnant years ago and decided to quit work, Peter assumed it was only temporary. Now, fifteen years later, he's very resentful. But he never said, "I assume you'll go back to work when the last child is in school—is that what you're thinking, Lynn?" If she had agreed, he could have gone back to her and said, "I thought we had a deal."

Whether it's a woman quitting work to stay home with the children, or a man quitting to go back to school or start his own business, expectations about how long your partner will not be contributing financially must be discussed. If you don't discuss the length of time, your mate secretly believes it's forever. That's what Ian must have thought.

When He Stops Working
▶ *Lana and Ian's Story*

Three years ago, shortly after they moved in together, Lana and Ian decided it was too much trouble to keep separate checking accounts so they merged their assets. From the start, it was uncomfortable for Lana, because she grew up in a very frugal home and never felt comfortable with the way Ian "threw money around." Whenever she raised the issue with Ian in the past, he replied, "I'm working hard enough. I should be able to spend at least some of what I make as I see fit. As long as the expenses are covered, it's none of your business." Lana could barely tolerate that when Ian was working, but then he lost his job over a year ago and he seems less inclined to find a new job every day. In the meantime, his spending hasn't slowed.

Lana's friends keep telling her that Ian is using her, but she doesn't see it that way. After all, when two people are in love, they help each other out. She would expect Ian to do the same for her if she lost her job. But she admits her patience is wearing thin and she's starting to wonder if she's being too easy on him—especially when he takes her credit card and goes to the mall while she's hard at work.

Lana is definitely enabling Ian and needs to stop, but her fatal mistake was not letting Ian know how long she would cover expenses while he's unemployed. However, it's never too late to set a boundary. Lana has to stop giving Ian money by weaning him off her assistance and letting him know that he will soon be required to contribute.

Using the Five Steps to Successful Negotiations, Lana told Ian:

- *I feel* angry that you're living off me and spending my money and don't seem to be trying to get a job.
- *I want* you to stop using my credit card, and in fact, I'm taking your name off of it, as well as the bank account. I also want you to get a job, any job, by the first of next month, so you can start contributing again.
- *Will you* start holding your own financially in this relationship again?
- I won't cut you off totally; I'll give you fifty dollars a week for spending money for the rest of the month, if you'll apply for five jobs each week (and show me). Also, I need you to start paying a quarter of the rent beginning next month, and the month after that I need your half of the rent and your half of all the other expenses. *Is that a deal?*
- *If not, I will* ask you to move out by the first of next month, and if you don't apply for five jobs each week, I'll deduct ten dollars (for each) out of next week's fifty dollars.

Lana's old behavior was enabling with no timeline. *Her new behavior* is to set very clear boundaries and a time frame.

Not Changing Deals That Aren't Meeting the Needs of Both

"But that's the way it's always been," is not a good reason to keep a deal the way it is if one mate is unhappy with it. People's needs change as they grow and time goes on. If you or your mate is unhappy with a deal, the deal needs to be renegotiated.

It's Her Turn

▶ Linda and Grant's Story

Five years ago, Grant and Linda started renting a mountain home for the summer months. At the time, their youngest child had just graduated from college, and they assumed they would eventually buy either this house or another in the area, and live there year-round. Grant, who is an accountant, plans on running a small accounting business out of their home.

About nine years ago, when the youngest was just starting college, Linda, who had never worked outside the home, began doing volunteer work at a home for disabled adults. Inspired by the satisfaction she got from the job and suddenly realizing how much she'd missed by not working all these years, she began studying to become a licensed occupational therapist. Now in the third year of her career and on the brink of an important promotion, she's had a change of heart about moving. She doesn't want to leave her job to live full-time in the mountains, beautiful as they are.

She reminds Grant that while they were renting the mountain house they never really sat down and discussed this as being their only option. Grant feels she's reneging on their "deal," when in fact, there never was a true deal. Linda's standing firm, but she's willing to consider moving to another location, as long as she'll be able to work at least part-time. She feels this is a fair compromise. Grant doesn't. Grant sees Linda's job as just a "hobby," and can't believe she'd let it stand in the way of their dreams.

Using the Five Steps to Successful Negotiations, Linda needs to explain:

- *I feel* cheated that you aren't supporting me in my career goals. I know we discussed early retirement plans, but I had no career then, and now I do.
- *I want* you to realize that my career is as important to me as yours was all those years to you, and now I want you to be as supportive of my career as I was of yours. I also want you to try to compromise with me.
- *Will you* be supportive and realize that it's not fair to ask me to give up my career? Let's look for a way we can both have what we want.
- I'll look for jobs in my field in mountain towns and then you look at real estate there until we find something we both love. *Is that a deal?*
- *If not, I will* continue on as I am without concern for the mountain house, and if you decide to leave to go live in the mountains, we'll just have a long-distance relationship—unless you can come up with some other possibilities for compromise.

Linda's old behavior was letting Grant have the control. *Her new behavior* is making herself a priority. *Grant's new behavior* is he will have to take her and her job seriously or risk losing her.

Depending on Him Financially

In a long-term marriage, even women who work sometimes find themselves in a situation where they are financially dependent on their husbands. It's a fact of life, yet it needn't be. When women don't work, the biggest problem is that those women don't make deals about it. Many women don't even assume that half of the money their husband earns is theirs. In most states, in a court of law, the assets are divided equally at the time of a divorce, so you need to realize that half of the money will be yours if you end up divorced—then act accordingly.

Whose Money Is It Anyway?

▶ *Mary and Patrick's Story*

Remember Mary (of Mary and Patrick in Chapter 5), who walked out of their family business and threw her husband out because he wouldn't negotiate household chores? Mary had helped her husband get their family business off the ground while she also raised their two boys, and then she stayed on in the business as the accountant. She, like many other women, felt as if she had two full-time jobs, because Patrick never helped with anything at home. When Patrick became critical and rude to her in the office, and when Mary finally reached the point where she walked out, she vowed never to return. Patrick was mad at first, but also seemed somewhat relieved to have her out of there. Running the business together had put a huge strain on their marriage.

Mary's been trying to decide what to do next. She knows she needs independence from Patrick, especially since working with him did serious damage to her self-esteem. She applied for a few accounting jobs and didn't get them, and is considering starting her own accounting firm although she's not sure she can afford to. "I want to do it without Patrick and his money," she told me. "Hold on," I said, "how did the money you and Patrick jointly created in the business become just his? You need to realize *and* remind Patrick that the money is both of yours, not just his. You've earned your part by raising the children, doing the housework, and helping start the business." Mary told me Patrick offered to give her some office space in his building to start her business, but he said, "That's it, however. You won't get a dime out of me for this project of yours."

I told her this was another control tactic of Patrick's. "He hopes to get you to back off your demands and let him move back in once he gets you back in the building and in contact with him again everyday. To think independently you need to get away from Patrick. Pretend that you're divorced, and that half of the family money is yours. Don't ask Patrick for money to start your business—see an attorney and figure out how much you can get." I cautioned her that if she shared an office with Patrick, he would have her helping in the business again, or at minimum she wouldn't break her dependency on him. "Tell him to rent it out and give you the money he makes to pay for your office," I suggested.

She began to create a vision of her new business and her financial independence from Patrick. Then we reviewed what she needs to say to Patrick:

- *I feel* pressured by you to take the office space in your building and I understand that financially it would be smart. However . . .
- *I want* to have my career completely independent of yours, so I need an office of my own somewhere else, and will need [a specified amount of] dollars to get started.
- *Will you* agree to support me financially and emotionally in making this happen?
- Why don't you rent out that space you were saving for me and let me use that money for my new office rent. *Is that a deal?*
- *If not, I'll* still look for my own office space and plan my new business independently of you, although it will still require financial backing from our joint funds. [And of course she always has the ultimate, "*If not, I will* divorce you and take my half of the money to start my business that way."]

Mary's old behavior was depending on Patrick and allowing him financial and emotional control over her. *Her new behavior* is to no longer ask Patrick for his advice about her financial future, and truly become independent of him, while holding him accountable.

Guidelines for Financial Equality

1. Keep three bank accounts: his, hers, and ours. Negotiate what percentage of each of your salaries goes into each account. If you don't work and both have agreed to that, decide what amount of money goes into your personal account each month as spending money, in trade for child care and household chores.
2. In deciding how much you each contribute to the family bills, you can use percentage of household income earned or number of hours each contributes to the household.
3. Share any resentments you have around work and money issues, remembering that changes just mean figuring out different tradeoffs.
4. Foresee upcoming changes in work schedules or income flow-and discuss ahead of time, making a plan now for how you will handle them.
5. You and your mate's philosophy about money do not have to match for the two of you to come to agreements on how you handle your finances together.
6. Each person should have a certain amount of money they do not have to be accountable for to the other.
7. It's good to say, "Let's make a deal that we have to check with each other on any purchases we want to make over $200."
8. You do not have a right to pressure him on any issue that you are not willing to do yourself, i.e., "I want you to work more and make more money," yet you don't work.
9. Know your joint financial worth at all times.
10. If you work outside the home, be sure he does his equal share inside the home.

Remember, deals that are "understood" are probably causing serious resentment in your relationship. All that is necessary to fix the problem is to talk through what each of you believes the deal to be and make any necessary changes.

◀ Points to Remember ▶

1. Financial *security* comes from your ability to create income.

2. Rescuing is just another form of controlling.

3. If you can't support yourself, you remain a victim financially.

4. Men resent that financial responsibility is ultimately always theirs.

5. A partnership is always negotiated, not demanded.

6. Both mates have equal rights and responsibilities (to provide for the family).

Chapter 9

Sharing Chores and Childcare

Do you play the victim or controller role when it comes to sharing chores and childcare? If you play the victim you may:

- Automatically assume that household chores are your job
- Handle all the household chores and childcare, then feel unappreciated and complain about it
- Nag your mate to help you, but go ahead and do it yourself when he doesn't
- Assume that your job (whether in or out of the home) is less valuable than your mate's
- Sacrifice your needs for your family's needs
- Believe that because you make less money than he does, most of the housework should still be yours
- Believe that you have to handle the children, because he is incapable
- Do everything yourself, because he doesn't do it right

If you play the controller, you may:

- Expect your mate to handle most of the household chores and childcare
- Assume that your work is more valuable than your mate's
- Criticize his efforts when he tries to help
- Insist that cleaning and childcare be done *your* way
- Assume that because you work outside the home, you shouldn't have to do anything else

But I Want to Do It All!

For many women, their homes and their children are their unchallenged domains. Although they usually won't admit it, most women will work themselves to exhaustion (and perpetual resentment) before they'll give up control of their "women's work." What better way to discourage your mate's involvement than to show him every day how well you do it all by yourself.

Women say, "If it were up to him, the kids would eat hot dogs every day and the house would be dirty all the time." I know that's what you truly believe, but have you ever tested your theory? It's often your attitude—that the home and children are more yours than his—that keeps him from believing he needs to participate equally. When he doesn't help around the house and you let him off the hook but feel resentful, the distance between the two of you grows, and the love diminishes.

"He Can't Handle the Kids"

▶ *Jane and Gary's Story*

My client Jane—the birthday story—(of Jane and Gary in Chapter 5) complained that her husband Gary never helps at home. She could never leave her children with him for five minutes because, "he wouldn't know what to do—I'd be afraid they might actually die in his care." I asked her how a father could be incapable of caring for his own children (if he truly was), and what she could do to change that. Like many women I have counseled, Jane admitted that it was difficult for her to hand over responsibility for their children, although she admits to resenting her husband's lack of participation. In some way she seemed to like the fact that she was the only good parent. She saw the children as *her* kids, not *theirs*. And although Jane played victim in many ways, with the childcare she had all the control. She actually had a very self-righteous attitude about what her children needed and didn't need, and believed that Gary was not capable of meeting those needs.

Once Jane focused on the controlling role she played regarding the children, she was ready to make some changes. One of her complaints was that she felt like she was in prison since she had the children 24/7, yet Gary felt free to come and go as he pleased. The few times she suggested he keep the kids, he, of course, said he didn't know how. Jane decided it was time to train Gary to be a father.

So she started by leaving the children with him while she ran to the grocery store. She didn't ask him if he would watch the children, she simply told him she was leaving the children with him while she was going to the store. She left emergency instructions for him—the way you would a sitter. Each time she left the children just a little longer. Gary finally began to ask questions like, "What do I do when the baby cries and how do I change a diaper?" Gary began to catch on because he had to.

Jane had difficulty with this at first because she took pride in being the one the children always came to. As the children bonded more with their father, she felt somewhat jealous. She had to remind herself that to get out of stay-at-home-mom prison, she had to share them with their father—this was the trade-off. Most important though, this truly is what's best for the children—to be involved with their father.

Stop Assuming It's Your Job

Almost every woman I know believes it's a reflection on her when her house is dirty. Seldom does anyone ever accuse a man of being a "bad" person for having a dirty house. In fact, if he's a bachelor, it's expected. And if he's a bachelor with a spotless house, he's often assumed to be gay. To get a man to help, you must first let go of the belief that it's your job, then change your behavior and stop doing it all (you may have to give up the idea of a perfectly clean house)— that's when you'll get him to change.

"But I Want It Done My Way! He Never Does It Right!"

It's true that he might not clean as well as you do, and he certainly won't do it the same way you would. He probably won't get all the crumbs off the counters or put the glasses back on the right shelves. But in the big picture, so what? That's the trade-off. He'll do it, but he won't do it your way. You may have to learn to live with the less-than-perfect results if your mate helps—without nagging, whining, or taking back the control (and the resentment that goes with it).

If the task at hand is something that has to be done in a certain way—like the baby's bottle—you can make a deal like, "Let me do the bottle while you get her diaper."

Five Things He'll Probably Never Do

- Scrub the kitchen stove
- Clean the crud around the sink
- Wash your delicates correctly
- Reorganize the kitchen
- Notice that the bathrooms need to be cleaned

You must be very careful with this, however. When you choose to keep a chore as yours, remember that it's a choice, and be sure you never complain about it. Be sure you don't teach him that if he does a bad job at certain chores, you'll eventually pick them up and do them yourself—it's an old trick used by children and husbands.

If You'll Do It, He'll Always Let You

He knows you want the house clean, so he'll let you keep it that way. He knows if he doesn't show up, you'll take care of the children. His attitude is: When it's important to you, you'll probably do it so he doesn't have to. But it's his home and his children too, and he benefits of course. This attitude about housework enrages every woman! We feel that men take advantage of our commitment to home and children. And they usually do because we let them.

That's how I felt when I was married years ago. I had tried and tried to get my husband John to help with the housework, and each time he did (about five times a year), he would say, "You didn't even thank me." My reply: "And you didn't thank me for doing it the other 5,000 times!"

"He Left His Dirty Underwear Next to the Hamper"
▶ My Ex's and My Story

My ex, John, always threw his dirty clothes next to the hamper, instead of in it. Of course, I nagged and bitched about it week after week and he just tuned me out. It wasn't until I set a boundary and followed through that anything changed. I told him that I'd wash only clothes that made it into the hamper—the others would remain on the floor indefinitely. That weekend we were having guests over and I knew it would be difficult for me to follow through, but I had to. John was sure I wouldn't. I cleaned the entire house that day, but I left

John's underwear next to the hamper in the bathroom for our guests to see. He put his dirty clothes in the hamper from that day forward.

The Understood Division of Labor

In the past, the man provided for the family and the woman took care of the house and children. The rules were pretty clear back then, and whether they liked it or not, each partner knew what was expected and what the trade-offs were. But today many women work outside the home and also do most of the housework as well. What's amazing is many women now accept both jobs. "But what am I supposed to do when the dishes have been sitting for a week and he won't do them?" My answer to this complaint is, "You don't have to cook him dinner the next night or do his laundry or pick up the dry cleaning for him. Take away something you do for him as the consequence."

"Until You Split Chores Fifty-Fifty, You Can Never Move Back Home"

▶ *Mary and Patrick's Story*

Mary (of Mary and Patrick in Chapters 5 and 8) finally got Patrick into marriage counseling while she continued to work with me privately by phone. She told him he could move back in only if he was willing to divide all the household chores and childcare duties. He fought her like crazy, arguing that they were in a traditional relationship, that he was the provider, and the household duties were hers. "After all, the business is mine!" he told her. Mary often let Patrick intimidate her with that. They had this discussion again and again, but Patrick still thought of it as his business. And now it was confusing to her because she's not working or bringing in money, so she wondered if he was right. Should she be the "housewife" now, even though she's looking for work and considering starting her own business?

Patrick always discounts Mary's efforts. In fact, during the time Patrick has been living in an apartment, she's had the children full-time and has had little time to find a job or start her business. He wants to move back in and argues that he shouldn't have to help around the house until she brings in equal income. She finally got angry enough to counter-intimidate him with, "Fine, I'll divorce you and take half of the business and then I'll be bringing in half of the income." Patrick finally backed down and agreed to negotiate.

They split up the chores and he agreed to handle the kids Mondays, Wednesdays, and Fridays. He moved back in but began resenting her. He had lost her as his bookkeeper and doubled his workload (housework and children) all at once, which meant he had very little time to drink with his buddies like he used to. Mary had trained Patrick to believe that he shouldn't have to help, so it didn't take long before he began to rebel and stay out all night drinking with his buddies like he used to, forgetting he had a wife and kids at home. They recently went away for a romantic weekend, but she couldn't let herself be sexual with him again because she's resented him for far too long to be able to get the passion back.

There's No Such Thing as an Understood Deal

Most couples don't discuss or negotiate how the housework and childcare will be handled because they make assumptions and have expectations they believe are "understood." The problem is, each person usually "understands" differently. Most men who are the sole provider believe that a stay-at-home wife has the responsibility to take care of the home and children—meaning everything in the home is her responsibility. Most women who are stay-at-home wives believe that since men live in the home too it's also their responsibility to participate in keeping the house clean and raising the children. Both end up feeling as if they've been cheated.

"I'm a Stay-at-Home Mom, but I Still Want Him to Participate!"

I hear this all the time: "Just because he has a job doesn't mean he shouldn't have to do anything around the house. I want him to participate!" A wife will tell her husband, "You live here too! Besides, you promised to clean the garage weeks ago." He'll respond with, "I'll pay someone to do it," which infuriates her. She'll usually respond with, "This is your family too and I want you to personally participate!" There's no "right" answer here; it depends on what deal was negotiated, and most couples haven't negotiated one.

Even if you have a traditional relationship and you've both agreed that he'll provide financially while you stay home with the children, the fine details of who does what and when must still be negotiated. Be careful not to argue who is right and wrong. Instead, simply create a deal you can both live with. It's advisable to make the deal before you get married while you still have power.

"But They're His Kids Too"

In a traditional relationship a man often believes he shouldn't be required to get involved in childcare. Everything he does with the children, as he sees it, should be optional. But when this happens, the kids unintentionally end up on the back burner of his priority list. He plans to play ball with the kids or take them to the zoo "some day"—his intentions are probably good—but he just never gets around to being the father he wants to be. Then one day the kids grow up and they don't know their father. Whatever deal the two of you make is up to you, but no matter what the deal is, his participation with the children should not be bargained away.

"Since I Make Twice the Money, You Should Do More"
▶ *Margaret and Donald's Story*

Remember Margaret (in Chapter 7) who was turned off sexually to Donald's half T-shirt, shorts, and belly hanging out? Even though Donald is now more careful about the way he looks when Margaret is around, her sexual attraction for him hasn't come back. This often happens when a woman is filled with resentment about household issues, and Margaret is no exception. Since her recent salary increase she's now making twice as much money as Donald, and she believes he should help more. What really bothers her is that Donald sees how stressed she gets but still doesn't help 50 percent with the children or household chores. Besides that, he gets upset when she tries to take time for herself to de-stress. When she stops at the athletic club to work out on her way home from work, Donald has an attitude when she gets home.

Donald feels as if Margaret has gotten uppity and selfish since her promotion. He was a beer-drinking kind of guy when she met him, and he hasn't changed, but she has! Now that she's hanging out with a wealthier crowd at work, he says she's trying to be somebody she's not. Donald feels he helps around the house much more than Margaret realizes or appreciates. After all, he's the one who takes the kids to day care and stays with them when she's in New York on business, eating at her fancy restaurants and going to plays. Donald believes that Margaret shouldn't have taken the promotion since it involves travel, and after all she is the mother of two children under the age of five. Sometimes she calls his bluff and says, "Okay, I'll quit and stay at home with the kids if that's what you want, but you'll have to find a way to earn a lot more money!" She knows Donald will always back down since her income has allowed them to buy the house of their dreams with a large backyard and pool, which they couldn't have afforded without the money from her promotion.

Margaret realizes that her resentment toward Donald is part of why she's been so turned off sexually. She admits she's losing respect for him as he produces less than half the income, yet criticizes her job, friends, and desire to work out. Here's what she told him:

- *I feel* so disappointed that you're behaving so badly with me since I got my promotion that I'm now starting to lose respect for you.
- *I want* you to be more supportive.
- *I want* you to accept that my travel and long hours are a trade-off for this new house and our lifestyle—that benefits the whole family.
- I *want* you to do a minimum of half the chores and childcare. In fact, what *I really want* is for you to do slightly more than half because I work more hours than you and bring in twice the money.
- *I want* you to be supportive of my trips to the athletic club and stop acting jealous of my new position and friends, and meet them and get to know them.
- *Will you?*
- *If not, I'll* continue to pull away from you, and our relationship will eventually end.

His Participation with the Children Must Be Spelled Out in Your Deal

Whether you work or not, you still need to be sure he participates regularly with the children. Get him to agree that his kids are a priority to him (which he probably will) and then present the issue for negotiation. You need to draw up a list of childcare duties and be prepared to negotiate deals with your mate that both of you can live with. For example, you could trade a night of romance for his promise to watch the kids on Saturdays. He'd probably be happy to chauffeur the kids around to their Saturday sports and social events for an evening of intimacy with you (or maybe even just an evening where you're not exhausted or complaining about how much there is to do). This is the kind of trade-off most stay-at-home moms need to negotiate with their husbands, explicitly and clearly. And, I should add, one their mates might even welcome.

What's a Fair Deal?

Remember that the only fair deal is an equal deal for both you and your mate. It's not really a win if you get him to do more than his share. Chores and childcare have to be negotiated in coordination with work and money issues to create a deal that's fair, whether it's within a traditional role or one where both parents work. If either of you contributes more than is fair, that person will feel victimized and resentful. Even if in reality he doesn't contribute more, but thinks he does, the two of you must talk and renegotiate until both of you believe it's a fair deal.

More often than not, when it comes to deals regarding housework, women get the short end of the stick. However, some women take the "princess" role and expect to get more than they themselves are willing to give.

She Acted Like a Princess, but Felt Like a Pauper

▶ Maria and Carl's Story

Maria and Carl met their last year in college when Maria was finishing her nursing degree and Carl was graduating with a degree in business. Maria was one of six children born to a poor Hispanic family, while Carl came from a wealthy family where he (along with nine brothers) ran the numerous family businesses upon college graduation. Though Maria was never a gold digger, she was excited that she met a man so financially secure that she wouldn't have to work. Besides, Carl was so giving that he was even willing to give money to her family in their times of need.

After the two dated for a while, Maria quit her job as a nurse and moved to Denver, beginning a traditional relationship where she stayed home and was supposed to be the homemaker. However, Maria, who was the youngest in her family, had been spoiled by her older sisters and brothers and came into the marriage with no cooking skills and minimal experience at performing other household chores. Her attitude was, "If I'm not good at it, I shouldn't have to do it." So Carl, who worked fifty to sixty hours a week, did most of the grocery shopping and quite a bit of the cleaning. He even started doing all the cooking on the weekends so the family would have some healthy meals. Maria even made numerous lists of chores for Carl to do and would criticize him for not getting them done in a timely manner. When Carl complained (which he seldom did), Maria would get angry and go to her room and pout. Carl continued to do more and more, while Maria did less and less. As his resentment grew, and nothing got resolved, Carl shut down and completely stopped communicating with Maria. Then he called me and set up their first appointment. (Find out in the next chapter why Maria feels like a pauper and victim, not a princess.)

"What about My Career?"

If a couple decides that someone should stay home with the children, it is, of course, sexist to think that it must be the woman. A possible solution to Donald and Margaret's hectic lifestyle might have been for Donald to cut back on his workload and settle into the Mr. Mom role, while Margaret earned the big money. But Donald's ego would never let that happen.

"It's My Turn"

▶ *Emma and Dwayne's Story*

Emma and Dwayne have what most people consider a traditional relationship: Dwayne works seventy-plus hours as a litigator for

175

a large law firm and Emma stays home to care for their twin four-year-old boys. Emma is a talented graphic designer who has continued working the occasional freelance project as time allows. Out of the blue, Emma was offered a part-time consultant's position with a new Internet start-up that would allow her to work at home, grant her stock options, and pay her a monthly retainer that would completely cover their mortgage and two car payments. The only hitch: Emma would need help with the boys for about sixteen hours a week.

Dwayne can't change his hours at work and he insists their kids should be raised by their parents, not "hired help." Emma says the boys are only a year from kindergarten anyway, that this is a great opportunity for the whole family, and she can't understand why Dwayne isn't willing to compromise. Dwayne says they had a deal that Emma would stay home until the boys got into school and that Emma is breaking the deal.

Deals are not forever because people change and so do their needs. However, in an out-of-balance relationship, the controller seldom wants to renegotiate the deal. Why should he? His needs are being met. Emma must make it clear to Dwayne, the controller, that she has as much right to pursue her career as he does. She can offer up possible solutions—to set up the sixteen hours of day care—or he can choose to back off of his work and stay with the boys if he feels they need a parent there. But, she will have to make it clear to Dwayne that resisting the change is not an option. If she lets him have his way, she will resent him and it will damage the relationship in the long term. Emma set a precedent by agreeing to a deal where her career was sacrificed. She has to now let him know she will no longer sacrifice her career or life for the sake of the family. Using the Four Steps to Powerful Communication, Emma made things very clear to Dwayne:

- *I feel* frustrated that you're being so rigid about this situation.
- *I want* you to work with me and respect my need to be productive

- *I want* you to accept that you're also a parent and that you may need to step in and pick up responsibility for the boys' care.
- *Will you?*
- *If not, I will* simply get a sitter and move forward with my plan.

Dwayne's response was:

- Can't you wait one more year until the kids are a little older?

Emma's response was:

- No, I can't wait. This job won't be offered to me a year from now. However, I might try to negotiate fewer hours with my boss or certain days so I can accommodate your schedule. I'm not willing to sacrifice, but I am willing to negotiate. Now I need you to do the same.

It took awhile and Emma had to hold her ground, but Dwayne finally negotiated with her and they sent the twins to preschool sixteen hours a week.

When He Won't Cooperate, Give Him an Ultimatum

Women ask, "What do I do when he won't make deals with me?" You go back to the Four Steps to Powerful Communication and make your own deal by giving him a consequence like Emma did. Call it a consequence or an ultimatum, but say, "If you don't help by doing the dishes, I won't cook." Or you can make positive trade-offs like, "I'll cook your favorite meal—fried chicken—if you'll give the kids their baths." He needs to know that not participating is not an option.

This Deal Is Fair to Both

▶ Gretchen and Art's Story

Gretchen and Art (from Chapters 5 and 8) brought in a list of all the household and childcare duties. Gretchen was tired of having them all dumped on her and wanted Art to participate. He agreed to take almost half, but since Art was bringing in most of the income, he wanted Gretchen to take on some extra chores. She agreed, as long as Art wouldn't expect her to sacrifice at the last minute and change her schedule for him. He agreed. They split up the vacuuming and dusting by floors; he took upstairs and she downstairs. She took the kitchen and he reluctantly took the bathrooms. He agreed to take the kids to school every other day and to stay with them and get them to bed on the nights she had classes. Both designated one night a week as their "personal" night—to go out or work in their respective offices or whatever they wanted to do.

◀ Points to Remember ▶

1. Women are often turned off sexually because they're resentful about household chores.

2. If you'll do the chores, he'll let you.

3. Just because he's not good at it doesn't mean he doesn't have to do it.

4. Make it clear that not participating is not an option.

5. Your mate's participation with the children should never be bargained away.

6. You will have to learn to live with less than perfect results if you want help around the house.

Chapter 10

How to Keep Family, Exes, and Stepchildren from Interfering

Do you play the victim or controller role when it comes to dealing with family, exes, and stepchildren? If you play the victim, you may:

- Sacrifice your needs for his family or yours
- Allow your family or his to control your relationship
- Whine about his involvement with his family
- Allow your mate's family to treat you or your children badly

If you play the controller, you may:

- Insist that he accommodate your parents, your ex, or your children
- Refuse to stop spending time with your ex
- Defend your family's control over your relationship
- Tell your mate how he "should" handle his relationship with his family, children, or ex
- Blame his family, kids, or ex for all your problems

When I talk with clients, I'm still surprised to learn how many couples are frustrated by, and seldom find solutions to, relatively minor, highly manageable situations with in-laws, exes, or stepchildren. We already know that our relationship with our parents, and their relationship with each other, have profound influence on how we think and behave with our mates. What we often overlook, dismiss, or don't see any way to change, is how our parents, in-laws, and exes affect our current relationship.

From the hard-drinking brother-in-law you never want to invite to another Thanksgiving dinner, to the ex whose very existence fans the flames of jealousy, in-laws and exes can be hard to keep out of your relationship. Whether your problems are with the in-law or ex directly or with how your partner deals with that person, you can change things for the better. First, accept that you don't have to love or even like everyone—or even anyone—who comes with your partner's "package." Second, accept that the same rule applies to your mate. While it can be uncomfortable and difficult when he dislikes someone who's close to you, there are ways to allow each of you to have your own feelings and relationships without causing problems between the two of you.

Handling In-Laws

When I was twenty-one and first married to John, we were having dinner at his parents' house, and I watched his mother cut his meat for him. I realized that she had trained him to believe that women are supposed to serve men. At one point I told her what I thought—that she had spoiled him and that it was a major cause of our problems. She turned to me and said, "Carolyn, why do you have to fight everything? You're just a rebel without a cause. You'll finally adjust and become a good wife, like I did. You're a sweet girl. I know you will." Instead, of course, I divorced her son three years later and she never really understood why. Many women of that generation don't get it and never will.

But it was naive of me to think that I could change his mother's point of view. And even if I did, it was too late for her to do anything about it anyway. John was already trained not to respect women, so if he was going to change, I would have to hold him accountable, not his mother.

"Your Mom Knows I'm Right"

▶ Mary and Patrick's Story

Mary (of Mary and Patrick in Chapters 5, 8, and 9), who made Patrick split the chores fifty-fifty before he could move back in, had a chat with Patrick's mom about his selfish, disrespectful ways. Surprisingly, Patrick's mom agreed with her and said, "It's my fault and I know it. Patrick's just like his father! Somehow I thought that if I put up with Patrick's father instead of divorcing him, it would help Patrick become a well-adjusted adult. I see now that all I did was help him learn his father's self-centered, disrespectful ways. I know Patrick is having trouble in his marriage with you because he doesn't respect women any more than his father does." Mary's mother-in-law even had a chat with Patrick concerning this, but Patrick just got angry with her and said, "You don't understand! How dare you take Mary's side!"

But, it's not just men who get bad relationship training. We women do too. Gretchen (Chapters 5, 8, and 9) modeled her mother's nagging and whining. Maria (Chapter 9) thought it was a woman's right to stay home with the children and that she shouldn't have to make deals or trade-offs with her husband. Jane (Chapters 5 and 9) thought that mothers are the only ones who know how to take care of children. We all have our baggage that we bring into our relationships. And yes, his baggage and our baggage interfere every day. (For more on how to deal with the baggage, see Appendix A.)

"Your Family Ruined Our Marriage"

▶ Maria and Carl's Story

When Carl, of Maria and Carl (Chapter 9), finally confronted Maria about their out-of-balance relationship, she finally shared what her resentments were. Maria told Carl, "You've let your parents run our lives since the day we were married, and I'll never forgive you for it." Maria felt victimized by Carl's family and believed she owed Carl (and his family) nothing for destroying her life. Once Maria moved to Denver as Carl's wife, she realized that she had also married Carl's family and the family business. It wasn't long before she realized that the ways of her "poor" family were totally unacceptable to him and his family, and his parents would now be calling the shots. And Maria simply let it happen. And her resentment toward Carl's family killed her love for him.

Maria's family may have been poor, but they were warm and emotional, while Carl's family was extremely unemotional and cold. She'll never forget that on his father's deathbed, she went to the hospital to say goodbye to her father-in-law, and Carl said, "No, my dad doesn't want to see anyone who's not immediate family." "But I am immediate family," she said. "No one except me and my mom and my brothers are allowed in, so just go back home," he said. She never forgave Carl or his family for that moment. Being the good Catholic girl that she was, she knew she wouldn't divorce him, so she shut him out and never participated again.

When I confronted Maria suggesting she had played victim to his family every step of the way, she responded, "No, it was Carl's responsibility to handle it and he didn't. He made his choice, and at that moment, I made mine." Maria couldn't see that the problem was also her fault because she had allowed his family to victimize her for the eight years. Actually, Maria was a controlling victim. Although she believed she had no real power, she controlled the relationship by keeping things from happening, instead of making them happen.

Maria had stopped cooperating with Carl altogether except for raising their son. She not only did very few household chores, she hardly ever talked to Carl, and when she did, it was only about their son or reminding him of household chores he forgot to do. She never had sex with him. And Maria felt entirely justified in her behavior. I told Maria, "Carl never knew until this moment what he was being punished for all these years." She insisted, "You're wrong—Carl knew exactly what his family did!" But he actually didn't. Maria never confronted Carl or gave him a chance to fix the problems in their relationship. Instead, she built an ironclad case against him and will probably never forgive him. Maria, like many women, allowed her in-laws to destroy her marriage instead of setting boundaries with Carl regarding them. What Maria needed to say years ago was:

- *I feel* upset that you're allowing your family and their beliefs to run our lives.
- *I want* you to stand up to them and defend *our* family.
- *Will you* tell them when they're out of line and let them know their way is not always the right way?
- *If not, I will* stand up to them myself, or never spend time with them again.

Maria, of course, never said these things. In fact, she never said anything at all. She simply sulked and withdrew more and more from Carl, creating her own world with her sons, friends, family, and hobbies. She told me she would never leave Carl because of her religious beliefs, but that she would never forgive him and work it out either. Carl's father was dead, but Carl agreed to confront his mother and brothers about the ways they had treated Maria, and Maria was glad. But she still said, "It's too little, too late." She expected Carl to stay and take care of her, accepting his punishment for the rest of his life.

"But Shouldn't We Like Each Other's Families?"

Let's be realistic. You know how your mom can be, how your brother or sister gets during the holidays, and how your dad is when someone has a difference of opinion. If these people were not your family, would you actually choose them as friends? You love them, but do you really like them? Yes, you must tolerate your family and his, and he must do the same. So don't worry about whether or not he truly likes your mother or bonds with your father. Do be concerned about how he treats your family when they're around and how he sets and holds boundaries with his. And don't let him have unrealistic expectations regarding how you will handle his family either.

"Why Can't You Be Friends with My Mom and Sister?"

▶ *Rosalind and Rod's Story*

Rosalind (of Rosalind and Rod in Chapters 3 and 7) has a real problem with Rod's mother, especially since Rosalind has become a mother herself. Rod's mother abandoned Rod when he was eight, leaving him with his father while she took off with another man. Rod says he's forgiven her and now wants Rosalind to be friends with her and his sister. Rosalind says to me, "She abandoned him and now she wants to be this big part of our family? She wants to see my baby when she abandoned her own? I don't think so! She wanted to spend a week with us right after the baby was born but she never helps and always wants to be waited on, and Rod doesn't help either, so I told her no. And as for his sister? She's a lesbian. I'm supposed to pal around with his lesbian sister? Is he crazy? I think Rod wants me to create the relationship with them he never had growing up. But that's his job, not mine. He doesn't get it though, he still says to me, 'I wish you got along with my family.'" I agreed with her that it's Rod's job to create the relationship with his own family. I suggested she set the following boundaries.

- *I feel* upset that you want me to take responsibility for creating a relationship with your family when you've never even had one with them.
- *I want* you to develop and maintain the relationship with your family yourself if you want one. I'll be glad to participate, but you have to be the one to handle them.
- *Will you* call your mother and develop your own relationship with her? Wait on your mother when she's here or tell her she has to help? Take time off from work to entertain your mom and sister when they visit? Explain to your mother that the reason she hasn't been invited to visit before is because you weren't helping around the house until now—and between the baby, the household chores, and my job, I had no time to entertain her?
- If you'll do what I ask, your mother is welcome in our home any time. *If not,* she isn't welcome here and *I'll* write her a letter letting her know why.

You Don't Have to Like Them, but You Do Have to Be Polite

If your partner has never been polite to your mother, lay down the rules: "You don't have to like my mother, but because she's my mother, you do have to be polite to her when you're around her." If that statement alone doesn't work, let him know what the consequences will be if his behavior doesn't improve. Remember to equalize the rules: All rules go both ways. "The deal is that I will be just as polite to some member of your family I don't like as you are to my mother. So let's decide how we're going to treat each other's family members." Then carry out the consequences. It's the only way he'll realize that you mean business.

The trade-offs don't have to be tit for tat with his family. You may like everyone in his family so you may need to make a different trade-off. For instance, if he doesn't want to have dinner at your mom's, consider offering something like this: "I'll go to that football game with you on Monday night if you'll have dinner at my mom's and be polite to her on Sunday." The rule of reciprocity means that you don't continue to give, or be nice, or do something for him, when he doesn't give back.

Don't Badmouth Him to Your Family

When you pour your problems out to your family about him, you're creating a wedge between your family and your mate—one that's very difficult to remove. Your family hears only what he did to you, not how you responded badly or what bad behavior of yours precipitated the fight. You're making them prejudiced against him, and giving them ammunition to help tear your relationship apart in the future.

How to Get Them Back on His Side Again

If you have been badmouthing him, tell your family in detail all about your own bad behavior, describing the dysfunctional fit between you and your mate in terms they can understand. Make them see that it took both of you working together to create these problems, and that working together, you'll solve them. This will help repair the damage you've done. If one of your family members won't get over it and still sees him in a negative light, set a boundary with that person like, "We're not going to discuss how bad you think he is. This subject is off limits from now on." Then promise yourself that you'll stop feeding them negative information about him.

Whose Job Is It to Handle His Family?

The general rule regarding most issues: If you have a problem with it, you need to handle it. But the rule changes when the problem comes from his family or friends—or from yours. He needs to handle *his* family and you need to handle *yours*. If you have to tell his mother that she can't come to visit, you'll look like the bad guy—she can assume it's just you (not him) who doesn't want her there. Whereas, if he talks to her himself, she's more likely to believe that it's a joint decision.

If He Won't Handle His Family, It Doesn't Mean You Can't

If the problem is with your mother-in-law who constantly criticizes everything you and your partner do, you might have tried ignoring it, telling yourself, "Well, she's his mother, and it's always been this way. I don't want to alienate her. I guess I have to live with it." No, you don't. If you don't deal with it, you'll probably resent her deeply and maybe even him—the way Rosalind did Rod—driving a wedge between the two of you. Instead, you need to first tell your partner how you'd like him to handle her: "Tell her to stop the criticism." Of course he may say, "That's just my mom. Just don't let it get to you." You then need to tell him that it's not an option for her criticism to continue. Tell him that you will handle it yourself if he doesn't (by leaving her presence, standing up to her, or staying away from her), then handle it if it comes down to that.

Rod agreed to talk to his mother about the problems surrounding her visit before the holiday. If he didn't do it, Rosalind decided that she'd write his mom a letter explaining that without Rod's help in the past she was too stressed to invite her as a guest. With Rod now helping with the baby and household chores, his mother is now invited as long as she works out her plans with Rod and his schedule.

"We Need Time for Us, Not Them"

▶ Deanna and Daryl's Story

Remember Deanna (of Deanna and Daryl in Chapter 8) who goes to school full-time while Daryl is starting a new business? They never have time together and Deanna resents Daryl's busy work schedule, but has learned to compensate by spending a lot of her time with her family.

Every Sunday, Deanna's whole family—her mom, dad, two grown sisters, their spouses, and three toddler-age nieces—arrives around noon for an afternoon get-together that never seems to end before eight at night (and later if there's a big football game on television). In Deanna's family, the Sunday dinner has been a long-standing tradition that she assumed responsibility for when her parents moved from their large home to a small assisted-living cooperative. Daryl has always liked Deanna's family, and he enjoys being around them. However, at this point in their lives, he feels that devoting an entire day to entertaining them—with the requisite shopping, cooking, and cleanup—takes away from them their only chance for quality time.

Daryl's resentment was building and last Sunday he exploded, right before the guests arrived. "I've had it up to here with your family! If you want to spend every free moment with them, go ahead, but I'll be damned if I'm going to!" Then he took off before her family arrived, without telling Deanna where he was going. He decided it was either that or create a scene during dinner. Deanna was rightfully upset and felt justified in badmouthing Daryl to her family during dinner, whereas she had made excuses for him in the past. When Daryl came home later, he apologized to Deanna and approached her in a healthy way, telling her what he wanted and looking for a solution. He said, "Let's not do this to each other. We're both really stressed and haven't had enough time for us lately. Let's try to work this out." He said the following.

- *I feel* resentful of this weekly commitment to your family since we don't have enough time for each other as it is.
- *I want* Sundays to be for us, not them. I want you to tell them that.
- *Will you* stand up to your family so we can preserve what little time we have together for us?
- I really miss spending time alone with you, Deanna, and I don't like feeling angry with your family about this. You can still see them all you want on other days. Since we chose this lifestyle and the schedule, I know this is our fault, not theirs, but I think my request is fair and reasonable.

Deanna argued with Daryl at first, saying that his workaholism was the real problem, not her family! But she does miss having quality time with Daryl, so she offered up a compromise.

- *Let's make a deal:* What if we host Sunday dinner every other week instead of every week, the other weekend we'll keep just for us. I'll tell them this Sunday and we'll start next week. Okay?

The following Sunday, after a wonderful summer meal out on the deck, Deanna announced to her family, "As you know, I love you all, and you know I love Daryl too. You also know what tremendous pressure Daryl and I are under right now. Because our lives are so stressful at this time, we need to change the dinner schedule to every other Sunday so we can spend some time alone with each other. I hope you'll understand." Then Daryl added, "Though we love spending time with all of you, some weeks I can't remember who I'm married to!"

Deanna's family was disappointed, and argued that they never had the opportunity to see Deanna either and that doing this every week has been the long-standing family tradition. Deanna stopped them cold with, "I don't think family tradition is more important than preserving our marriage!" "Besides," she joked, "if you ever want to have any grandchildren, we're going to have to have time for us!" They agreed.

Family Differences Need to Be Respected

When Alan and I were first together, I tried to get his mother and daughter to celebrate holidays the same way my family does. My family seldom misses a holiday together and I believed his family shouldn't either. So one year I got quite upset when his daughter called the morning of Thanksgiving saying she was in a bad mood and decided to drink a bottle of wine instead of coming to dinner. Then his mother canceled on us one Christmas morning because she decided she'd be uncomfortable since too many people were invited. Needless to say, I wasn't happy about his family's handling of holidays and I let everyone know it. This caused a huge fight between Alan and me. When we finally talked it out calmly, he said, "I've tried to explain to you that my family couldn't care less about the holidays. It's no big deal to them. They agreed to come over in the first place only to please you!" This was so completely different from my family that I couldn't understand it. But I finally realized I wasn't respecting his family's differences. So we made a deal. I said:

- *I feel* frustrated when I try to plan these events and your family backs out.
- *I want* us to stop planning to have your family over if it's no big deal to them.
- *I want* you to check in with them every holiday and make sure that not getting together is really okay with them.
- *Will you* take it upon yourself to handle this with them?
- *The deal is:* I won't worry about your family during the holidays and you'll make sure they are really okay not spending

time with us. And if they do want to get together, I want you to coordinate with them. Okay?

- *If not, I'll* just make plans for us with my family and not worry about them.

Alan agreed and we made that deal about seven years ago, and we still follow it. Usually his mother and daughter don't want to celebrate the holidays with us, and it actually makes my life easier now that I've accepted it.

When the In-Laws Are Truly a Bad Influence

There are truly bad in-laws—people who are dangerous, who might hurt your children, who are crazy, who are drug addicts, who constantly mooch, who come on to you, or whatever. Of course very strict boundaries must be set with these particular people. For instance, if your brother-in-law comes on to you, you need to tell your husband that he makes you uncomfortable and that you don't ever want to be left alone with him. Whatever the issue is, and whatever bad behavior the in-laws have, the two of you need to realistically discuss the situation, agree on a plan, and both follow it—instead of defending your family member just because he's a family member.

"Does Grandpa Molest?"

▶ *Kristi and Gavin's Story*

Remember Kristi (of Kristi and Gavin in Chapter 7) who was upset at Gavin because he watched porn and masturbated? Gavin suspects that Kristi's father might have sexually abused Kristi, and that's why she is so uptight about sex. Gavin says all the signs are there, so he confronted Kristi, and she responded, "Don't be silly, my dad would never do that!" Gavin was not convinced. But since they've decided to get a divorce, it's not really Gavin's business at

191

this point except that Gavin is concerned that Kristi's father might be touching their daughter inappropriately. He saw him place her hands on his penis once, though he was fully clothed.

Gavin has insisted that their daughter not be left alone with the grandfather. This is a serious concern and requires extreme boundaries to be set. A guardian ad litum has been appointed and will make sure that whatever happens is in the best interest of the daughter.

"Whose Mother Is Worse?"
▶ *Tami and Brandon's Story*

Tami is black and Brandon is white. They appear to be a happy, successful couple, and they're planning to marry in the fall. But, they have serious in-law problems.

Brandon's family comes from a wealthy background and a long line of racists. Tami says Brandon's mother controls him, because when his mother told him, "Marriages are difficult enough without adding the race card," he broke off the engagement. Now they're back together, but Tami doesn't trust him.

Brandon says that Tami's mom is the worst mom he's ever known and that she doesn't deserve the warm, loving treatment she gets from Tami. Not only does he believe her mom is a loser for leaving Tami when Tami was a teenager so she could work and travel in Paris, but her mom is always broke and wanting a handout as well. Tami let her mom live in her house when she moved in with Brandon; charging her only half the house payment, but her mom didn't keep up the payments. Tami didn't say a word about it, much less consider booting her out. In fact, Tami lent her mom even more money and Brandon went through the roof when he found out. Brandon fears they'll be supporting her mom for the rest of their lives if they don't stop now—along with Tami's loser brother who's a druggie and has been in and out of jail numerous times. Brandon says her family is disrespectful with money and don't understand privacy, since they also stop by regularly unannounced. Brandon can't understand why Tami would be so nice to a mother who abandoned her, but Tami says, "I love my mom and she's just going through a hard time."

Brandon says the real reason he canceled his engagement to Tami and pulled away was because of her family, not his. He was afraid that he was marrying into a family of losers who have their hands out! Brandon and Tami both needed to set some very strong boundaries with their families to keep their families from destroying their relationship. Tami never stopped to think how much money she was losing by letting her mom live in her house or how upsetting this was to Brandon. Brandon didn't realize that by confiding in his mom about how Tami's mom and brother were such losers, he was promoting her prejudice against blacks.

These are Tami's requests:

- *I want* you to stop telling your mom bad things about my family, and in fact, *I want* you to go back and tell her we have those issues now worked out.
- *I want* you to stand up to your mom the next time she brings up the race issue and tell her, "We're not going to discuss race again, Mom. I love Tami and I don't care what color she is."

These are Brandon's requests:

- *I want* you to tell your mom and brother they can't stop by whenever they feel like it without calling first.
- *I want* you to not lend more money to your brother because he probably spends it on drugs. Tell him the only money he'll get from us is to pay for drug rehab.
- *I want* you to give your mother notice to vacate your house so you can rent it out and keep up with our bills. If you feel you need to help your mother financially, help her pay for a one-bedroom apartment instead of your three-bedroom house.

- *I want* you to tell your mother that you expect her to set up a payment plan with you to pay back her loans or you won't lend her any more money.

They both agreed, set the boundaries with their respective families, and were married a few months later.

Deals to Make Regarding In-Laws

- Neither of us talks badly about the other to our families or in-laws.
- We don't discuss with either of our families how we spend our money, unless it's money they have given us.
- We must check in with each other before committing to plans with them.
- When our families visit, it's each person's job to take care of or entertain his or her own parents.
- Both sets of parents have equal rights when it comes to spending time with our children.
- When there's an issue involving our families, each person has to handle whatever it is with his or her respective parents.
- We don't allow either of our families to run our lives or control us in any way.
- We don't have to like them, but we will both be polite and considerate to both sets of parents no matter what.

Stepchildren—"Don't Be Mean to My Kids!"

Parents usually fight about how to raise their own children, so when you add stepchildren into the mix, the war is on. Usually one parent is too easy and the other is the disciplinarian. In some ways, parents seem to try to balance out each other, sort of like "good cop, bad cop." However, all this really does is keep the children confused.

The solution is to negotiate a set of rules that take both parenting styles into consideration—and then stick by those rules jointly (for all the children) and no matter what.

"Your Son Is Mean to My Daughter"

▶ *Krista and Eugene's Story*

Krista and Eugene fight regularly over their two sets of children. Eugene says that Krista's son treats one of his daughters disrespectfully and that it's Krista's fault because Krista herself is disrespectful to his two girls. Recently Krista told his daughter, "Stop acting like such a little princess!" Then Eugene heard her son call his daughter a princess and was really upset at Krista. Krista says that if Eugene hadn't spoiled his girls so badly she wouldn't be calling her a princess. Besides, Krista says Eugene makes her look like the bad person because she's the one who always has to reprimand the kids while he lets them get away with everything.

"I have to be extra nice to them because you're mean to them," Eugene responded. Krista reassured Eugene that she loves his two little girls, but that they definitely need discipline. However, she is tired of being the bad guy, so either they will have to figure out a joint plan they both can enforce, or he will have to begin disciplining the girls himself. Once Eugene understood that Krista wanted to be warm and loving with the girls again, he was ready to make rules for all the children that they could both enforce. Krista had to set a consequence for Eugene, however, for the times he doesn't enforce the rules.

"It's All His Fault"

▶ *Sue, Ryan, and Stepson Cory's Story*

Sue and Ryan's relationship (of Sue and Ryan in Chapter 2) was volatile enough without adding Sue's seventeen-year-old son

Cory to the mix. For Ryan, it was like adding fuel to the fire. Cory wasn't about to let some strange man come into his home and treat him and his mom like crap after he'd been the man of the house most of his life. And of course Ryan, who felt like he was rescuing them both, wasn't about to put up with Cory's back talk, so Sue was continually caught in the middle of the ongoing war between her son and her new husband. But when Cory got in trouble with the law for aggression toward a classmate and his marijuana use came out, Ryan decided he'd had enough and said, "Cory is our problem! You and I could have a great relationship if Cory wasn't living here. I'll only stay married to you if you'll send Cory back east to live with your parents."

Sue responded with, "I can't believe you're asking me to choose between you and my son—because if you are, you will lose!" That was the final straw for Sue—the day she decided to stop playing victim to Ryan. Like a mother bear, she defended her cub to the end, walking away from Ryan when in the past she was never able to leave to protect herself. She said:

- *I feel* appalled and disgusted that you have the guts to ask me to give up my child and that you actually blame him for our problems.
- *I want* you to apologize to me for even suggesting such a thing. And I want us to make some rules and guidelines not only for Cory and his behavior, but also for you and your behavior with him.
- *Will you?*
- *If not, I will* end this relationship with you once and for all.

Sue filed for divorce, and moved out immediately. Ironically, Cory decided on his own to leave and go live with his grandparents for a while. But as Sue said, "That isn't the point. No man should ever ask a mother to give up her child." I agreed with her.

Rules for Handling Stepchildren

- Decide ahead of time how much authority you will allow your mate to have over your children and if punishments will be carried out by you, by him, or by both.
- Discuss together what behaviors irritate you the most about the children—yours, his, and ours. Then set up a chart of rules and consequences you both agree on.
- Post the rules (making sure they apply to all the children in the household—no exceptions) and have a family meeting explaining how things will work from now on.
- Never allow a child or stepchild to have the power to come between the two of you, and never ask your mate to choose between you or his child.

Handling Exes

The older you get, the more likely you'll end up with a man who is divorced with an ex who claims his time and attention, especially if there are children involved. You may also have an ex—boyfriend or husband—who has difficulty letting go of you. The way you or your mate handles an ex can be one of the most important issues you deal with. You may believe that treating your ex with warmth and respect shows what a great person you are, but your mate probably sees it very differently. If an ex is treated as a priority or has the power to come between you and your mate, emotions of jealousy, revenge, hurt, and anger come pouring out and have the potential to destroy your new relationship.

If your mate has a problem with your ex, don't say, "So what am I supposed to do? He's their father." Instead say, "He's going to be in our lives for a long time because he's their father, so how do you think we should handle him? Any suggestions? I'm willing to try to figure out a better way of handling this situation."

"You Bought Her a House, but You Didn't Buy One for Me"
▶ Misty and Gordon's Story

Remember Misty (of Misty and Gordon in Chapter 8) who lost her power with Gordon when she moved from California to Denver so he could be near his children? One of her regular complaints was, "You must have loved your ex more than me. You bought her a house and haven't bought me one." Gordon tried and tried to explain, "I married her and she was dependent on me, so I started resenting her. When I divorced her, I wanted out so bad that I let her have the house. When I met you, I was excited to finally meet a strong, independent woman I wouldn't have to support (and resent). That's why. Why can't you get over it? It's not about loving her more. It's just the opposite!"

Let's All Be Friends

Many people don't see why they can't remain friends with their exes. He may say to you, "We were married all those years and had three children together. I don't hate her! There's no reason we can't be friends and talk or have coffee together once in awhile!" But there is. Just because two people get a divorce doesn't mean they don't still have a dysfunctional relationship with each other. Misty was upset with the way Gordon let his ex call all the shots about their kids. Misty wrongly assumed it was because he still loved her in some way. Actually it was because he felt guilty for not loving her anymore, for cheating with Misty, and for leaving her. Instead of acting like a victim, and complaining about the house he bought the ex, Misty needed to set boundaries with Gordon regarding how he handled his ex: "Since we can't seem to get an answer from your ex regarding whether or not we'll have your children at Christmas, I'm going to go ahead and book a flight to California to be with my family."

When You Think He's Still Interested in Her

People stay too involved with their exes for many reasons, but remaining attracted to or still being in love are only two of them. More often than not, continued involvement with an ex has more to do with not being able to let go of the dysfunction the two of them played out. If she broke up with him, he may still feel rejected and need to win back her approval, which is really about his own insecurities, not his love for her (but it may look the same to you). Maybe he feels sorry for her and believes it's his duty to listen to her problems or give her extra money, since he, like Gordon, has guilt over abandoning her. Maybe he has pressure from his friends, family, or children to be nice to her. Whatever his (or your) issue with the ex is, it's probably just old dysfunctional baggage still being played out. It really needs to be cleaned up (see "The Separation Process" in Chapter 14 to learn how) or at least ignored—but it shouldn't be allowed to be played out like it was when they were still married. In many ways, it's irrelevant what the baggage is because setting boundaries is still what you need to do regardless.

He Won't Give Up His Friendship with Her

If he says, "I don't know why you're making such a big deal about this—my ex and I are just friends," make it clear that if he insists on remaining friends with his ex, then all three of you will have to be friends. Alan used to get little cards from his ex saying, "Let's just have a cup of coffee and talk." I suggested he call her and say, "Carolyn and I would love to have coffee with you any time. Let us know when." Instead he just never responded—which was also fine with me.

If your mate does want to see his ex, reply with, "That's fine. Let's invite her over. But it's not okay with me for you to spend time alone with her." If this friendship is truly important to him, you'll get a feel for how innocent it is or isn't when she comes over. And if he still insists on seeing her alone, tell him, "If you refuse my request, just remember it goes both ways. I'll call an ex of mine or develop some male friends and spend time with them when you're with her."

What's Not Appropriate with an Ex

- It's not appropriate to spend time in your ex's house.
- It's not appropriate to listen to your ex's personal problems.
- It's not appropriate to allow your ex to discuss his or her romantic feelings toward you.
- It's not appropriate to celebrate your ex's birthday or other holidays with him/her.
- It's not appropriate to have any sexual contact with your ex.
- It's not appropriate to give family funds (besides alimony and child support) to your ex without getting an okay from your mate.

"Stand Up to Her—Or I Will!"

▶ *Myra and Joseph's Story*

Myra couldn't believe how Joseph let his ex push him around regarding his children, child support, phone calls to the children, and so on. Myra ragged on Joseph about it constantly until he finally came in for my help. The problem at this point was greater than just his ex—Joseph couldn't stand up to any woman. He admitted that his ex was extremely controlling, and he was just beginning to figure out that Myra is just as, if not more, controlling. Myra had even talked Joseph into putting all of his assets into her name to make sure his ex didn't get them. So now, every time they fight, Myra has all the power and threatens to leave him with nothing if he doesn't handle his ex the way she thinks he should. Joseph has two women he needs to stand up to.

With my help, Joseph finally said to Myra, "I have two women controlling me and that's not okay. I'll handle my ex and children and you can be involved in the decision-making, but ultimately, it's my problem to deal with and I'll handle my ex and my children my way!"

Boundaries for Exes

- Don't call me except to discuss the children.
- No secrets will be kept from my mate.
- Whatever you want to say to me, you can say to both of us.
- Nonurgent communication doesn't justify a meeting with you. Use the mail, fax, e-mail, or voice mail.
- Visitation is for me and my children only, and doesn't include you.
- Anything that occurs at my house is none of your concern and vice versa, unless it involves our children's safety.

When Your Mate Is Too Attached to Everyone

Sometimes one of you gets so overcommitted to everyone else that you seem to lose interest in the person most important to you. That's what happened to Britney and Kyle.

"My Parents, Children, and Ex Come First—and Always Will!"
▶ Britney and Kyle's Story

Britney (of Britney and Kyle in Chapters 1 and 7) is part of a very tight, close-knit Jewish community. She and her extended family have lived in the same town for decades and are part of the

Jewish social elite. Britney was married years ago to an abusive man and had two children with him. Over time, her ex has changed and sincerely regrets losing her. Although Britney says she loves Kyle more than anything and wants to build a life with him, her life is really already full of family members, children, friends, ex-boyfriends, and an ex-husband.

Britney works every day in her father's business and spends enormous amounts of time socializing with the rest of her family, her two grown sons, and her numerous friends. Kyle goes with her to most of the social events, but they spend very little alone time together. On top of this she spends time with her ex on a regular basis, even going on exotic trips with him. She tells Kyle she never has sex with her ex (he's gained 150 pounds), but her ex is very wealthy and Kyle knows he would do anything to get her back. When Kyle tells Britney it's inappropriate for her to spend all this time with her ex, she says, "Well, if I had a normal man [referring to his lack of sexual desire] who acted like he adored me and wanted to have sex with me, maybe I wouldn't. But that's not the case now, is it?" Kyle then feels bad, becomes the victim, and backs off. And heaven forbid he even suggest she's too attached to her family—because when he does she gets self-righteous and reminds him that he had a mom who abandoned him—how would he know what a healthy family relationship looks like?

Kyle shuts up, shuts down, and pulls away sexually—often not understanding why he does this, himself. When Britney asks what's wrong, he just tells her he's tired, hoping she'll figure out that he means that he's tired of going with her to parties, weddings, and other social events every night of the week. He thinks she'll finally understand that they're doing too much. But she doesn't.

Kyle is starting to realize that Britney's overcommitted life is what exhausts him—and his anger about it turns him off sexually. Kyle needs to set boundaries with her about their lack of quality time together and Britney needs to start respecting those boundaries if the two of them are ever going to move forward and finally marry.

◀ Points to Remember ▶

1. If he insists on being friends with his ex, insist you all become friends.

2. It's your responsibility to handle *your* parents, and his responsibility to handle *his*.

3. If you've badmouthed him to your family, go back and clean it up by admitting your part.

4. Do not allow either ex to get in the way of your relationship.

5. You do not have to like each other's families, but you must be polite to them.

6. Staying close to an ex is unhealthy and inappropriate.

7. Divorce often does not stop the dysfunctional relationship between exes.

Chapter 11

When You Don't Like Each Other's Friends

Do you play the victim or controller role when you don't like your partner's friends? If you play the victim, you may:

- Whine about it when he goes out with his friends
- Stay home and feel bad when he spends time with his friends
- Accuse him of caring more about his friends than you
- Guilt-trip him about having friends because you don't have any

If you play the controller, you may:

- Pressure him to choose between his friends or you
- Badmouth his friends
- Argue that your friends are better than his
- Guilt-trip him that he should be mature enough not to need to party with his friends

When it comes to friends and associates, we bring two poisonous myths to love. One is that because two people love each other, they will both like the same people to the same degree. The second is that once we find love, we don't really need other people. Both ideas are false. In fact, a key ingredient to a healthy relationship is for both of you to have friends of your own, as well as friends together. The solution to handling respective friendships without resentment is negotiating differences and setting—and holding—boundaries. These can be as simple as following mutually agreed-upon house rules such as: No phone calls from friends before nine in the morning or after ten at night; neither of you will make last-minute plans without checking with the other first; each of you sets aside one night each week to do what you choose with whomever you choose without checking in; and both of you agree to be home before the bars close.

You Don't Have the Right to Choose Your Mate's Friends

Telling your mate who he can be friends with, or vice versa, is overstepping his personal boundary and is disrespectful. You have no right to control his friendships, nor does he have the right to control yours. If you try to control his friendships, you're trying to take away his personal power and that threatens his identity. Remember—we aren't trying to change your mate's entire personality—only his bad behavior with you.

"But Why Does He Still Need His Single, Drinking Buddies?"

Women often think that once a man has "settled down" with her, he should no longer have any need for partying, carousing, and drinking with his buddies. But he does need friends, and so do you. Remember, marriage is not death and if you make him feel he can't have fun, he will resent you and/or eventually leave. Certainly if he's out every night, partying like he did in college, he may have a problem accepting adult responsibilities. Finding a happy medium is the goal. If his partying is affecting his responsibilities at home, start by setting boundaries and ultimatums regarding his work, chores, and the children—which should then affect how much he sees his friends. If his partying is out of control, you need to let him know how his behavior is affecting your relationship, but be sure you don't scold him or tell him he's immature, because that puts you into a controlling role.

Outgrowing a Friend Is Different from Giving Up a Friend for Your Mate

I've given up most of my male-bashing and "desperate for a man" friends—by choice. Since I'm now in a happy, healthy relationship, I have little in common with those women. However, I still have many single friends and so does Alan, and we both agree we don't want to give them up.

Some people pride themselves in keeping the same friends for twenty years, while others make friends easily and let them go just as easily. Alan's the type who keeps friends for the long term, while I move on more quickly as I grow. Neither one of us is "right" about how we deal with friends—we just see it differently—and we both respect the other's point of view without judgment.

How to Handle His Most Obnoxious Friend

I remember asking Alan, "What could you possibly see in a friend like Sam? He's a rude, obnoxious jerk!" The answer? Alan liked Sam because they've been friends for years, they love to go to Vegas and gamble, he's very funny when he's drunk—and Sam is a man's man! None of these traits endeared Sam to me.

"You Need to Protect Me from Your Friends"

When Alan's friend Sam gets drunk, he becomes verbally abusive and critical. He criticizes everything from my hair to my weight, which makes me go ballistic. Alan would defend Sam by saying, "Why do you let Sam get to you? Just let his insults roll off your back like the rest of us do." To which I would respond, "I'm not letting it roll off my back! Sam is abusive, and if I ignore it, he gets away with it. I don't let people treat me like that! In fact, I don't understand how you can let him talk to you that way! I can't believe you don't stand up to him!" Alan believed he was acting strong because he didn't let Sam's insults get to him. I believed he was weak because he didn't stand up to him. This is a classic argument between men and women.

We spent hours debating our different perspectives on what constitutes strong, and finally negotiated a deal that worked for both of us. I said, "There's only one thing that would make me stop going off on Sam when he's rude and critical and that's if you handle him!" Alan said, "But you're a strong woman and pride yourself in handling people." "I know," I replied, "but my way of handling an abusive man like him is to cut him out of my life—but I can't do that because he's your friend. Since he's your friend, I need you to protect me from him. I want it to be your job to handle Sam when he says something insulting, nasty, or abusive to me. I'll look at you, and all I want from you is to say, 'Sam, that's over the line. Stop it!' He respects you and I believe he'll stop. If he doesn't, I want you to be prepared to leave with me if I want to leave. Will you do that? If so, I promise to stop going ballistic and making scenes when he insults me."

We made the deal. I believe Alan must have immediately had a talk with Sam and told him to stop it because it happened only about two more times over the last ten years. When it did, Alan kept the deal, and Sam backed off. Alan didn't have to give up his friendship with Sam—and I didn't have to let Sam treat me badly. It was, and still is, win/win! In fact, I now look at Sam and several of Alan's other weird friends as interesting characters in the story of our life together. And now—Sam doesn't get to me.

When He Hates Your Friends

His reasons for disliking your friends could be valid or something he's created in his own mind. Your friends may be a threat because they may badmouth him and try to sabotage your relationship (in which case you need to set some boundaries with them). Or he may just feel jealous of your time with your friends, jealous of the closeness you have with them, or just think your friend is an awful person.

"Mildred Didn't Cause Our Divorce—You Did!"

▶ *Sandy and Jimmy's Story*

Sandy's husband Jimmy told her she had to choose: her friend Mildred or him! Sandy, a very successful yet shy, thirty-seven-year-old corporate executive who worked her way up the corporate ladder, felt victimized by Jimmy's ultimatum. Sandy, who finds it hard to make friends, has one close friend of eight years, Mildred, whom she sees once every ten days or so and talks to her almost every other day. Her time with Mildred is not excessive and the two of them never do anything that could cause Jimmy to be jealous, like go out drinking or manhunting.

About eight months ago, Mildred and Jimmy got into an argument over something silly, and afterwards Jimmy (the controller in the relationship) told Sandy she wasn't allowed to see Mildred anymore. Sandy (who usually played victim) said she wouldn't give up the friendship. "So you're choosing her over me then, huh?" Jimmy asked. "No, I'm not choosing anyone. I can see why you thought she was rude to you, but I thought you were nasty to her too. I see both sides—and I hope the two of you will work it out—but I'm not giving up either one of you over this!"

This issue is what brought Sandy into my office. She was shocked that Jimmy wanted to control her friendship with Mildred but as she looked back she realized she had let Jimmy control her friends before. He had come between her and her brother years ago, and he had insisted that she give up several of her other friends—which she did. When I suggested that Jimmy was a controlling person, she said she had never thought of him that way, but she guessed that he was.

After much soul-searching, Sandy began to realize that she's been controlled most of her life, playing victim to her overpowering mother, who was critical and cold. That, combined with the fact that Sandy felt sorry for Jimmy, made her an easy target to be dominated by him. Jimmy has had problems with work over the years, and now Sandy's income is more than twice Jimmy's.

Jimmy is a mildly successful car salesman with a huge chip on his shoulder. He believes he was fired from several jobs just because he's black. When Jimmy was fourteen, his mother ran off with his stepfather, ultimately giving Jimmy up to his dad. He never forgave her for that and never stopped feeling like a victim in life because of it. Jimmy is a grudge holder, has major abandonment issues, and is a manic-depressive. I suggested Sandy stop feeling sorry for a man who takes his anger at the world out on her. (No wonder she had trouble seeing him as controlling—he plays a controlling victim.)

When she brought Jimmy into my office he immediately told me, "Sandy obviously doesn't really love me if she won't give up Mildred." To Jimmy, Sandy was abandoning him just like his mother had. I tried to work with him on his issue with his mom, but he resisted. He rejected every compromise I suggested to resolve the Mildred issue and finally said, "I will not compromise. She gives up Mildred or we get a divorce."

After four joint sessions with no sign of Jimmy being willing to negotiate or look for a compromise Sandy said, "Have it your way. You want to believe that Mildred is the reason we're getting divorced, go ahead and believe it. But the real cause is your controlling attitude. I've let you have your way for seven years, and now you believe it's your right to continue to have your way. I can't do this anymore. I'm moving out! Go ahead, tell everybody it's Mildred's fault we got divorced. But I know the truth!"

How to Preserve Your Friendship with a Friend He Can't Stand

Just like Alan did with Sam and me—Alan protected me from Sam—you have to protect your mate from your friend and your friend from your mate. For instance, you should try to keep your quality time with each one separate, never insisting that the three of you must spend time together. Your friend and your mate should only have to be in each other's presence at big events where there are numerous other people around as buffers. In a situation like your birthday, you may want to have drinks with her after work and then dinner with your husband. While asking him to respect your right to the friendship, you need to also show respect for his feelings about her.

When You Hate His Friends

Suppose some of your mate's friends are people you just don't like—people you believe aren't particularly good for him or for your relationship. What do you do about those cheaters and interfering lowlifes your mate wants to call his friends?

When His Friends Are Lowlifes

When he has a lowlife friend, boundaries are necessary. Note that I still didn't say this gives you the right to demand he give up his friend—although I know that's what you want to do. Your mate is a big boy and if he decides to do drugs or stay out late or behave like he's single, your issue still needs to be with his behavior, not his choice of friends. You can negotiate a deal such as:

- *I feel* upset that you promise me you'll be home at midnight, yet every time you go out with Gary, you always break that promise. I've set a consequence that you have to do the dishes for a week, but clean dishes is not what I'm looking for.
- *I want* you to promise me you'll stop going out with him in the evenings because this behavior is ultimately going to destroy our relationship.
- *Will you?*
- *If not, I'll* do what you do. The rule you seem to be following is "No matter what we tell our mate, we'll just come home when we feel like it." If that's the rule you're following, then I will too.

Our Best "Cocaine Friends"

▶ *Brandi's and Colin's Story*

Colin and Brandi met in college and drank and partied every night with their best friends Keith and Renee. Eventually the two couples got married and Keith and Colin went into business together. Their business was immediately successful and the money began pouring in beyond their wildest dreams. Both couples bought new homes and new cars and plenty of toys. Life was great!

With all the money coming in, these partiers soon moved from beer parties to cocaine parties. At first, all four of them used on a regular basis. Then, one year into the marriage, Brandi got pregnant—and everything changed! She and Renee decided they should stop using cocaine but the guys had trouble stopping, blaming each other for continuing to use. After the baby was born, Brandi and Colin appeared in my office.

Brandi told Colin it was time to grow up and act like a father now or she'd take the baby and leave. Out of fear of losing his son, he agreed to stop. Brandi didn't trust him and began checking up on him, interrogating him and accusing him of still using cocaine, even though he really wasn't. Colin rebelled against her control and secretly started using again. The more she nagged him, the more he rebelled; the more he rebelled, the more she nagged him.

I helped Brandi and Colin make this deal: That Brandi would stop nagging Colin if he would submit to random drug tests. To keep the deal, Colin realized he needed to spend less time with Keith since their friendship seemed to revolve around cocaine. But pulling away from the friendship had to be *his* decision, not Brandi's.

When His Friends Cheat on Their Wives and He Defends Them

There seems to be a code among men that they cover for each other's cheating. To me that's condoning it. Even Alan sometimes protected the confidence of his cheating friends until one day we fought because I chose not to protect his cheating friend Ted when his girlfriend asked me for the truth. That obviously caused problems between Alan and Ted, but Alan stood by me and my right to tell the truth. And Ted, of course, became careful of his behavior in front of me. Although Alan and I had discussed the cheating issue thoroughly (more on this in Chapter 12) and had made clear deals about it, I knew that his friends and their "manly man" value system regarding cheating was always there pulling at him. I had to comfort myself by remembering that my deal was with Alan, not them. Interestingly, over the years, his buddies stopped cheating and many of them have developed healthier, more equal relationships. It seems like Alan's values rubbed off on them instead.

When His Friends Interfere

You know which friends of his wish he wasn't with you. Maybe it's because they want him to stay single and be available to them. Maybe it's because you're strong and they're used to submissive women. Maybe your personalities just clash. They may tease him and say he is "whipped." They may even try to break the two of you up. It often feels like things would be fine if it weren't for "his friends." But instead you need to look at him and his behavior, not his friends'. Is he defending you and the relationship? If not, ask him to say something to them like, "Hey, back off you guys. I'm happier than I've ever been! You guys are just jealous because you go home alone every night."

After my numerous confrontations with Alan's friends, most of them couldn't stand me. They nicknamed me Pit Bull and Attila the Hun. One night they even gathered together and took Alan out to a bar for a verbal "blanket" party where they confronted Alan, telling him they hated me and that he had to make a choice between them or me. He told them, "I'm happier with Carolyn than I've ever been. Trust me, you don't want to make me have to choose." Once he set that boundary, everything changed. The power struggle ended and they adjusted to me being part of his life.

Milt Stirs the Pot

▶ Marion and Tom's Story

When Marion first met Tom's friend Milt, she heard negative things about him—that he was underhanded in business and chauvinistic with women—but she didn't really believe it because he seemed quite nice. As time went on, she realized that every time she and Tom had a fight, Tom had just played golf or had drinks with Milt. She began to put the picture together: Milt was causing problems in their relationship.

Tom would come back from a night out with Milt, saying things like, "I don't see why I have to answer to you about when I'll be home—you don't own me. You think because I sleep with you, you can start telling me what to do!" Marion would argue that when people live together, they owe it to each other to check in about when they'll be home. "Who says?" Tom would reply, and then he would purposely stay out late the next few nights and not call her, thinking he was asserting his independence. Marion would be angry when he got home and would rag on him. The next day Tom would tell Milt and Milt would say, "See, I warned you! Marion's turning into a real bitch! Don't let her do this to you—this is just the beginning. That's what women do—try to control you!"

Tom was feeling more and more justified in his bad behavior because of the way Marion was acting. I told Marion, "Don't rag on him. If he wants the rule to be that there's no checking in to tell you when he'll be home, then you just have to follow that same rule too. But you'll follow it to the nth degree, beating him at his own game—until he doesn't like it and wants the rule to change. Don't nag him anymore and don't try to punish him; just be sure you come home later than he does several nights a week. Be vague about where you've been—like he is. Yes, it's much like playing a game or giving him a dose of his own medicine, but not quite as punitive. Remember, he said that just because a couple lives together doesn't mean they need to answer to each other. Let's see if he still feels that way when you're the one not coming home!"

Marion had lived in Denver only two years and didn't have as many friends as Tom, so it was hard for her to do. She also didn't like having to do it, but she did agree to try it. She went to the mall, saw some movies alone, went out drinking with friends sometimes, and went over to her friend's apartment to watch television until midnight a few nights, making sure she came home after him. Tom would ask where she had been, but all Marion would tell him was that she was out with friends, and no more.

Tom began to suggest they stay home more and more, but from time to time his chats with Milt still made him rebel and stay out late again with no phone call. When he did that, Marion would go to her friend's house and watch TV until midnight several nights in a row to prove her point. In fact, one weekend she spent most of her time there. Finally, Tom confronted her, "What's going on here? Are you cheating on me?"

At that moment, Marion had the power and it was time to try to negotiate: "No, Tom, I'm not having an affair. I love you and want to be with you, but your friend Milt has convinced you that I'm trying to control you, so you're constantly fighting with me and fighting against our having a normal life together."

- *I feel* frustrated that you think I'm trying to control you each time I try to make plans with you.
- *I want* us to plan our lives as a couple, showing mutual respect with phone calls, and coming home at reasonable times, and planning meals together.
- Marion had "equalized the rules" and told him: "Since you wouldn't work with me in the past, I decided to try it your way. I don't make any assumptions that we'll be together each night. And since you don't try to coordinate with me, I'm spending time with friends who will. It's not really what I want to do, but you leave me no choice."
- *Let's make a deal* that two nights a week we don't have to check in, but the rest of the time we do. And also, I want you to tell Milt that you're choosing to do this the next time he says I'm trying to control you.
- *Will you?*
- *If not, I'll* simply continue planning with my friends every night like you do and we won't have much time together.

Tom was so relieved she wasn't cheating, he gladly agreed to the deal; besides, he was starting to miss Marion and looked forward to having a home life again.

If "equalizing the rules" hadn't worked with Tom, her next step could have been to confront Tom directly regarding whether or not he really wanted to be a couple and live together. She could have said:

- *I feel* frustrated that you asked me to move in and now don't seem to want to be a couple.
- *I want* you to work out a deal with me regarding our time together versus your time with your friends.
- *Will you* do that?
- *If not, I'll* start looking for my own place.

Your Man-Hating Friends

If you talk to your male-bashing friends on a regular basis, it may be a key reason you're not in a healthy relationship. I know from first-hand experience. Years ago, when I lived in Aspen, I had a large group of man-hating, single friends, and on Sundays before we went skiing, we had what we called "Bitch Brunch." We sat around expanding on the latest episode of what some man had done to us. I never really realized how much those friends held me back from finding a healthy relationship, until after I had met Alan and began to rekindle my friendship with Judy from that group. Alan and I were getting along well when Judy and I met for a drink one night. Although she was now married, we somehow got right back into our "men are jerks" conversations. I went home to Alan that night and unknowingly picked a fight. The next day Alan said something to me I'll never forget. "What happened with you and Judy last night to put you in such an angry mood? I can hardly wait for you to go out with her again! Can I have advance notice so I can get the boxing gloves out and be ready next time?"

When Friends Come First

I often hear from both my male and female clients, "I want to be number one on his (or her) priority list. His friends are number one—and that's not right!" By the way, this seldom improves after marriage, so it's important that you resolve this issue before you marry him. Once you're married, you have less power to move up on the list. And what's more, although you might think the opposite, you're even less likely to be a priority once you've had children—not because of the children, but because he knows you're less likely to leave him.

If he's first on your list and you're fourth on his, you have to move him down and make him fourth on yours—like Marion did with Tom. You'll need to "uninvest" and become less interested. You need to become more involved with your friends, family, work, or hobbies to equalize the power and help him identify with your feelings. Being too available to him has enabled him to keep you a low priority. So change it. Even if he is number one in reality, start treating him as if he's not. I promise you he'll notice. Then and only then will you have enough power to get him to negotiate with you.

"Your Time Is Really Spent with Them, Not Me"
▶ *Britney and Kyle's Story*
Kyle (of Britney and Kyle in Chapters 1, 7, and 10) says that Britney's friends always come first. "Even when we're out for a romantic dinner or at her house cuddling on the couch, she answers her phone and talks to her friends for thirty minutes to an hour. She's so rude! Then she wonders why I'm not feeling amorous when she gets off the phone. I usually start packing up to leave while she's talking. You'd think she would get the hint!"

Opposite-Sex Friends (Yours and His)
It's your responsibility to keep your mate aware of who your friends—and close acquaintances—are, including (and especially)

those of the opposite sex. If this person is a secret friend, he's probably not just a friend. Not letting your mate know about him leads to trust issues, jealousy, and often even the beginning of an affair.

Basic Rules for Conducting Friendships (Yours and His)

- Don't criticize his friends or hold his friends' beliefs against him.
- Never demand he end certain friendships.
- Neither is allowed to have secret friends, especially of the opposite sex.
- Never spend time alone with opposite sex friends you are attracted to.
- Don't badmouth your mate to your friends.
- Don't tell your friends information about your mate that is embarrassing or considered "private."
- Neither should defend a friend's bad behavior.
- If either of you wants to be friends with an ex, the ex must be friends with both of you.
- Both must be polite and tolerant of the other's friends even if you don't like them.
- Both are allowed to set boundaries regarding certain behaviors when your mate is out with his friends.
- Always protect your mate from a friend's bad behavior.

When You Know She's Interested in Him—and He's Too Blind to See It

Call it women's intuition or knowing your competition, but women know when another woman is a threat. Alan played golf with a woman named Ellen, who'd just come out of a ten-year relationship with a married man. When we were out one night, I happened to overhear people talking about several of them going to Ellen's for drinks after golf on Friday (I was leaving town for business on

Friday). When we got home, I asked Alan about it, and he said yes, that was the plan. I told him I wasn't okay with that because I could tell that Ellen was interested in him. He said he couldn't believe I was acting so jealous, especially since he wasn't interested in her. After a half-hour arguing back and forth, I played "equalize the rules" and said, "Okay, I'm not saying you can't go. I just want to know what the rule is. If I've got it straight, I can go to the house of a man who is interested in me, at night, and drink alcohol with him—as long as I'm not really interested in him? Okay, I just need to know what the deal is before I leave for L.A. tomorrow." He looked at me in disbelief, then said with tenderness, "Let's not do this to each other." I said, "Let's not." He never went.

Dating While Married Is Not Okay!

▶ *Gretchen and Art's Story*

Gretchen and Art (of Gretchen and Art in Chapters 5, 8, and 9) have a deal whereby they are allowed to have friends of the opposite sex. It was Gretchen's idea to make the deal because Art actually doesn't have any female friends, but Gretchen wanted to keep her friendship with Todd, her hiking buddy, and a man she admits being attracted to.

One week Gretchen announced to Art that Todd had invited her to his high school reunion next Saturday night. "What? An event like that and on a Saturday night? Isn't that a date? That doesn't seem right to me," Art replied. Gretchen agreed that Todd's request seemed awkward to her too, especially since he had asked her not to wear her wedding ring that night so he could pretend that they were together. Art told Gretchen, "It's obvious you've gone too far with this friendship, and you need to set some firm boundaries with Todd or stop seeing him." She agreed not to go to Todd's reunion, but still planned to hike with him once a week.

A few weeks later, purely by accident, a woman at work who

had wrecked her car asked Art to give her a ride home from work, so he did. Gretchen threw a fit when she found out! Art accidentally used the "competition" technique from Chapter 5 which changed the power structure in their relationship, giving Art more power than he ever had. Gretchen finally heard Art and he was finally able to get Gretchen to back off from her friendship with Todd. Who knows how far Gretchen's flirtatious friendship with Todd might have gone otherwise. When a mate understands that all rules apply to both of you ("equalizing the rules" technique), he (in this case she) is more likely to think through the consequences of his actions.

◀ Points to Remember ▶

1. You don't have the right to choose your mate's friends.

2. Don't tell friends anything about your mate that you haven't told him.

3. It's important to have friends of your own as well as friends together.

4. Protect your mate from friends he doesn't like, and require the same from him.

5. Male-bashing friends keep you from finding the man of your dreams.

6. It's okay to outgrow friends and move on.

7. If he doesn't make you a priority, don't make him a priority.

Chapter 12

Accountability for Flirting, Cheating, and Jealousy

Do you play the victim or controller role when you encounter flirting, cheating, and jealousy? If you play the victim, you may:

- Feel insecure every time someone is friendly with your mate
- Constantly fear that your mate will find someone better than you
- Ignore the signs that your mate is cheating
- Know about, but put up with, your mate's indiscretions

If you play the controller, you may:

- Constantly need to attract the attention of the opposite sex
- Flirt with others in front of your mate
- Cross the line with flirting and collecting phone numbers of "potentials"
- Make scenes because of your jealousy
- Constantly accuse your mate of cheating
- Have cheated in the past, cheat now, or consider cheating an option for the future

Growing Apart and Infidelity

Partners often feel pulled apart as they try to balance time between their individual pursuits and their partner. As they drift apart, each one is a prime candidate for an affair with anyone who appears more understanding or attentive to them than their mate. For approximately 50 percent of couples, one or both partners have cheated at some point in their relationship. Have you drifted apart? Ask yourself these questions:

- Do I believe he's happy?
- Am I really happy?
- Are we still kissing on the lips; and if not, why not?
- Do I still want to have sex with him; and if not, why not?
- Do I more often try to look my best when he's not around? (Maybe I need to dress up for him tonight.)
- Have our lives grown boring? If so, what can we do to change that?
- Have we drifted apart since the kids were born? If so, what can we do to fix that?
- Am I emotionally and sexually satisfied in this relationship? Is he? If not, what do we need to do?

When these questions aren't addressed, flirting, jealousy, and cheating can become serious issues in the future of the relationship.

Why People Cheat

Couples decide to break their vows and cheat for two reasons. First, the passion, romance, and sex have fizzled away in their present relationship. Second, they've built up resentment toward their mate because of unresolved issues. Instead of working on the relationship and resolving resentments, people often feel justified in looking outside their relationship to meet their needs. Infidelity starts long before the first affair.

Each criticism you can't forget, each time he feels he can't win, every fight that doesn't get resolved are the beginnings of infidelity.

People Cheat in Sexless Relationships

About five years into our relationship, Alan became upset with me, wouldn't tell me what it was about, and withdrew from me sexually. After asking the usual questions, "Is it me? Are you no longer attracted to me? What is it?" and getting no real response from him, I began to fantasize about other men. Luckily, I did something that's very hard to do—I told him. With huge tears in my eyes, I said, "I have to tell you that since we haven't had sex for a while, I'm starting to fantasize about other men. I want you to know this now while my fantasies are about movie stars—men who are out of my reach. My fear is that if we don't work out our sexual issues, I'll soon be fantasizing about men who *are* available to me, and then I'll start acting out those fantasies." Alan immediately became sexually attentive again (and we did ultimately work out the issue that made him withdraw from me).

"It's His Fault I Cheated"
▶ My Ex's and My Story

When I was twenty-two and married for only a year, my husband John was already paying very little attention to me emotionally or sexually. I was in college at the time, getting my M.S. degree in counseling psychology, spending time around many attractive male classmates and professors. Several men came on to me in a therapy group where I opened up about my sexual problems with my husband, but the man who broke through my "I'm married" barrier was my psychology professor, the leader of the group. He gave me attention, spent quality time with me, and made me feel special. Before long, I was in bed with him. I knew it was wrong at the time, but justified my affair because John was ignoring me. I now know that his bad behavior did not justify mine. I should have confronted my husband about his cold, unemotional ways, telling him how unhappy I was and giving him a chance to fix it before I moved on—that would have been the fair and healthy thing to do. Of course my psychology professor certainly should have guided me on how to do that rather than sleeping with me, but that's another story.

Who We Cheat With

Many of us find it easier to share our issues about our mate with anyone except him—and that's our first mistake, especially if we confide in a male friend or coworker. It may start innocently. We're frustrated and need someone to talk to. The male friend or coworker assures us that we're underappreciated, and he strokes our ego. We don't stop to think about his ulterior motives. The more we talk to him and the more he understands, the worse our mate looks and the better he looks to us.

We're afraid of confrontation, so we don't tell our mate—the one person who needs this information the most—what's wrong. When you tell your friends but not him, you're not doing everything you can to save your marriage. Later, when the confidences you share with a male friend turn into an affair, you'll probably naively say to your friends, "The affair took me by surprise," or "It just happened!" Not true. You made a decision to break the bond when you chose to discuss your problems with someone other than your mate.

If you're cheating, know that the reason this new lover "understands" you so well is because you've communicated all of the information to him that you should have shared with your mate. If and when you divorce and start a relationship with this new person, you'll probably repeat the same pattern: when there are problems, you'll tell others, instead of him. That behavior will destroy your relationship no matter which man you're with.

Men Who Cheat

We all assume that when men don't get sex at home, they will eventually cheat to get it, but what's up with men who cheat even when they have a good sexual relationship with their wives? Many old-fashioned men believe it is a man's god-given right to have more than one woman, especially when he brings in most of the money. He may believe that an added benefit to being a good provider is that he's allowed to get a little on the side. My client Bill believed this, and he just didn't understand how his attitude kept him single.

"It Would Kill Me to Think of Her with Another Man, but I Always Have Women on the Side"

▶ *Bill's Story*

Bill, a thirty-year-old man who says he longs to be married and have a family, definitely has a double standard when it comes to cheating. He justifies his cheating (and doesn't even call it cheating) by telling himself that the woman he's with doesn't really love him, so he has to keep other options open. In each relationship, Bill is the classic obsessive, jealous male who always wants to know where a woman is and what she's doing at all times. He projects his own promiscuity onto the women he dates, acting like an obsessive, jealous fool, pressuring and controlling the woman he is with—while he's the one sleeping around. By the way, it's not unusual for a man to project his own desire to cheat on to you by acting overly jealous.

Who He Cheats With

The difference between cheating women and cheating men is that men don't need to have issues with their mates to cheat. Their cheating is often just about sex—not love—and they often cheat because they can, with anyone they're attracted to. They may even really love their wives, which is difficult to understand because they certainly don't consider their wives' feelings. Men who feel entitled to more than one woman (womanizers) also seldom consider their cheating "affairs." They consider their sexual trysts as simple indiscretions or innocent mistakes or one-night stands—something that's no big deal. When dealing with a man who has this attitude your only protection is to remember to "equalize the rules". Tell him, "That's good to know. Then you won't be upset when I make 'an innocent mistake.' So we both can have one-night stands and not consider it cheating? I'm just clarifying the rules."

Women Who Try to Steal Your Man

Some women have no boundaries when it comes to men, and wedding bands don't seem to affect them. In fact, it's often the challenge of taking another woman's man that intrigues them, and these women know how to seduce your man. While you're pressuring him about his honey-do list, she's telling him how wonderful and smart he is and inviting him to the hot new "in" spot for a drink. If you're taking your mate for granted, it's only a matter of time before some woman will move in on him. She counts on the fact that you're always angry at him, your lives are boring, and you seldom have sex. She knows he's vulnerable to any positive, sexual attention she gives him. If it's any consolation, statistics show that a man very seldom ever leaves his wife for the mistress. But a mistress will wreak havoc in your lives for several years before she gives up. So don't ignore the problems in your relationship to the point that cheating becomes an issue.

"He Spends More Time with Me Than Her!"
▶ *Kirsten and Sheldon's Story*
Forty-two-year-old Kirsten, a gorgeous blonde neurologist, began seeing Sheldon, a married man, seven years ago. They were coworkers when Kirsten began to pursue Sheldon, a well-seasoned

doctor—first as her mentor and then as her lover. Kirsten asked for Sheldon's help with several patients and he was flattered and pleased to help her. Kirsten dressed especially sexy on the days they had their lunches discussing cases, and she stroked his ego every day. It wasn't long before other things were being stroked too. But Sheldon told her from the beginning that, although he was bored with his stay-at-home wife and loved being seen with gorgeous Kirsten in her sexy clothes, this was just for fun because he still loved his wife and would never leave her and the children.

Kirsten came in to see me right after she turned forty and had been with Sheldon for over five years. She, like most women, wanted marriage and children, and knew that if she stayed with Sheldon, she would never have it. But she couldn't understand why he would never leave his wife. "He spends much more time with me than he does her. We travel together; he buys me gifts and calls me seven times a day when we're apart. He has to love me! What's going on? What should I do?" Kirsten couldn't understand how Sheldon's wife wouldn't know about their affair after so many years—his wife knew they spent a lot of time together—but she has never asked Sheldon about Kirsten or accused him of cheating with her.

Both Kirsten and Sheldon's wife were the victims of a controlling womanizer. Every time Kirsten got depressed and whined to him, he paid for her therapy or bought her something expensive. Every time his wife acted unhappy, he took her on a trip. Neither woman held Sheldon accountable, and both were enabling him.

Sheldon's wife needed to confront him on her suspicions. But Kirsten needed to confront Sheldon as well, which she finally had the courage to do when she got wind that he had a new girlfriend. With the help of a friend Kirsten found out where the new girlfriend lived and paid her a visit. On the way over, Kirsten dialed Sheldon on her cell phone and started an intimate conversation. As she walked in the door, she handed the phone to his new mistress as she said to Sheldon, "Say hello to my new friend." Finally, Kirsten faced reality and ended it.

Don't Bury Your Head in the Sand

We all hate bad news, especially when it's regarding someone we love. Many women, like Sheldon's wife, are prone to burying their heads in the sand when it comes to a mate's cheating, and stay-at-home wives are usually the worst. They've built their lives around their husbands and are reluctant to confront a situation that will possibly cause an upheaval in their homes or lifestyles. These women often ignore the truth until there's no turning back. That's what happened to Stacey.

"The Kids Are Grown, and I'm Gone"

▶ *Stacey and Dean's Story*

Forty-eight-year-old Stacey has been married to Dean for twenty-seven years. Their twenty-five-year-old daughter moved away a year ago, and their eighteen-year-old son is going away to college next week. Last Friday night, Dean announced to his wife that he was moving out and moving in with his girlfriend. Stacey was shocked, but shouldn't have been. Dean had cheated on her numerous times before. Each time, she forgave him, and he promised never to do it again.

Dean has had the same girlfriend for the last five years, and Stacey even admits there were many clues, but she chose to ignore them. Dean was a great father and she wouldn't have divorced him despite his indiscretions, and Dean knew it. Stacey says she stayed for the sake of the children, but the truth is, she stayed because she had grown comfortable playing the role of the victim, which she had played throughout the entire marriage.

Stacey should have confronted Dean the first time she caught him cheating. But instead she let it go, because she was afraid of what she might find out. Stacey should have asked Dean if he loved the other woman. If he did, Stacey should have told him to leave; if he didn't, Stacey should have insisted on marriage counseling to work out the problems between them. Now it's too late, and Dean in his usual controlling fashion has made the decision for them.

Deal with the Possibility of Cheating Before It Happens

If you aren't happy or you suspect he isn't happy, you need to talk to each other about why. If you don't, you're choosing to watch your relationship die. Just because he never brings up issues and never complains doesn't mean he's happy. He could be stifling a lot of resentment, and so could you. And if he seems like a great family man it doesn't mean he isn't cheating. He can love his kids and still cheat. There are always clues. Don't ignore them until it's too late.

"You Slept with Her after I Followed You to Kansas!"

▶ Melanie and Jackson's Story

Melanie and her husband Jackson were having some problems in their relationship when Jackson got a big promotion and a transfer to Salt Lake City. Financially, they couldn't turn it down, so Melanie quit her job to follow Jackson. Melanie helped Jackson get settled in Salt Lake City and then returned with her son to Denver for a month to sell their house and wrap up loose ends.

When everything was completed, she and their son headed back without announcing their exact arrival time, only to find another woman in their new house. When Jackson came home, he admitted he'd been having an affair with Mary for over six months and that she had spent the last month in Salt Lake City with him while Melanie was back in Denver. He said, "Mary knows I'm married to you and she's okay with that. I wish you could be as open sexually as she is." Melanie put her son in the car and headed back to Denver, moving into her parents' basement with her son.

After several visits to my office, Melanie began to realize that Jackson's attitude about everything had worsened since their child was born. He had become more cocky and controlling. I asked Melanie if she herself had changed. "Of course," she said. "I'm a mom now. I've stopped going out with my friends because I'm totally dedicated to my child. Jackson knows I want him to be more of a responsible father and

229

he seems to be acting worse, not better!" "Are you nagging him to straighten up?" I asked. "Of course I am. Somebody has to." I assured her that I wasn't blaming her for his affair, but pointed out how she has been acting like a victim since the baby was born. She had given away more and more of her power to him—and once she quit her job and moved to Salt Lake City, he had all the power, and she had none. That's why he thought he could get away with his cheating and his cocky attitude that she should accept it.

I helped Melanie get her power back and she began to hold her boundaries with Jackson. Within a month he was begging her to come back, promising he would never cheat again. The last I knew she had a new job in Denver and certainly a new attitude! She told him, "You want me back? You find another job in Denver, move here, and work at winning me back!"

Once a Cheater, Always a Cheater?

Do all cheaters cheat again? They do if they think they can get away with it. Cheaters usually have a pattern of avoiding emotional issues in relationships, choosing to move on to someone new instead of addressing their problems. Then they do the same thing in the next relationship, and the next one, and the next one . . . They continue to cheat because they never learn to resolve issues. Jackson, of course, needed to talk to Melanie about her nagging and how the relationship had changed since the baby, instead of acting like a rebellious teenager.

"He Cheated *with* Me—Will He Cheat *on* Me?"
▶ *Lindy and Anthony's Story*

Lindy and Anthony were both engaged to other people when they met. Lindy continually told Anthony how badly her fiancé was treating her (which put her in the victim role), and Anthony slipped right into the rescuer (controlling) role. After two years of secretly seeing each other, they both agreed to end their engagements to other people and get married.

Now that they're married, Lindy is constantly accusing Anthony of showing interest in other women—which he does. Anthony has always been a womanizer and is proud of it. He tells Lindy, "I've always been a big flirt—you know that!" Lindy's greatest concern is that he'll find a new woman who needs him more than she does—and she should worry because rescuing damsels in distress is a long-time pattern for Anthony. Feeling needed feeds his ego. And now that Lindy has started her own business and is feeling happier, stronger, and more equal, they've started arguing about little things. Anthony's beginning to see her as an adversary instead of that weak little woman who needed to be rescued.

Lindy says Anthony has changed since they got married. They no longer have the deep emotional talks that made them so close. But when she thinks about it, those talks were all about how badly her fiancé was treating her, and Anthony would empathize and advise her on what to do. They no longer seem to have much to talk about. She'd like to talk to him about *their* problems, but Anthony refuses.

Will Anthony probably cheat? Yes—because he cheated in the past, he has a self-righteous attitude about cheating, his relationship with Lindy has been out of balance since the beginning, his ego isn't fed by her anymore, the relationship wasn't built on solid ground to begin with, and, most important, he refuses to deal emotionally with issues in their relationship.

What Constitutes Cheating

When the Clinton/Monica scandal erupted, the nation debated whether having oral sex was really cheating. Mistresses had heard this argument from the men they were cheating with for years, "We can only have oral sex so when my wife asks if I've cheated on her,

I can still say 'no.'" Most couples never considered having a conversation about what constitutes cheating before the Clinton scandal. Discussing what is and isn't sexual and then "equalizing the rules" is extremely important in every relationship. If your mate says he doesn't believe that oral sex is cheating, all you have to say is, "So if it isn't, then we're both allowed to have oral sex with others and it won't be considered cheating?" You can laugh as you say it if you want, just so he gets the point. Most men never stopped to consider that their wives or girlfriends could follow the same rule.

"Sexual Massages Are the Same as Cheating!"

▶ *Misty and Gordon's Story*

Gordon (of Misty and Gordon in Chapters 8 and 10) traveled for business and often got sexual massages while out of town. One day Misty got suspicious when she saw some strange charges on Gordon's credit card, so she decided to call the number. Once she realized it was a massage parlor and what kind it was, she accused Gordon of cheating. He said it wasn't cheating; she said it was. They argued "right and wrong" to no avail. Finally, Misty said, "I don't care what you think. It's not okay with me for you to get sexual massages. And if this is something you can't give up, then you'll have to give up our marriage." There would be no negotiation because, for Misty, this was a deal breaker. Gordon agreed to give up the massages, but he didn't really believe he had done anything wrong, and this damaged Misty's trust in him.

Emotional Cheating

Is an emotional relationship with the opposite sex cheating? Most women yearn for an emotional connection with a man and are therefore vulnerable to almost any man who plays the emotional trump card. To decide if your emotional connection with a man is cheating, ask yourself: "If my mate had the same relationship with another woman, would I be okay with it?" Probably not. If your mate is emotionally unavailable and you're vulnerable emotionally because of this, you need to confront your mate. Make it clear to him you'll get your emotional needs met elsewhere if he doesn't come through for you, but give him a chance to fix it before you cheat on him emotionally.

"Is He a Cheater or Am I Just Overly Jealous?"

Sometimes jealousy can distort our view of things and we can't tell for sure if we're showing our own insecurities or if we really have reason to worry. Usually men argue that looking at women is as normal for a male as watching football. Women say these men are being disrespectful when they can't take their eyes off attractive women. Both sides are valid.

"You're a Flirt and I'm Jealous!"

▶ *Rose and Terry's Story*

Rose is a tall, striking, thirty-two-year-old blonde bookkeeper who has been dating (and fighting with) Terry for seven years. Rose admits she's insecure, but she says that Terry eyeballs every attractive woman he comes in contact with. And besides just staring at other women, he flirts—with waitresses, wives of friends, and female coworkers. Rose believes that Terry has cheated on her, but she can't prove it and he'll never admit it. But she's found what she considers clues: a matchbook in his car with a woman's phone number written on it; he shuts off his computer quickly when she walks into the room; and he often refuses to tell her where he's been, saying he won't play into her insecurities. She often feels crazy with jealousy, and then makes a fool of herself by searching his car and house for phone numbers and other clues. The more Rose acts like a victim with her jealousy, the more Terry rebels, puts her down, acts controlling, and disrespects her—making him more likely to cheat.

Here's what I told Rose to do:

- *Develop an attitude* of, "If you want to be with someone else, go for it. But if you want to be with me, stop this disrespectful behavior now or I'll leave. This is not okay with me."
- *Set boundaries* around his flirting with consequences, such as, "I want you to stop staring at other women when you're with me and I'm going to fine you five dollars every time I catch you doing it. And when I actually see you flirting with another woman, I'll say you owe me five dollars and I want you to not only give me the five dollars but also stop giving that person attention at that point and instead reassure me. Will you? If not, I'll leave your presence."
- *"Equalize the rules"* by no longer reporting to him where she's going and what she's doing. Once he gets upset and wants her to share again, let him know, "I will if you will."
- *"Use Competition"* If Terry is chatting it up with some girl, walk away and chat it up with some attractive guy, or disappear and let him wonder where she is.

Is Flirting Wrong?

Smiling, talking, laughing with someone of the opposite sex, but always letting him know you're not really available can be fun, healthy, and harmless. The person you're flirting with can know that you find him attractive, as long as he knows you don't intend to do anything about it. But Terry crossed the line, however, when he exchanged phone numbers and had secret conversations with coworkers he was interested in. When Rose got jealous, he never reassured her that she was the special woman in his life. In fact, he did the opposite—he used his flirting and her insecurity to keep the power in the relationship.

Handling His Jealousy

Jealousy comes from insecurity. Extremely insecure men (and women) believe that keeping their mate in a box and never allowing them to be exposed to anyone else is what is necessary to keep them. They don't realize that controlling their partners this tightly will only cause resentment and rebellion. The more tightly you try to hold on to someone, the more likely you are to lose him.

The Dancer and the Harley Rider

▶ *Shara and Lucas's Story*

When Shara and Lucas came in to see me, Lucas was so jealous that he was holding Shara captive in her own home. All Shara wanted was to get out of the house to go to school or work. Lucas, a very large man who owns a Harley Davidson motorcycle shop, got tears in his eyes when he told me that he felt that Shara was too good for him. He feared that if he let her out of the house, he would lose her forever. I tried to help Lucas understand that if he didn't back off on his jealousy and possessiveness, he would surely lose her. I tried to help Shara see that Lucas couldn't stop her from going to school or work and that she needed to do these things and not ask for his permission. Neither changed their behavior, and they quit therapy after only a few sessions.

One year later, Shara came back to see me—alone this time. Her life had changed dramatically, and the power in the relationship had flipped 180 degrees. Lucas's greatest fears had come true. Shara had not only gone back to work, she was now working as a topless dancer! Plus she was blatantly cheating on Lucas while still living with him. I helped her see that she had gone from obedient little girl to rebellious teenager. She knew she had, but couldn't stop herself because Lucas was acting like the victim and letting her get away with it.

Let's back up. Instead of having an affair and taking a job in a dance club, Shara should have said the following to Lucas.

- *I feel* angry that you try to control me because of your own insecurities. I love you but I won't let you keep me from having a life.
- *I want* you to stop acting so jealous and treat me with the respect that I deserve.
- *Will you* back off and not try to stop me from going back to school and getting a part-time job?
- *If not, I will* do it anyway, and if you fight with me about it, I'll move out.

What Not to Do

Here are some guidelines to help you navigate the murky waters created by flirting, cheating, and jealousy.

Don't Believe the Agreement Not to Cheat Is Understood

It's understood in most relationships that "you do not cheat!" However, don't trust that this boundary is understood by the both of you. Remember, people will try to get away with whatever they can. He needs to clearly know what the consequences will be if he cheats. One client of mine made her fiancé sign a prenuptial agreement that she will own their half-million-dollar house free and clear if he ever cheats on her.

Don't Say You'll Leave If You Won't

Most women who find out their man has cheated, not only don't leave, but fight to keep him—and men count on it. Why don't women leave? Because when he chooses someone else over us, it makes us feel rejected. When we feel rejected, we're likely to want to prove to our mate that we're good enough for him instead of pulling away from him like we should. So be very careful, whatever you do, to set a realistic consequence you know you can keep.

Don't Teach Him to Lie—Always Give Him Credit for Honesty

If you explode every time he tells you the truth, you're teaching him to lie. If you can tell when he's lying, but you let it go, this also enables him to keep lying. You need to give him credit for honesty. Make it clear that if there's a problem, and he tells you the truth, you promise you'll try to work it out. But if he compounds the problem by lying, you won't forgive him for that.

Don't Tell Him That Other Lovers Have Cheated on You

The worst thing a woman can tell a new man in her life is, "Men always cheat on me." She doesn't realize that she is possibly setting a precedent for the future since she is pointing out to the new man that she usually plays victim in her relationships. Indirectly she's telling him that she allows men to cheat on her—which basically gives him permission to cheat.

Don't Play Good Wife If He Isn't Playing Good Husband

Don't sit at home while he goes out—go out as much as he does. Misty sat home with Gordon's kids while he went out to "business dinners" every night. How comfortable for Gordon to be out flirting or maybe even cheating (or getting sexual massages) while he knows exactly where his wife is—home with *his* kids. I talked Misty into going to an evening business meeting with the guys from work (thereby "equalizing the rules"). When Gordon found out she was with a group of men from work smoking cigars and drinking cognac in a cigar bar, he went through the roof! However, he was finally willing to negotiate with her about what was appropriate behavior in their marriage. Once he had to worry about what she was doing, she had more power in the relationship to negotiate boundaries around his behavior.

If He Cheats, Don't Take the Blame—Make Him Take Responsibility for His Actions.

Don't believe for a moment that it's your fault he cheated on you. You may have contributed to the problems in the relationship, but it's his fault he chose to break the bond rather than try to work out the issues.

Guidelines to Keep the Two of You from Cheating

- Be sure your mate feels loved and special to you, and expect the same in return.
- Don't allow any bond with anyone outside the relationship to be stronger than the bond you have with your mate.
- Mark your territory with coworkers, friends, or anyone who could be after him, and allow him to do the same.
- Maintain a good sexual relationship.
- Don't allow someone you find intriguing to regularly flirt with you.
- Don't spend alone time with someone you find attractive.
- Don't have friends of the opposite sex that your mate is not allowed to meet.
- Don't stay in a loveless relationship—fix it or get out.
- Promise to discuss any problem you have with your mate with him, before you tell anyone else.

If He Cheats, Don't Forgive Him until He Explains

People seem to believe that you should be able to forgive someone just because it's the right thing to do. But that's not true. Forgiving him before you've held him accountable enables him to repeat his behavior and is destructive to your self-esteem. He has to earn your forgiveness. To do that he must do the following.

- Be honest about what he did (but don't give the actual details).
- Explain why he did what he did.
- Explain what he would do differently if he had it to do it over.
- Make a promise that he not only won't do it again, but explain how he'll handle any similar issue in the future.

◀ Points to Remember ▶

1. When you feel jealous, make him jealous instead of acting jealous.

2. Womanizers believe it's their inherent right as a provider to cheat.

3. Confiding problems to others about your mate breaks your bond with him.

4. The tighter you try to hold on to someone, the more likely you will lose him.

5. Set a real consequence about cheating that you know you can follow through with.

Chapter 13

Handling Irritating Behaviors and Extenuating Circumstances

Do you play the victim or controller role when you're annoyed with his irritating behavior? If you play the victim, you may:

- Nag or complain about his lateness, sloppiness, or unfinished projects
- Ignore his irritating behaviors, assuming there's nothing you can do
- Call him numerous times when he doesn't respond to you
- Coddle him when he sulks, withdraws, or is irritable
- Assume you have very little power in the relationship because of some extenuating circumstance
- Agree to change one of your irritating behaviors even though you don't intend to

If you play the controller, you may:

- Defend your irritating behaviors by insisting, "that's just the way I am!"

- Justify your irritating behaviors as being normal
- Demand that your mate stop certain irritating behaviors
- Blame him for things that really are beyond his control

Handling Irritating Behaviors

Sometimes it's the little things that get on our nerves the most. Maybe you're a neat freak and he leaves the cap off the toothpaste or crumbs on the kitchen counter. Such behaviors irritate us even though we sometimes think they shouldn't. However, the reality is they do affect your relationship with him in a negative way. His irritating behaviors originally required conscious, deliberate choice on his part, but now they're so ingrained, they seem beyond his control—or so he tries to tell you. You need to warn him, "If you continue to do that, I'll at least get some remuneration for your bad behavior. Let's start with you treating me to a full day at the spa for every time you [forget a special occasion, or act out some other chronic, irritating behavior]."

"Shouldn't I Try to Overlook Those Irritating Behaviors?"

Sometimes small behaviors can be overlooked, but others can't. Alan always uses fresh lemon when he cooks, then predictably leaves it on the counter to dry up, which really irritates me. I could set a boundary with a consequence for the next time he leaves it out, but I probably won't, because I love it that he cooks and will put it away myself when I clean up. It's not a big deal and I've decided to let it go. If you decide to overlook an irritating behavior, have a chat with yourself to be sure it really doesn't bother you. And once you decide it doesn't, you must promise yourself to never bring it up again. Saying you've let it go while continuing to nag him about it is not an option.

Irritating behaviors should not be overlooked if they upset you, turn you off, or seem disrespectful. You need to set boundaries and consequences that are as serious as the behavior warrants. For example, if your mate promises to lower the seat each time he uses the toilet but constantly forgets, you could say, "Okay, each time you don't put the seat down, you owe me a dollar. Okay?" On the other hand, if he believes he shouldn't have to put the toilet seat down, you could ban him from your bathroom (if you have two) or search for something to trade to get him to agree such as, "I'll promise to always put the pliers back if you'll put the toilet seat down. Is that a deal?"

Be Sure You Don't Overstep His Boundaries

If your mate leaves the cap off the toothpaste and you share the same bathroom and the same toothpaste, you have the right to set boundaries around the issue because it affects you directly. However, if it's his bathroom and his toothpaste, it's his business whether or not he leaves the cap off. You don't have the right to set boundaries on issues that don't affect you directly. If he's a slob, that's who he is; he just can't leave his things around for you to pick up without facing a consequence. I have clients who get upset because their mates eat with their mouths open, or bite their fingernails, or talk too loud. If someone doesn't want to stop biting his fingernails, there's not much you can do, although you can try to negotiate the issue if your mate is willing—anything can be negotiated. You could try something like, "I won't hold your hand if you have chewed-up nails," but it seems rather silly.

The Cell Phone Debate—Who's the Rudest?

▶ Misty and Gordon's Story

Remember Misty (of Misty and Gordon in Chapters 8, 10, and 12) who lost her power in the relationship with Gordon when they moved to Denver? One of the most irritating and controlling things Gordon ever did was to grab her cell phone and shut it off while she was talking to a girlfriend. They were sitting at the bar in a nice restaurant when Misty took a call on her cell phone, which irritated Gordon, so he grabbed the phone out of her hand, turned it off, walked to his car, threw the phone in it, and locked the car door. Misty followed after him, berating him all the way. She then went to her own car and drove to the house of the friend she was talking to. Later that night they had a huge fight when she finally came in two hours later. "Where have you been?" he asked. "None of your business," she replied, "and if I had my cell phone you would know!"

Gordon justified his bad behavior because he felt Misty was being rude; Misty justified hers because he acted controlling. Neither handled the situation in a healthy way. Here's what Gordon should have said:

- *I feel* irritated that you're talking to your girlfriend when we're out having drinks together.
- *I want* you to tell your friend you'll call her back because this is not a good time to talk.
- *Will you* do that?

If she ignored his request, he could say:

- *If you don't* end this conversation, I'm not having dinner with you. [Or] I'm going to the other side of the bar. [Or] I'm leaving and going home.

Here's what Misty should have said:

- Gordon, *I feel* angry that you felt you had the right to take my cell phone because you didn't like me talking to a friend!
- *I want* you to give me my phone back right now, and *I want* to call my friend back and have you apologize to her.

- I promise I'll cut my conversations short in the future if you promise me you'll never do anything like that again. *Will you? Is that a deal?*
- *If not, I will* leave and finish my conversation with my friend at her house.

Pet Peeves

It's important to know your mate's pet peeves and for him to know yours, and for both of you to be respectful of them. I have two major pet peeves: when someone says he or she will do something and doesn't following through; and when someone takes the last of something—butter, toothpaste, coffee—and doesn't replace it, or at least put it on the grocery list so I know I'm out. Alan knows this and is great at following through on both these things. Alan's a neat freak (lucky for me), and his pet peeve is seeing dishes sitting around the house. So before I leave each day, I do a quick sweep and pick up any dishes I left lying around and put them in the dishwasher. These small acts of kindness have become ways we show respect for each other.

Quick Solutions to Irritating Behaviors: What to Do When . . .

Different things bug different people, and there's no firm rule about what's right or wrong. It all depends on what bothers you, how badly it bothers you, and whether or not you believe it's something you can live with or something worth changing. Here are some ideas on how to deal with behaviors that some people find irritating.

When His Irritating Behaviors Are Disrespectful

Sometimes irritating behaviors, such as not replacing the toothpaste cap or throwing wet towels on the bed, are symptoms of bigger problems in a relationship—a power imbalance and a sign of disrespect. Standing up to him on major issues may help change his behavior on these minor issues. But for immediate changes, if he does something that truly irritates you, make a deal to fine him a certain amount of money, or get him to agree to do a chore he hates every time he acts out the behavior that irritates you.

Often people don't even realize they're being disrespectful until and unless someone points it out to them. I shared a hotel room with a girlfriend last summer and she seemed extremely irritated with me when I woke up. When I asked why, she said, "You just came in here and scattered your makeup and hair things all over the sink without concern for me!" I'm not used to sharing bathrooms, and was totally oblivious that I'd done something wrong. I apologized and cleaned up my stuff, but explained to her she could have just told me up front instead of sulking. I hadn't meant to be controlling (but I was); on the other hand she shouldn't have played victim with me, acting irritated and not letting me know what the problem was until I asked. My friend should have said:

- It bothers me *(I feel)* that you've put your makeup all over the counter in the bathroom and not left me any space.
- *(I want)* Please come in here and move your stuff to one side.
- *Will you* do that?
- *Let's make a deal:* Anytime in the future that you act inconsiderate when we're together, you have to buy me lunch, okay?

I would have agreed, but added:

- *If I forget* and I'm not here or asleep, you have my permission to shove it all over—and then I'll still take you out to lunch for forgetting.

245

When He Curses, Brags, or Teases

Remember it's his right to do those things unless it affects you directly in some way. When you're with him and he's cursing, bragging, or teasing, you need to tell him you're bothered and then set very clear boundaries and consequences. You can set boundaries such as: "If you curse in front of my family [or brag in front of my friends, or tease me about my weight], I'll first say a code word that only you and I will understand. Then, if you don't stop your behavior, I'll say, 'Don't go there,' and if you still continue, I will leave your presence."

When He Invades Your Privacy

Boundaries need to be very clear when it comes to your privacy—not because you have secrets, but because it's invasive and rude for him look through your purse or check your phone or e-mail messages. That of course means you must respect his right to privacy as well.

He Checked Her Personal E-mail

▶ Phyllis and Keith's Story

Phyllis met Keith recently on the Internet and they began dating. One night at her house, she left her computer on when she left the room, and Keith read an e-mail she had sent to another man. Phyllis had been sexually explicit with this other man and Keith was extremely upset—but so was Phyllis. Although her first instinct was to defend her right to send that e-mail, she stopped herself and instead confronted him about invading her privacy, making it clear that he had no right to open the letter. Phyllis's stand was basically, "This is not okay with me," and rightly so, especially with a man she barely knew. She made him promise he would never do anything like that again. If Keith does invade her privacy again, Phyllis probably needs to end the relationship because such behavior indicates controlling behavior.

Again, rules go both ways. If something like this happens in a longer-term relationship, "equalizing the rules" can work. You can agree that both of you either have the right to check each other's voice mail or e-mail—or neither of you does.

When He's Habitually Late

Sometimes people who are habitually late are actually intentionally inconsiderate of other people's time—which is a control tactic. Other people just have time management problems, seeming to always overbook their lives—usually victims who need to "people please." You don't need to psychoanalyze your mate to solve the problem, although it's interesting to note whether his lateness comes from a controlling or victim role. Either way, however, you need to set boundaries to teach your mate to respect your time.

One simple boundary is to charge a dollar for every minute he's late. Another is to let him know you'll throw his food out if he's over fifteen minutes late for dinner. Or if you've made plans to go out together, you can say, "If you get home late, I'm going to the party without you and you'll have to come alone later by yourself." Or, "If you're home by six, I'll help you take your car in, and if not, you'll have to find someone else to take you." Just make sure you follow through on whatever consequence you set.

When He Doesn't Return Your Calls

It feels rejecting when someone you love or deeply care about doesn't return your phone call when he says he will. Our instinct is to keep calling him. Realize that continuing to call is chasing him and that causes you to lose your power and give him the control. Fight the urge to call him. If you must call because you're supposed to meet somewhere and aren't sure whether you're still on, then leave him a very businesslike message. Otherwise just go about your business and become unavailable to him so that he has to wonder where you are—this is a natural consequence to his bad behavior. Just remember that every call you place to him after the first one makes you look weaker and takes away your power.

"I'll Track You Down"
▶ Shonda and Lawrence's Story

When Lawrence doesn't return Shonda's phone calls, she goes ballistic. She keeps calling and calling him, leaving nastier and nastier messages, then heads to his place of work or his home to track him down. Instead of behaving so obsessively (which makes her look psycho), Shonda should call once and leave a message. If Lawrence doesn't call back, she should call again a few days later and set a boundary like, "Lawrence, I called yesterday and didn't hear back from you. If I don't hear from you by six this evening, I'll assume our plans for tomorrow night are off and I'll make other plans." Then if he calls before six, she can go with him, and if he calls after six, she can't—no matter what. If Shonda holds the boundary, Lawrence will eventually learn to be more respectful by returning her calls sooner, and asking her out in advance.

When He Doesn't Finish What He Starts

I hear wives complain that their husbands start projects around the house and let them drag on for months, sometimes years, without any end in sight. Maria had this problem with Carl.

"If It's Not Done by Monday, I'm Calling a Landscaper"
▶ Maria and Carl's Story

Maria, as I said in Chapters 9 and 10, gave Carl lists and lists of projects to do and felt resentful that Carl never finished them, even when the projects were his own idea. Carl may not have been finishing them because of his resentment at Maria for not doing her share of household chores. However, Maria could have changed his behavior, no matter what the reason was. For instance, he wanted to do a big backyard landscaping project. Three weeks ago Carl dug several big holes but never bought the trees that were supposed to go into the holes. He says he's too busy at work so why doesn't Maria just order the trees? Maria says she wouldn't get the exact trees he wants and then he'd be upset.

Maria believes Carl enjoys irritating her by leaving projects half done (and he probably does). I questioned Carl and he denied getting pleasure out of upsetting her with unfinished projects (he may just not be aware of his passive/aggressive behavior). He said he's just trying to do too many things because he hates to pay someone to do work he can do himself.

To solve Maria's problem, she needs to set boundaries by giving Carl a deadline by which projects have to be done—or else. "What's the 'or else'?" she asked. First of all, they need to discuss a realistic finish date for each project; this alone may deter Carl from taking on a project he can't finish. Then, since Carl hates paying plumbers and construction workers, the best consequence is, "If it's not finished by Monday (the deadline he agreed to), I'm calling someone to come and finish it."

She discussed this new plan with Carl and he didn't really like it. "Would you rather I resent you, nag you, or sulk like I have in the past?" she asked. He said no, especially since these are the key behaviors he wants her to change. So together Maria and Carl came up with a deadline for the backyard landscaping. By the day of the deadline, Carl had barely touched the project, and the truckload of dirt was still sitting there piled high. He made several excuses as to why he hadn't had time to do it but Maria simply said, "A deal's a deal. Shall we discuss which landscaping company to call to finish the project?" He reluctantly agreed.

When His Behaviors Are More Than Irritating: What to Do When . . .

When his bad behavior affects your quality of life, you must no longer put up with it. Maybe he damages your financial future by gambling the money away. Maybe he gets drunk every day. Whatever his bad behavior is, when it damages your relationship on a large scale, you've got to make sure it stops.

When He Takes His Bad Moods Out on You

We all get in bad moods, but some people seem to hold on to them longer than others. When I tell clients that they can choose not to stay in a bad mood, and choose not to stay around someone else who's in a bad mood, they seem surprised. But solving the problem is as simple as that—making a choice.

"He's Always in a Bad Mood and That Affects Me and the Kids"

▶ *Lynn and Peter's Story*

Peter (of Lynn and Peter in Chapters 6 and 8) gets in a bad mood and won't get over it. For example, Peter got in a bad mood because he had to stand in a long line for an extra ticket to a hockey game, and he stayed upset all evening, making Lynn wish she hadn't gone to the game because he ruined her whole evening. Peter felt justified in his anger, and he was. But he wasn't justified in holding on to it and ruining Lynn's evening.

I asked Peter how he thought his angry moods affected his wife and children, and he said, "It never entered my mind." "Well, let me tell you," I said. "They feel they have to walk on eggshells. They're afraid to get near you because you're always angry. They never know when your mood will ruin an evening!" Peter seemed surprised. He had never really thought about it. He was so focused on his feelings that he never thought about his family. Because Lynn had never confronted Peter, or expected him to behave differently, he didn't have to think about it. I asked Peter, "Would you behave like this if you were just dating Lynn?" She quickly replied, "If he did, it would be our last date!"

I helped Lynn understand that by not saying or doing anything to Peter, she was enabling his bad behavior and continuing to act like a victim. I told her, "When you're not happy and you're not having fun with someone—even your husband—it is your responsibility to change that and not to put up with it.

Lynn developed a strategy for handling Peter's bad moods. She would first say "bonsai," the code word they had agreed upon earlier to clue him in that he was talking nasty to her, only now we added that it's also a warning about his bad moods. If he didn't catch on, Lynn would continue with:

- *I feel* concerned because you seem to be in one of those moods again where you stay irritated all night.
- *I want* you to try to get over it so we can have a good evening.
- *Will you* calm down and not let this situation spoil our whole night out together?
- *If not, I will* leave your presence until you get over it. (If they're at the athletic club she might leave the weight room and go swim instead. At a game, she might move to some other seat. At a restaurant, she could go sit at the bar or take a cab home.)

Peter fought back by saying he should be able to feel his feelings and share them with his family. I agreed. "But for how long? All night? Weeks? At what point are you simply being inconsiderate of others' feelings? What about Lynn's feelings?" Peter agreed that I had a point so I suggested he try talking to himself in the following way.

- *I feel* stressed and irritated because of whatever happened today.
- *I want* empathy from my friends and family but I also want to get beyond my bad day.
- *I will* express myself honestly to them, but then try to control my own behavior—for their sake, and for mine.
- *If not, I* need to do my sulking or feeling sorry for myself alone.

Then he should learn to say to his family and friends:

- I had a really rough day and I'm stressed out because of these things, but I'm here to have fun now so give me just a few minutes and I'll be in a better mood.

When He Drinks Too Much

It is possible to live with an overdrinker or even an alcoholic and set boundaries so that you don't enable his drinking or let him destroy your life. It's certainly not easy, nor is it something I'm recommending. But it is possible.

"When You Get Drunk and Embarrass Me, I'm Leaving"
▶ *Marion and Tom's Story*

Marion (of Marion and Tom in Chapter 11) had a bigger issue to face than Tom's friend's interference in their relationship. Tom is clearly an alcoholic. But Marion has decided that she's not going to leave Tom over this at this time, and, instead, is learning to set boundaries with him. Instead of continuing her usual ragging on Tom, she told him:

I can see it coming when you start going over the edge with alcohol and your behavior begins to change. The next time

I see it starting, I'm not going to get upset or try to get you to leave; I'm simply going to say, "Tom, it's happening again and I'm leaving now." Then I'll leave. This will be our deal because I refuse to stay around you when you're drunk. I may go home or I may go with a friend to a different bar. I won't wait up for you and I will sleep in the guest bedroom that night. I agree not to be mad at you and I don't want you mad at me because I left. I'm not trying to change you. You can still get drunk, just not with me around. I've made a decision not to ever be around you when you're drunk again. Deal?

Because he hated the ragging and fighting so much he agreed, and the deal has worked unbelievably well. They've stopped fighting over Tom's drinking, and often when she says she's leaving, he'll say, "I think I'll go on home with you." And when they get home, if he's drunk, she still sleeps in the guest bedroom. No nagging, no fighting—just, "That's our deal."

When He Uses Drugs

Drug use is certainly a deal breaker for most people, and should be. However, many women, who love a man and have his children, don't leave when they find out he's using drugs. Kyla left Brock many times but always came back. This time she meant it.

"Go into Rehab or We're Through"
▶ *Kyla and Brock's Story*
Brock married Kyla and had three children with her. When they began fighting, he started hanging out with the wrong crowd and started using rock cocaine. This made everything worse, of course. Kyla threatened to leave Brock numerous times, and each time he'd

stop using and try to get his act together. That would last a month or so. As soon as they began fighting again, he'd go back to using, telling her it was her fault—that she drove him to it. Finally Kyla got an apartment, took the kids, and gave him the ultimatum: Get into rehab and stay there until you come back to me and the children clean—and know you can stay that way. This time she meant it and he knew it. He followed through and was successful. He then worked with me in therapy for six months to try to stay that way. You have a right to any boundaries you want around the issue of drugs. What's important is that you don't set a consequence you won't follow through with. Since this is an issue that affects you and the health of your family, you have a right to protect yourself in any way you want.

When He Smokes and You Don't

The decision to quit smoking is a very personal choice. It's not a decision you can, or should, make for the man in your life—or he can make for you. If your man won't quit, then try to work out a compromise. That's what Alan and I did.

When I met Alan he was a smoker. I hate smoking and have never smoked myself, but I knew nagging about his smoking wouldn't make him stop. I told Alan I wish he didn't smoke because I want him to live longer. He felt flattered, not nagged, but didn't stop smoking of course, although he did cut back somewhat. We made a deal, however, right after one of my nonsmoking Aspen girlfriends insulted him (she said, "if you're going to smoke, I'm going to fart.") and it started a fight. We knew this could become a bigger issue for us if we didn't try to work something out. The deal was this: He would be especially respectful and considerate in his smoking, always holding his cigarette away from me (and anyone else who didn't like smoke), and opening windows when he lights up—without me having to remind him. In exchange, I wouldn't nag him about his smoking. We've followed this deal successfully for fifteen years.

When He's Critical

When someone criticizes you, the basic message is: Something is wrong with you. That's why it hurts so much. However, when your mate shares his feelings (following the Four Steps to Powerful Communication in Chapter 5), he's admitting that something is bothering him and he wants to find a solution to the problem. Telling you how he feels about an issue requires vulnerability on his part. It's scary for him and forces him to actually face the issue head-on so it can be resolved. If he says, "I feel turned off to you because you've put on so much weight," you won't like to hear it, but now you know what the real issue is and the two of you can deal with it. This is a lot different from his saying simply, "You're fat!"

Criticism is someone else's judgment of you and is only meant to hurt. It is seldom constructive. However it's much easier for someone to make an offhanded critical comment than it is to really communicate with you about the problem. But it offers no solution. And the mistake most people make when someone criticizes them is to defend themselves instead of telling the other person to stop criticizing and mind their own business. For instance, if you tell me I'm fat and I argue that I've lost weight, I'm fighting your criticism and showing acceptance of your right to accuse me of being fat. Whether or not I am fat is none of your business. My response needs to be, "I didn't ask you to evaluate my weight. It's none of your business and I don't want you to bring it up again!" I need to address your bad behavior of being critical instead of defending myself. It doesn't matter what the particular criticism is, you've overstepped a boundary by criticizing me and I need to say so. Maybe you think you're doing me a favor (as if I didn't know) or being honest about something that's bothering you. My response is, "You can tell me how you're feeling about it, such as, 'I'm worried about your weight gain,' but you are not allowed to criticize me." Unfortunately, many people don't know the difference.

Here are three rules to follow.

1. Do not ever allow anyone to criticize you without that person owning up to his or her personal feelings about how or why it's affecting them.
2. Be careful not to ask your mate questions that elicit his judgment or criticism of you.
3. Do not stay in the presence of anyone who criticizes you. Criticism is verbal abuse, should be seen as such, and never allowed.

Often your mate criticizes you to punish or hurt you because he's upset about something totally unrelated. If you don't allow the criticism, he may eventually figure it out and tell you what he's really upset about. You can say, "I won't allow you to criticize me, but if you want to tell me what you're really upset about, I'll listen." Criticism if not stopped in the early stages often turns into physical abuse. Ultimately if he will not stop his criticism, be prepared to counter-intimidate him by saying, "If you continue doing this, I have a long list of your faults that I'm ready to tell you about. Let's see how well you handle constructive criticism." If he doesn't stop, tell him what's wrong with him and walk out the door—still not defending against or validating his criticism against you.

When He's Physically Abusive

There is no one who believes that a woman should stay in a physically abusive relationship—except, often, the woman being abused! The main reason women stay in abusive relationships is because they only know how to play victim. Usually, through a family history of abuse, they don't feel "good enough" and believe problems with a man are always their fault. They end up making excuses for their mate because at times they see glimpses of his warmth, pain, and vulnerability and they are easily convinced they are to blame. But the two of them are in the worst kind of dysfunctional fit of all—he plays a physically threatening controller and she plays a "scared little girl" victim. If this describes your relationship with your mate, just remember that his behavior will never change as long as yours doesn't.

Do Physically Abusive Men Ever Change?

It's not impossible for a wife beater to change, but it's highly improbable. One thing's for sure: He won't just wake up one day and stop abusing. He will need help, and here's what you have to do:

- Leave him and stay in a safe place.
- File charges and get a restraining order against him; you need the courts involved to regain your power.
- Have your attorney tell him or his attorney that you won't discuss reconciliation until and unless he completes a domestic violence class.
- Once he has completed his class, don't meet him anywhere but in a therapist's office for the first four or five times you see him.
- In the therapist's office, ask him to explain to you what he's learned about his behavior and how he plans to change it ("I'm sorry" isn't good enough).

Here's what to look for to see if he has truly changed:

- His understanding about how his childhood teachings caused his bad behavior
- A new level of respect for women
- His understanding about why he explodes in anger
- An acknowledgment that no bad behavior of yours ever warrants his physically harming you
- A new plan for how he will deal with his emotions in the future, especially his anger (Do not accept "I won't get

angry at you" or anything that shows more denial.)
- His plan for dealing with the people in his past who taught him violence (He needs to confront them. See Appendix A for more on this.)
- An agreement that he will participate in relationship counseling with you for three to six months before you move back in

If he can't or won't do these things, he doesn't get it and he hasn't changed, so you can't go back.

What to Do When There Are Extenuating Circumstances

Sometimes there are extenuating circumstances surrounding problems in a relationship that need a little extra work or several levels of negotiating. Communicating with power, negotiating deals, and setting boundaries still work in these cases, but figuring them out often takes more finesse.

Extenuating circumstances involve circumstances beyond your control such as: a terminally ill husband, a disabled child, extreme religious differences, he is certifiably crazy, he really prefers men, it's hard to get a restraining order against him because he's a cop, he slept with his patients and will lose his medical license (cutting you out of alimony) if you don't stand by him, he's suicidal, he'll lose his trust fund if you divorce him.

Many of these topics sound like topics for the next Jerry Springer show; however, they are all true situations of clients I've worked with. All of these clients had relationship problems that were compounded by these extenuating circumstances, but most were still able to resolve their problems by setting boundaries.

Many couples with religious differences work them out, and many don't. A friend of mine married a Jewish man who didn't want her or their child to celebrate Christmas. They negotiated deals about having a small tree as long as there are no wreaths or outside decorations.

One of my clients had a terminally ill husband, so she never confronted him on any of their relationship issues, giving in to him and doing whatever he wanted right up to the end. And although she really did love him, her love was tainted with resentment by the time he died last year. Along with her grieving, she also felt a sense of relief. Had she dealt with the issues, she and her husband may have been closer right up to the end.

"My Husband Is Truly Crazy"
▶ Crystal and Brett's Story

When Crystal came into my office, she told me, "My husband is crazy." I assured her that most women who are unhappy in their relationships feel that their husbands are crazy. And in their first two joint sessions together, he appeared normal to me. Then in a session alone with Brett, he insisted that his mother-in-law used witchcraft to put spells on him and that Crystal was trying to poison him. Then he talked about buying guns to protect himself from them. Crystal was right—her husband was truly crazy—a paranoid schizophrenic whom I immediately checked into a hospital psych ward. Crystal asked me, "Do I have to stay with him because he's sick? I don't love him anymore and I want to divorce him, but is that fair?" Brett had been very controlling and mentally abusive with her for the last year, yet Crystal was feeling guilty about abandoning him because he was mentally ill. There is no negotiating with a truly mentally ill person. Brett got help in a psychiatric hospital, he was medicated, and then released to his mother afterward—and Crystal filed for divorce.

When He Irritates You on Purpose

As much as some couples try to be considerate of each other, your mate may actually sometimes try to irritate you. One male client told me once, "I know that getting her messages is extremely important to her. Maybe that's why I screw them up all the time—it's the only power I have." Victims often act passive-aggressively without ever realizing it, to try to hurt those they believe are hurting them.

Handling His Passive-Aggressive Behaviors

Passive-aggressive behavior is the most difficult kind of bad behavior to deal with. When you confront a passive-aggressive person and accuse him of being angry with you, he almost always denies it. He wants to avoid confrontation at all costs, so you can never figure out what he's really upset about. Having an affair or a one-night-stand often comes from passive-aggressive behavior. When confronted, the passive-aggressive person will rarely ever connect his bad behavior to his anger toward his mate.

The only thing you can do in dealing with a passive-aggressive person is take away his power to hurt you (which angers him more, of course). If he bounces checks on your account and you believe it's his way of "getting" you, remove him from the account. If he forgets your anniversary to punish you, you make plans with someone else on your next one, assuming he'll forget. If you can take enough things away from him that he uses to hurt you with and withdraw from him when he's treating you badly, he'll become so frustrated that he may finally agree to tell you what he's angry about so you can work it out with him. If not, you'll finally have to end the relationship with him because he leaves you no choice.

"This Is Not Okay with Me!"

When an issue is of great importance to you, you need to make it clear: "Your behavior is not okay with me!"—under any circumstances or for any reason. Practice, "This is not okay with me!" as your new mantra.

Possible Consequences for Irritating Behaviors

- Assessing your mate a financial penalty
- Setting deadlines with consequences for when he must come through
- Getting him to agree to do any chore he truly hates every time he does his bad behavior
- Allowing you to do something he'll hate—like painting the living room purple
- Equalizing the deal by copying his bad behavior, such as staying out until 3:00 A.M. or leaving the dishes in the sink

◀ Points to Remember ▶

1. Don't overlook irritating behaviors that cause you resentment.

2. It's overstepping to try and control anyone's behaviors that don't affect you directly.

3. Set boundaries to protect yourself from issues that do affect you directly.

4. When you ignore his irritating behaviors, you are enabling them to continue.

Chapter 14

When He Won't Change

Do you play the victim or controller role because you assume he won't change? If you play the victim, you may:

- Believe him when he says it's your fault the relationship isn't working
- Feel guilty that you don't love him anymore (since he's hurt you so bad)
- Beg him to stay or take you back even though you know it won't work
- Play on your children's or friends' sympathy so they'll try to get him to change for you
- Try to be overly fair as you end it

If you play the controller role, you may:

- Regularly threaten divorce to your mate
- Blame him for everything that's gone wrong (not acknowledging your part)

- Try to hide assets and/or take him for everything you can financially in the divorce
- Tell your children and friends everything he did wrong to try and turn them against him

I never said that changing you to change him would be easy. Most people don't like change, because we're creatures of habit. Most men don't even like the furniture moved around in the living room, so why wouldn't he resist when we try to make changes in who makes dinner, puts the kids to bed, or does the laundry?

When He Refuses to Cooperate with You

When our mate won't cooperate with us, he leaves us little choice but to remove ourselves from the situation. It is not possible to create a healthy, equal relationship when your partner is fighting you every step of the way. That's what Mary finally realized.

Alcoholics and Family Values Don't Mix

▶ *Mary and Patrick's Story*

Mary (of Mary and Patrick in Chapters 5, 8, 9, and 10) desperately wanted to keep her family together and had a hard time giving up. Mary herself had come from a broken home, and her father left when she was twelve. She feels like her parents' divorce almost destroyed her life. She went wild as a teen, getting involved with sex, drugs, and alcohol before age thirteen. Once she grew up, she longed to have a normal family life and swore that she would provide one for her children. Family values are at the top of her priority list. The only problem is that they're not at the top of Patrick's.

In fact, Patrick's behavior seemed antifamily. Although after she confronted him, he did his chores and picked up the kids, he'd go out every night drinking with his buddies, sometimes not even coming home. Mary knew Patrick was a sober alcoholic when she married him and now it appeared as though he was back to his old behavior. Mary said, "That's not okay with me!" and threw him out again. He left and she didn't hear from him for weeks. Once Patrick moved out, he ignored all of his responsibilities. He stopped picking the kids up from school, put no more money in the bank account, and stopped all communication with her, his children, and his own parents.

Mary went to Al Anon to try to understand what's going on. As badly as she wants a stable family life, she's beginning to realize that it's completely impossible to force an alcoholic into being a good family man. Understanding this is helping her let go. Though neither she nor Patrick have filed for divorce yet, she's moving on with her life. She's made some headway with her own accounting business, but realizes that it won't produce money immediately, so she's applied for several jobs. She knows now that she has to get out of the house and meet people and stop allowing her life to revolve around Patrick's. She's gradually letting go of the fantasy that she and Patrick (and the children) will ever be "one big happy family."

Six Possible Reasons He Won't Change

1. He doesn't really believe you'll leave him if he doesn't change.
2. He's an old-style man who has no concept of an equal relationship.
3. His family and/or friends are just like him and enable his bad behavior.
4. He's too angry and resentful to care anymore.
5. There is not enough warmth left between the two of you to motivate him to try.
6. He has serious personal problems that keep him from being able to change.

When someone is used to having things his own way for a long time, it's sometimes impossible to ever get that person to see your side of the situation. It may be because his issues are so deep, he can't see beyond them to work with you to find the love you once shared. You may have tried to make too many changes too quickly and he became overwhelmed. On the other hand, maybe he never felt sufficiently threatened. Maybe he thought he could outwait you and you'd eventually come back to his way of thinking. Maybe he's so stubborn he'd rather lose his marriage than his pride.

That's what happened in Sue and Ryan's relationship (of Chapters 2 and 10). In marriage counseling, they would work out several deals regarding their issues, then a few days later, one or the other would say, "No, I'm not agreeing to that. I know I said I did, but I changed my mind." By sabotaging the deal, Ryan (or Sue) felt in control of the relationship, as if he (or she) was winning. Each person's individual goal was to win the war at any cost—which became more important than working out issues or saving the relationship. When this happens, ending it and moving on is the only option left—Sue finally filed for divorce.

Setbacks: How to Recover

We all have setbacks from time to time. Perhaps you were holding him accountable for the housework until your mom came to visit and started picking up after him. Getting your power back could be as simple as saying, "I know I let you off the hook last week, but we need to get back to our deal now." It is possible to get back on track and turn a relationship around in the eleventh hour. Once you seriously consider ending the relationship, you have nothing to lose. Oddly enough, letting go can actually be very positive for a relationship. When there's nothing left to lose, couples often become more honest with their partners and themselves, more apt to speak their minds, and less likely to deny their feelings or true issues.

Sometimes it becomes necessary to take drastic measures—you may need to move out and separate before he truly believes you're serious. If he has felt content, believing all along that you will never leave him, actually leaving him may be the only way you can gain enough power for him to finally work with you.

Don't Forget the Power of Rejection

It seems crazy, but the best way to get your power back—and maybe him—is to reject him. That means pull back in every way possible: Stop doing anything for him, don't show him you love him in any way, stop calling him, don't make plans with him. Basically—stop being nice to him! Let him wonder where you are, what you're doing, and whether or not you still care. If he hasn't been cooperating with you, pulling away is healthy and natural, and smart.

Whose Fault Is It?

Regardless what roles you and your mate played in your particular dysfunctional fit, you both contributed equally to the problems—one of you acted as the controller, while the other enabled the controller by playing victim. By the time you tried to change it, the dysfunctional relationship had a life of its own. It takes two people to have an unhealthy relationship, but only one can stop the dysfunction. Without it, though, he may decide not to play.

"Why Couldn't I Be Stronger with Him?"

Changing someone else's behavior often feels impossible, but changing your own is probably the hardest thing you'll ever do. Why? Because you've been acting this way over and over your entire life. Part of your heart probably still believes you need to "kill him with kindness," you ought to "treat him the way you want to be treated," you must "give more than 50 percent," and you should "never give ultimatums." The part of you that believes any of those teachings is fighting everything you're reading in this book.

Don't Beat Yourself Up

If you take on all the blame for the breakup, you're acting like a victim and setting yourself up to fail in future relationships because you're carrying around too much guilt baggage. It's healthy to look at the part you played and vow to yourself that you will not behave like that in the future. But then you must look at the part he played and get angry with him; this will help you let go. If you get angry at yourself, you'll become self-destructive, which disempowers you and causes you to become depressed. Anger at yourself starts a downward spiral of low self-esteem which leaves you vulnerable to his (and everyone else's) control.

"Why Was I Such a Jerk?"

If you were the self-righteous controlling partner, who held on to the belief that none or few of the mistakes in the relationship were yours, you've been in denial and need to change your behavior. You need to learn to treat your partner respectfully, negotiate, process your emotions, admit your part, and vow to change in the next relationship, and move on!

If you use your anger to protect yourself (which is healthy), you stay empowered. In fact, the mere act of standing up to (or admitting your part if you were the controller) someone who has harmed you will put you back on the upward spiral of high self-esteem. Staying focused on feeling anger toward those who have hurt you will keep you empowered and able to walk away. (For more on this subject, see Appendix A.)

Do You Still Win Even If the Relationship Ends?

Ironically, it's possible to view the ending of a relationship as a personal success, even though that's not how our culture usually sees it. Guard against seeing it as a failure because it can put you back in the victim role. If you've stood up for yourself, communicated openly, negotiated fairly, and done all you can to establish a balanced relationship, you can't be a failure just because your partner refused to get with the program. You have grown.

How to Know When It's Time to Let Go

There are times when we know it's over. Cheating, habitual lying, stealing, physical violence, blatant flirting with a friend or family member, trying to jeopardize your career, asking you to give up your child (and maybe even your pet) are all deal breakers for most people. He has crossed the line and there is no turning back.

"You're Catholic!" "You're Violent!"

▶ *Marilyn and Larry's Story*

Each time Larry (of Marilyn and Larry in Chapter 7) broke up with Marilyn, he told her it was because she's Catholic. He's Protestant and wants his future children raised that way. Each time it happened, she said she wasn't going to change her religion for him. However, he continued to come back again and again, trying to convince her that Catholicism was wrong—every time threatening her with, "You know that's a deal breaker for me!" However, after he broke into her apartment and destroyed her most valuable things following a huge fight, Marilyn told Larry, "Your violence is the real deal breaker." She finally walked away for good.

Letting Go Is Hard to Do

We often believe how attached we are to a man relates to how much we love him. Attachment and love are two very different things. What usually keeps us tied to a man is our emotional dependency on him. It's not really about him. It is about us, our emotional strength, or lack thereof, and our inability to separate from others and stand on our own independently.

"He Loves Me, He Loves Me Not"

▶ Janis and Tyler's Story

Janis, who's forty-three, and Tyler, who's thirty-four, met seven years ago and immediately fell in love. Janis was divorced with two children and Tyler had never been in a long-term relationship before. They dated two years and then moved in together. Tyler seemed to be an equal partner at first, because he was involved with both Janis and her kids. Then one year later, out of the blue, Tyler announced that he was taking a job in Oregon. He said it was only temporary and that he'd be back in a year or two. Janis was surprised, hurt, and didn't understand how he could do that without talking it over with her and the children. But Janis was used to being abandoned since her ex had walked out on her years ago, her dad had left when she was ten, and her mom had always been unavailable because of her alcoholism. Janis was used to accommodating others' needs by playing victim. She never stood up to, got angry with, or held anyone accountable—for fear of losing them. This time was no exception.

By the time Janis walked in my office, Tyler had already been in Oregon for four years. She knew it was time to admit to herself that Tyler wasn't coming back. However, she and Tyler still saw each other three or four times a year and he called often, which gave her hope. However, Tyler had bought a house in Portland, had developed a large circle of friends, and had no plans for moving back (even though he had quit the job he moved there for). Janis finally gave Tyler an ultimatum—"Come back or we're through." He said he couldn't make that promise, so Janis ended the relationship and moved on with her life.

Six months later when she was dating someone new, Tyler called to say, "I miss you; can we talk?" Janis was so excited because she had never stopped loving him. They talked and she was smart enough to set her boundaries, telling him, "I'll get back with you only if you're willing to go to therapy with me and do some work on yourself." He eagerly agreed. She also asked for a commitment about the future. His reply, "As long as things are going well with us, I'll sell my house next spring and move back to Denver."

Tyler kept all of his therapy appointments with me, but never really worked on himself. He really didn't believe he had any problems—and he certainly didn't think he had a commitment problem. As long as he was in therapy with me, Janis continued to spend time with him, assuming he was resolving his commitment issues. When he was in town, they came in together for sessions a few times. At my urging, Janis would ask him if he was committed yet. He always gave the same answer, "I am right now, and as long as things are going well for us."

Four months later in my office, again with no warning, Tyler announced, "I can't do this anymore. I have to be honest. I love you and love spending time with you, but I can't see myself in this relationship with you ten years from now." Janis couldn't believe what she was hearing. Tyler was a classic commitment-phobic. No one is ever perfect enough for them (because they themselves are so insecure, yet hide it from themselves). They're always looking for someone to make up for their own imperfections, and at the sign of any flaw, they bail. Tyler has never committed to anything and Janis knew this, so she shouldn't have been surprised that he couldn't commit to her either.

Tyler never really intended to change. He just wanted to buy more time with Janis, enjoying the relationship the way it was before—on his terms. Janis felt extremely angry, tricked, and abandoned once again. She felt like she lost, when in reality, she had finally won back her freedom. Janis knew for sure this time that it would never work between her and Tyler. She also learned a valuable lesson: She had made a deal with Tyler, but hadn't really checked in with him regularly to see if it was working. Instead, she relaxed and enjoyed their time together (hoping that I was fixing him), denying to herself that Tyler was still a serious commitment-phobic.

This relationship with Tyler finally forced Janis into working on her own personal issues. Janis has a pattern of denial—she overlooked her mother's alcoholic problems and denied the truth about her cheating, abusive father, who abandoned Janis as a child. She did the same with her first husband—ignored signs the marriage was over and felt surprised when he walked out one day. Before she's ready for the next relationship, Janis has some personal work to do regarding staying in touch with and expressing her emotions, and confronting a man when his actions don't match his words.

How to End It and Move On: The Separation Process

When we think about separating from a husband or boyfriend, we usually think about living apart, but it is also necessary to separate emotionally. Some of us are better at detaching than others. Men can usually let go more easily than we can. Women often say to me, "How can he just walk away and not look back?" We hate him for it, but feel envious that he can do it.

Men detach more easily—not because they're born that way—but because they're taught at an early age to detach from their mothers so they won't become sissies. An ability to detach easily is not necessarily healthy. Many men who do this are simply in denial and have all emotions blocked. We women, on the other hand, are often overattached. Neither extreme is healthy. However, learning to separate and move on when a situation is bad for us is a necessary part of adult development.

"I Have All My Friends Since Grade School"

▶ Britney's Story

Britney (of Britney and Kyle in Chapters 1, 7, 10, and 11) prides herself on keeping in touch with all her friends and past lovers, but in truth she has a problem letting go of anybody. Part of her problem is that she's an approval seeker—she's still trying to win her father's approval at work, her mother's approval as the best daughter, and trying to be the "best" friend anyone could have. She plays this out by taking on too much, overbooking her time, and letting everyone else (her sister and employees) off the hook. She won't ever say no to any of her friends, her adult children, or to her family. Kyle says he gets the brunt of Britney's overbooked life. Not only does she have no quality time to spend with him, but she expects him to keep up the pace with her. Britney has never even let go of her best friend from high school, although she admits to me the woman is a pest and gets on her nerves. Britney is often overwhelmed and becomes ill because she's stretched too thin. Her life's cluttered with people who are no longer of any value to her and who demand more from her than they give back. When I confront her on this, she agrees with me, but does nothing to change it. Britney doesn't want to learn how to separate from others— she'd rather feel popular than improve the quality of her life.

Setting "Life" Boundaries

Imagine making a movie of your future life. If your life is to be a happy, nonstressful one, you have to keep the size of the cast down. Acquaintances and friends who aren't extremely close, and people you know but aren't really close to you, should appear only sporadically. Britney's story is overcrowded with characters who want major roles in her life, but some should be cut or the story will be chaotic (just like Britney's life already is). Your life may be packed with too many characters also, or maybe the wrong characters. Do you need to recast the story of your future life?

Learning to Separate Begins in Adolescence

As we become adolescents, we begin to look at our parents differently—we evaluate them as people, not parents, and as we see their negative traits, we begin to separate our own identities from theirs. The more we can differentiate our own personalities from our parents', the clearer our identity becomes. I remember thinking, "I'll never be a doormat to a man like my mom is!" That was a healthy thought, a "separating" thought.

The process of separation from our parents is one reason adolescent years are filled with so much turmoil. Neither we nor our parents really understand it. Those of us who make the break are less likely to play victim to our mates in the future, more likely to have high self-esteem, less likely to be approval chasers, less likely to obsess or be addicts, and better able to cope with life. But many of us never finish the separation process, which is why patterns of dysfunction pass from one generation to the next. When we don't complete it, we're confused about our identities, and much more likely to doubt ourselves and allow a mate to control us.

Divorce or Separation?

When you know it's over, of course, it's time to get a divorce and a separation would just postpone the inevitable. People often separate instead of getting a divorce because it sounds less serious and less frightening. But remember, separation puts your life on hold. If you can't imagine fixing the relationship, if you have more resentment toward your mate than warmth, or if you have fallen out of love with him, the relationship is over, and it's time for a divorce. You need to get on with your life.

However, if the two of you still love each other but aren't together because you constantly fight and can't agree on how to resolve issues, separation could be an option for you. While separated, you need to work on yourselves individually, hoping to come back smarter, stronger, and more able to work out your issues. If you separate be sure you make agreements about the following separation issues:

- Are you allowed to date others?
- How often should you see each other or call each other? (I believe only a couple of times a week is best.)
- Are you committed to individual therapy and how often?
- Should you have joint therapy sessions together? When?

When There's No Turning Back

Once you know the relationship is over, you need to move on. To do this, you must say goodbye and let go, even if you secretly want him back. You need to write him a goodbye letter to separate your identity from his and rid yourself of the baggage from that relationship. If you're having difficulty getting in touch with your anger to write your goodbye letter, call some of your friends or family—they'll remind you why you should be angry. It's often difficult for people who play the victim role to get angry, and if that's true of you, go to Appendix A for help; but you may need to see a therapist to help you unlock your anger.

Writing Your Goodbye Letter

The goal of your goodbye letter is for you to look at him for who he truly is, warts and all. Once you can see him with your eyes wide open, see how different you are from him, and realize what a jerk he has been to you, the stronger you become and the easier it is for you to let go.

Express to him that he has had no right to criticize you or treat you the way he did. Be sure you come from a position of strength as you start the letter. Tell him you're angry or repulsed, because of his bad behavior, and that he had no right to do that.

Tell him that he's wrong about you. State positive things about yourself without sounding as if you're trying to win his approval. Tell him how you are better than he is: "I am not as stupid or naive as you may think. I'm smart enough to figure out what a jerk you are."

Blast him with his negative traits. Let him know you see through him. Criticize and scold him. Be aggressive and accusatory: "You're a cold, inconsiderate jerk. No wonder you have no friends." Think of every single negative thing you can. If he lets his mother control his life, tell him he's weak. If his breath smells, tell him that, too. And tell him you now see why his last girlfriend broke up with him.

Clarify how you are different from him and proud of these differences. Make the point that he was never good enough for you anyway. "No wonder you didn't appreciate me—I'm a person who cares about people and you have a heart of stone. I'm successful and you're a loser!" It's important that you make it clear to him (and yourself) that he was not good for you.

Tell him the kind of man you want is different from him. "I don't know what I was doing with someone like you when I want a man who is warm and can express himself." Or, "I want a man who knows where he is going in life."

Make it clear you will never allow him or anyone else to treat you like that again!

Close the letter with some final goodbye phrase that shows it's really over, like "Grow up!" or "Have a miserable life—that's what you deserve!" The letter is more for you than him, and that's why you must be angry, aggressive, and negative about him. Your self-esteem is at stake here! Once you've written the letter, you can either say it all to him or send it to him. If it seems too vicious, take a few parts out before you send it, but send it. (Unless you're in the middle of a divorce, in which case, wait to send it until after everything is finalized so you don't jeopardize your case.)

Keep a copy of the letter and reread it anytime you start to reminisce about good times, have regrets, or feel positive toward him for any reason.

"You're a Passive-Aggressive Jerk!"

▶ *Janis and Tyler's Story*

After Janis finally realized it was over between her and Tyler, this is what she told him in her goodbye letter: "God I hate you! Now I see your true colors. You're mean, you can't be trusted, and you don't know how to love. This has nothing do with me. I realize now that you have a deep-seated anger at your older sister, which you never deal with, that makes you secretly hate women and want to hurt them. I should have realized how emotionally dead you are when I watched your parents come to town and blow off your party, and you acted like it didn't affect you at all. In fact, you pride yourself on being easygoing when really what you are is passive-aggressive. You're not really a warm person at all. I am, and I don't know what I was doing with someone as emotionally shut down as you are. You don't feel anything—anger or love. Yet your anger comes out in very underhanded ways. I want a man who can share himself, who knows what he wants in life. You're always wandering around and acting as if you want to figure yourself out, but you're just fooling yourself. I'm glad I know now what you're really like—instead of suffering with your inability to feel any longer. Guess what? I could never see myself with *you* ten years down the line! Goodbye and good riddance!"

Starting Over

This is the time to go out and experiment with your new skills. First, try applying the principles and techniques you've learned here to your other, nonromantic relationships. Before you become too deeply invested in a new relationship, practice behaving in a way that commands respect. Set boundaries and carry through with everyone. Let others know how you feel, what you want, and negotiate with them. Concentrate on developing within yourself the "mirror" qualities you want to see in your next relationship. Train yourself to ask for and get what you want, not just what others may feel like giving to you. Approach your next relationship—even if it's not someone you're really interested in—as a laboratory experiment, where you will practice setting and holding boundaries. Practice being the healthy equal partner you plan to be in your next relationship so you'll be ready when that special someone comes along. And trust me he will.

◀ Points to Remember ▶

1. Stop analyzing your relationship and change it.

2. Sometimes letting a relationship go, empowers you to save it.

3. Beating yourself up when you made a mistake disempowers you further.

4. Learning to separate and move on is a healthy and necessary part of adult development.

5. Let go of people who no longer add value to your life.

6. Do not become who others say you are.

7. Expressing anger is a requirement of letting go.

8. When you become healthy, others must choose to change or get away from you.

Chapter 15

How the Two of You Can Stay in Love Forever

In the exciting first stages of a relationship, your love was fresh and without resentments—and that was good. But it was probably more out of balance than you realized. You may wish your relationship could be exactly the way it was back when the two of you first met. But the way it was then is probably what started your dysfunctional fit. His love may have been based on taking care of you and you may have looked up to him (a parent/child dynamic). Maybe you were both needy and insecure and developed a codependent relationship based on your insecurities. The beginnings of adult love (involving respect and admiration) are different from the early stages of an out of balance relationship. That's not to say that adult love can't be wildly exciting, but it does show more restraint. The addictive behaviors are not allowed—sex too soon, constant contact, suffocation. Instead, both you and he are trying to be healthy and protect the relationship for the long term to create a relationship that is much deeper. It is this deeper love, respect, admiration, and equality in the relationship that are the basis for a long-term happy, healthy relationship.

Staying in love isn't easy. No matter how much in love two people are at the beginning of their relationship, love doesn't ensure long-term success. In fact, love has very little to do with success. Instead, it's how well two people can resolve issues so that they can maintain their love. Remember: The key to keeping him in love with you forever is to keep his respect—and to keep his respect, you must maintain equality in the relationship.

You many not have every issue in your relationship resolved, but the emotional climate at your house should have warmed up considerably, communication should be improved, and many issues that tormented you in the past have hopefully found resolution.

Why Wasn't I Taught This Before?

There isn't a woman alive who hasn't humiliated herself with a man because she didn't know better—including me. Remember, we were given the wrong information from our parents and society about how to behave in relationships, and most of us had no healthy role models showing us the way. We can't be held responsible for something we never understood. But from this day forward, having been given the information you need to keep your relationship in healthy balance, you no longer have an excuse for your bad behavior or for allowing his. Here is a quiz to test your new understanding of how to maintain a balanced relationship.

Quiz:
Is Your Relationship in Balance?

Question   **Yes or No**

1. Do both of you try to control yourselves and your own behavior rather than each other's?   _____

2. Do both of you take blame for the part you've played in damaging the relationship?   _____

279

Quiz:
Is Your Relationship in Balance?
(continued)

Question	Yes or No
3. Do both of you give the relationship your best, but not your all, compromising but never sacrificing?	_____
4. Have you created fair deals regarding housework, childcare, and money, and do you both try to renegotiate when you realize you are resenting a deal you've made?	_____
5. Do the two of you face issues head-on and work them through, as quickly as possible rather than avoid them?	_____
6. Do you treat each other with respect and stop yourselves if you start to act like a parent or a child with each other?	_____
7. Do both of you feel free to express your true personalities, and feel accepted for who you really are by your mate?	_____
8. Can you both communicate to each other in a loving, respectful way without fear of surrendering your power?	_____
9. Are you both able to acknowledge and respect each other's differences, instead of being critical or judgmental?	_____
10. Do the two of you show affection, share interests, profess your love, and set aside quality time?	_____

It would be great if you answered "yes" to all of these questions—and that is the goal. But every relationship is different and each one improves on its own timetable and in its own way. This quiz can act as a guide for the two of you in how to continue developing your healthy, loving, and equal relationship.

"Watch Out! I'm No Longer a Victim!"

A controller can't control if he has no victim. As many of the women, whose stories appear in this book, began to grow and change, their mates didn't necessarily become super-enlightened men who said, "Oh, I get it now. I have to stop trying to control you!" In fact, some resisted and walked out, and many resisted but could find no way to continue their bad behaviors. If you set a boundary, and ultimately don't stay in your mate's presence when he treats you badly or controls you, he can't continue his bad behavior toward you. Here's a quick quiz to test your (or his) progress at becoming an equal partner.

Quiz:
Am I Behaving Like an Equal?

Question	Yes or No
1. Do I take responsibility for my own life, knowing how I would handle it if he were not in it?	_____
2. Do I have career goals, and am I reaching them and moving forward with my life?	_____
3. Am I able to tell my mate what I need and want?	_____
4. Do I look for win/win situations rather than whine or expect him to read my mind?	_____
5. Am I setting clear boundaries with him?	_____
6. Do I share my feelings—good and bad—with him?	_____
7. Do I have a plan for how to financially provide for myself in the future?	_____

Quiz:
Am I Behaving Like an Equal?
(continued)

Question	Yes or No
8. Am I making sure I get as much from this relationship as I give?	_____
9. Am I supportive of him when he's vulnerable?	_____
10. Do I play fair when it comes to money?	_____
11. Am I willing to negotiate with my mate when he's unhappy with my behavior?	_____
12. Do I allow my mate his differences instead of trying to prove I'm right?	_____
13. Do I carry my weight with household responsibilities and childcare?	_____
14. Am I able to share information about my life with him and require that he does the same?	_____
15. Am I able to reciprocate warmth and vulnerability as well as anger when appropriate?	_____
16. Do I monitor my bad moods and not take them out on my mate?	_____
17. Do I include my mate in decision-making?	_____
18. Do I listen carefully to my mate's point of view?	_____
19. Am I respectful of his feelings when he's hurt or angry?	_____
20. Can I admit when I'm wrong?	_____

The more "no's" you answer to questions 1 through 10, the more likely you are still playing the role of victim. The more "no's" you answer to questions 11 through 20, the more likely you are still playing the role of controller. And of course, the more "yes" answers you gave to all twenty questions, the more you've given up the controller/victim dysfunctional behaviors and are behaving like an equal in your relationship.

Facing a Crisis Together

The true test of the strength of the bond between two people often comes during a crisis. The crisis can come in many forms: the death of a parent, the terminal illness of a loved one, or a major loss of income. For example, the loss of a child can be devastating, and you often hear of a couple splitting up after their child's death. Sometimes it's because they can't stop blaming themselves or each other, and sometimes it's because their emotional bond as a couple was not strong enough for them to work through it. On the other hand, my sister's crisis ended up improving her relationship with her husband. Once she was diagnosed with cancer, her upscale, "everything for show" lifestyle no longer mattered when she could be dying. The priorities in her life changed completely, and it was no longer okay with her that she had a workaholic husband. She stopped playing victim and confronted him. They went to counseling, worked it out, and today, twelve years later (after twenty-five years of marriage), they have a much healthier, equal relationship because of her crisis. In a crisis like that you find out whether you can work together as a team, putting the immediate goal first and other issues second, and the two of you reprioritize your lives instantly.

Don't Trust Him 100 Percent

It's not always a crisis that causes your mate to regress. We start to relax, he's doing his share of the housework, he's picking up the kids, things are going well. You feel like he "gets it" and you can now trust him. Then the holidays come around and he becomes the jerk you thought he was six months ago. He's watching football while you're slaving over the stove for his family or he's on the golf course when he promised to get the groceries for the party. Sometimes he's just saving face and acting macho around his friends and family, and sometimes he does selectively "forget" certain things you've talked about. Count on him forgetting the promises he made. That's why writing out your agreement is a good idea. Don't take it personally when he regresses (remember people will get away with whatever they can), just remind him (but don't nag), and let him know you expect him to follow through.

The Ten Commandments of Keeping Personal Power (and Keeping Him in Love with You)

1. **Be confident:** I like who I am and you should like me too.
2. **Tantalize him:** I know you want me.
3. **Be mysterious:** There's a part of me you may never know.
4. **Raise your market value:** Others like me and want me.
5. **Remain independent:** I want you, but I don't *need* you.
6. **See behind his mask:** I know you better than you think I do.
7. **Keep him off the pedestal:** You're not all that!
8. **Fight your own dragons:** I've got it handled, honey.
9. **Know how to be a bitch:** Don't even think about it!
10. **Know when to pull away:** Call me when you get a clue.

When You Are an Equal Partner

When you're an equal partner you have accepted the fact that your happiness is your own responsiblity. You know what you want and where you're headed. Even though you may make wrong turns at times, you know you have the strength to handle your life without leaning on your mate. The following are the characteristics of a woman who is an equal partner to her mate.

- She controls her own destiny—she knows what she wants in life, has goals, and is taking steps to reach them.
- She knows who she is and is proud of herself; she defends her beliefs when attacked, and is secure enough not to let others bring her down.
- She is exciting to be around because she's full of energy and has a good sense of humor. When she's passionate about something, nothing can stop her.
- She would rather be in *no* relationship at all than in one that holds her back in any way.
- She knows that her parents, siblings, friends, and mate may view the world differently, but she allows them their differences as long as they don't judge her.
- She deals with all levels of her life, ignoring none—money, her man, her education and career, her family, and her friends.
- She enjoys an active social life but also loves her alone time.
- She communicates with power. She lets others know immediately how she feels, what she wants, and what she'll do if she doesn't get it.
- She feels a sense of passion for her work as well as for the people she loves.
- She's selfish, i.e., takes care of herself first, treating herself with the same consideration and respect she wants from others.
- She values her time and spends it only with others she enjoys and who treat her with respect.
- She is her authentic self with others, not allowing *their* expectations to affect *her* behavior.
- She confronts others head-on, setting boundaries, yet gives them a chance to redeem themselves; if they don't, she pulls away from the relationship.
- She follows her own values instead of the "shoulds" of others, and stands up for those values, without trying to push them on others.

285

- She looks as good as she feels, because her image reflects her self-worth.
- She has a full range of emotions and behaviors from tears and vulnerability to anger and aggression.
- She compromises but doesn't sacrifice.
- She is a risk-taker.

When He Becomes an Equal Partner

These are the characteristics of a man who is an equal partner. He, too, realizes that his happiness is his responsibility, not yours. He has no desire to lean on you, or control you—only to be with you.

- He has no expectations about who does what according to gender.
- He respects you and your needs the same as his own.
- He treats you as well or better than he treats his friends.
- He values your love and returns it eagerly.
- He listens to your feelings and expects you to listen to and respect his.
- He considers quirks in your personality as cute and knows they're part of what makes you unique.
- He is emotionally honest, even if it hurts you, knowing that's the only way to keep a close emotional connection with you.
- He stands up for himself and confronts you when you aren't being fair.
- He handles all areas of his own life—career, money, friends, family, and his emotions.
- He enjoys social activities, but also enjoys his alone time.

His list may seem too short, but actually both lists are interchangeable—in a truly equal relationship, both of you will have all of the characteristics for male and female equal partners.

"I Want Him to Adore Me"

Remember how he loved and adored you when you were first dating? Remember your attitude and how you expected to be treated as special? Whether or not a man adores you has mostly to do with the way he views you. And the way he views you has more to do with your attitude about yourself than anything else.

Adoration requires a delicate balance of love, power, respect, attraction, mystery, unavailability, and challenge. Remember that to have a man's respect, you must love and respect yourself, and to do that you have to keep your personal power. For him to be and remain attracted to you, you must be able to be vulnerable, soft, intimate, and loving *without* giving your power away. Being adored also requires mystery, unavailability, and challenge. For him to never take you for granted, he must always fear losing you—just a little bit. He must know that you value yourself and demand to be treated well above all else. He must know that if he does not treat you well, you will leave and find someone who will.

My Long-Term Loving Relationship with Alan Today

Alan and I have a very unusual relationship in that we have chosen not to marry, although we've been together for over fifteen years. I was thirty-nine when we met and he was forty, and we both knew that we never wanted to get married again. I had decided not to have children and Alan already had a daughter, so marriage for the sake of children was not an issue. We have intentionally kept much of our lives completely separate, although we believe that we are more committed to each other than any married couple we know. We live together in our two homes that we own individually, living in his home in downtown Denver during the week and in my home in the mountains on the weekends. We have signed legal "power of attorney" documents for medical purposes, and have our wills made out to each other.

We keep all of our finances separate (no joint bank accounts) and split all grocery, entertainment, and travel expenses equally. We each pay our own house and car payments and other personal bills. We both work hard and spend our money however we please with no restrictions by the other. Although we often cook together, our latest deal is that Alan does most of the cooking (because he chooses to), and I do most of the kitchen cleanup. Each of us does our own laundry and basic housework, and each of us has a housekeeper who comes in every other week. (I proudly state that I have never dusted, vacuumed, or cleaned any room in his house.) Our families seldom interfere with our lives. Alan's mother lives in Denver and he visits her every Sunday night, and he talks to his daughter on the phone frequently. Both of them come to my house for special occasions. We fly to see my family once or twice a year and they adore him.

During the week we both drink socially and spend quite a bit of time with mutual friends, having dinner and going to parties. Alan often plays golf with his friends (even Sam) and I often hike or sing karaoke with my girlfriends. We hide out at the mountain house on weekends and spend Saturday and Sunday mornings sleeping in, lying in bed talking, catching up on the week. We're now quite compatible sexually, although we had some problems early on.

We've negotiated and found solutions to our many issues. I tell people, "Alan and I no longer have anything to fight about." We have no resentments toward each other and are incredibly loving and warm when we're together. Both of us are completely committed to the relationship and feel happy with our lives together. Our relationship is equal and respectful. We've both changed our behavior and have become better people since we've been together.

The Eight Key Ingredients of Love

1. **Common relationship goals** regarding the present and the future including (but not limited to) emotional intimacy, quality time together, pursuit of interests, marriage, children, social life, a home, financial security, sexual intimacy, and companionship.
2. **A feeling of goodwill** that comes from warmth and truly wanting the very best for your mate.
3. **Excitement and interest** created by bringing your separate and unique personalities to the relationship.
4. **Freedom** to be yourselves and follow your own interests resulting from both feeling secure in yourselves and the relationship.
5. **Ability to search for and find solutions to problems** because you respect each other and your differences, and seek solutions that meet both your needs.
6. **A deep bond** between you that others can't penetrate.
7. **Security** that comes from trusting your mate and knowing that you are both equally committed to the relationship.
8. **Commitment** to, and a vision of, your future together for many years to come.

◀ Points to Remember ▶

- A man must respect you to stay in love with you.
- You must keep separate identities to keep sexual attraction.
- It's your job to tell others when they hurt you so they can stop.
- You must participate like an equal partner if you want that from him.
- When a man has the power to make you feel good, he also has the power to make you feel bad.
- By setting boundaries with him, you show him how to win with you.

Appendix A

Emotional Work

It is possible to change the way your mate (and others) treat you simply by changing your own behavior. However, to keep your own behavior in check and healthy, you need to work through your emotional baggage from your past. When two people enter into a relationship, they bring with them all the baggage of their past relationships: their hurt, anger, disappointment, and defensive behaviors they've used to deal with those feelings of rejection. If you don't clean up your past issues, you'll constantly have to work at overriding your instinct to act dysfunctionally.

Handling Your Emotions

Most people don't understand how to deal with their emotions. We often think that "handling" emotions means ignoring them, pushing them away, or not letting them affect us. To the contrary, handling our emotions actually means feeling the pain and working through it to find resolutions so that our problems don't recur. When we don't deal with our emotions we find ourselves reliving our problems again and again, whether in an old relationship or a new one.

Having a full range of emotions is normal and natural, and experiencing those feelings is healthy. It's when we stifle, ignore, or avoid our feelings that we become victims or controllers in our relationships. For instance, if you deny feeling hurt by someone's behavior, acting as if his bad behavior doesn't affect you, you don't let him know he's hurt you, which then allows him to continue his bad behavior. You either behave like a victim by allowing it, or act like a controller by blowing up. Issues left unresolved turn into resentments, keep us behaving defensively, and cause permanent damage to our self-esteem. Our damaged self-esteem keeps us either acting like victims, chasing someone's approval, or controlling others to make sure no one can hurt us again.

Dealing with Your Emotional Baggage

We all have emotional baggage we bring into our relationships. Emotional baggage consists of personal issues that haven't been resolved or worked through in a way that ensures they no longer affect us. These feelings of hurt, anger, sadness, embarrassment—pain of all kinds—often rear their ugly heads as distrust, anxiety, frustration, insecurity, confusion, or overwhelming guilt in our relationships, causing our behavior to be inappropriate. It's difficult to constantly override these feelings in an effort to keep our own behavior in line. Avoiding these feelings and pretending they don't exist only intensifies them and keeps us from resolving issues in our relationships.

Who Has Hurt or Rejected You?

Feeling hurt and rejected in our past is what causes most of our dysfunctional behavior. Guilt and fear of hurting others causes the rest.

We have all felt rejected at some time in our lives. It's what we do with those feelings that counts. Most of us do nothing, which leaves us feeling overly sensitive to feeling unloved by our mates and others. When we never resolve our rejection issues, we're more likely to assume that we're not loved, even when we are. Then our dysfunctional behaviors kick in: Our fear of rejection makes us doubt ourselves, edit ourselves, fear being intimately known, and even sabotage our own lives. To let go of our feelings of rejection, we must confront the key people in our lives who have hurt us, or apologize to those we have hurt.

Emotional Baggage from Parents

Our first dysfunctional, out-of-balance relationship started with our parents. As children, we were naturally victims of our parents' control. Some parents withhold their love and approval, which sets up their children to act like victims, people-pleasing to try to win their love. Other parents give too much love and attention, often spoiling their children and showing them how to control relationships. Either way, a dysfunctional role of controller or victim begins here.

If your parents gave you the control, you probably assume you know what's best for others and ignore your mate's values and needs. If you were constantly seeking your parents' love and approval, you probably put your mate's beliefs and needs first, ultimately trying to control your environment indirectly, playing victim as you seek the approval of your controlling mate, as you did with your parents.

We also learn from modeling our parents behaviors as we watch them interact as a couple. You may nag your husband just like your mother nagged your father, or explode in anger like your dad did when he was frustrated with your mom. You may have learned to avoid confrontation or to fight viciously, depending on what your parents did. These bad behaviors seemed normal to you, which is why there's often a tug-of-war going on in your head regarding behaviors that feel right versus behaviors you know are healthier.

You Can Rid Yourself of Dysfunctional Behavior

If you clean up your emotional baggage with your parents first, you'll be better able to rid yourself of dysfunctional behavior in other parts of your life. When you stop playing victim or controller with your parents, it will be easy to stop playing those roles with your mate.

Step One: Look at Your Parents Realistically

You are an adult now and are legally equal to your parents. To become emotionally equal, you have to look at your parents realistically, simply as people—people with good and bad traits, people you may like or may not like, people with personality traits you admire or traits you abhor. Ask yourself: Would I choose to live my life just like theirs?

- **What beliefs and values do I have that are different from theirs?** Which of their beliefs are valid for me and which one's aren't? Stop thinking of your parents as a part of you, but instead as people separate and different from you.
- **Do I want to be like them?** Think about how your parents deal with problems, how they show love, honesty, and vulnerability. Do you want to behave in the same ways? Decide exactly which traits you want to copy and which ones you want to discard. How do you want your life to be different from theirs?

Step Two: Withdraw and Separate Your Identity from Your Parents

You can be whoever you want to be, no matter who your family is, how dysfunctional they are, or who they believe you are. To do this, you must separate your values and beliefs from theirs, and demand their respect for the way you see things. Don't allow them to talk down to you—no matter what. Don't let them believe they're "right" in their judgments about your life, whether it's how you spend money, who you date, or whether or not you go to church on Sundays. Express your anger to them without fear of losing their love. By telling your parents *your truth*, you separate your identity from theirs and no longer need their approval—or anyone else's.

If you're still living with your parents, or talking to them every day, or asking them for money, or whining to them about your life, or listening to them whine, or using your mother as your best friend, or asking your dad for advice—you're too connected to them, and are probably acting like a victim, allowing them to control you. You must break your dependency to become an equal adult. Borrow from a bank before taking money from your parents; don't tell them how badly your life is going, cut back the frequency of "checking in" phone calls, and stop asking them for advice on how to live your life.

Step Three: Stop Seeking Your Parents' Approval

The concepts of seeking approval and being respected are mutually exclusive. Approval seeking happens in an out-of-balance relationship, while mutual respect exists only in an equal relationship. All of us want our parents' love and respect. However, if our parents don't respect our right to have values and beliefs different from theirs, we must have enough self-respect to pull away and stop seeking their approval.

- **Stand up to your parents.** When your parents criticize or judge you, stand up to them by telling them: "You're wrong about me. I'm smart, even though you don't seem to know it since you criticize every thing I do. From now on, if you criticize me, I'll tell you to stop. And if you don't stop, I'll leave your presence. Besides, I no longer allow your criticisms to affect me."

- **Criticize your criticizers.** If your parents won't let go of their control, you may need to fight aggressively to stop playing victim with them. You may need to point out their flaws: "You say I'm lazy, but, Mom, when did you ever hold a real job?" "Dad, you question my integrity when you've cheated in business for years."

Step Four: Confront and Purge Past Anger Toward Them

To equalize the relationship, you need to take your parents off their pedestal and hold them accountable for their bad behaviors. Confront them about ways they've hurt you in the past, giving them details of major painful incidents, letting them know the damage they caused to your self-esteem and how they still affect you today. Don't behave abusively toward your parents, but in no way allow them to intimidate you either. If they won't listen and cooperate, pull away and refuse to spend time with them until and unless they are willing to work through these issues with you so that you can equalize the relationship. Make it clear that you'll no longer accept the out-of-balance relationship you once had with them. Either they begin to treat you respectfully as an adult (equal), or you won't spend time with them. Setting boundaries with them will give you the strength to do the same with your mate.

Step Five: Set Guidelines to Be Treated as an Adult

It's important that you create new rules for your relationship with your parents if you want to get rid of your emotional baggage. Here's what I suggest you tell them:

- I will not allow any more criticism and you can no longer tell me how I should live my life. If you try to, I'll tell you to stop, and if you don't stop, I'll hang up or walk away.

- You must accept that many of my beliefs and values are different from yours and that your way isn't always right. We'll have to agree to disagree on many things.
- You will need to be supportive of my choices and decisions or I will stop sharing information about my life with you.
- You will need to be warm and loving with me or I won't spend time with you.
- I will no longer try to please you or make you happy, but instead will concentrate on my own happiness.

To be strong enough to maintain control over your own behavior, you need to clean up your emotional baggage with others, especially with your parents. To become a healthy adult you must equalize the relationship with your parents. Once you've done that, all other relationships become easy and most of your dysfunctional behaviors will cease. You'll stop chasing approval, feeling insecure, rescuing others, and acting self-righteous. Instead of seeking and participating in relationships built on dysfunctional fits, you'll find that happy, healthy relationships become the norm. Then you'll find it more natural and easy to enjoy a healthy, equal relationship with your mate.

For more information on how to clean up your emotional baggage, separate your identity from others, and equalize your relationships, see my book *Loving Him Without Losing You: 8 Steps to Achieving Intimacy and Independence,* CBPA Psychotherapy Publications, 2001.

Appendix B

Update on Characters

The couples in this book were all encouraged to do individual emotional work to make themselves healthier and stronger in their relationships. Each person grew at his or her own pace. Some individuals did enormous work on themselves, others barely scratched the surface. Here are their updates. (Names are arranged alphabetically by the woman's first name.)

▶ **Alexis and Raymond** had been together for three years and were talking about living together and eventually marriage and children. But each time she says she's giving up her apartment, Raymond finds an excuse for her to postpone. She's realized he's almost as commitment-phobic as Carlos was. She gave him an ultimatum last week and he didn't respond so she's once again moving on. However, Alexis now realizes that she needs to work on her emotional baggage stemming from her childhood before she gets into another relationship. She still chooses unavailable, yet controlling men like her father and five brothers.

▶ **Allison and Sid** dropped out of therapy because Allison had trouble believing she was controlling and didn't think she should have to change. The last I knew they were still playing out their dysfunctional relationship, regularly breaking up and then getting back together. Both did some emotional work on themselves, but not enough.

▶ **Bethany and Nick** are very happily married. Bethany worked on herself emotionally for years to resolve her "unavailable father" issues—which is what made her available for this healthy relationship.

▶ **Bill** (one of the two men in our stories without a mate) has been in and out of therapy with me for years every time another woman left him. Each time, I pushed the emotional work he needed to do, but he refused. Finally, twenty or so women (who'd rejected him) later, he confronted his stepfather three weeks ago. He has hated his stepfather for being cold and controlling and keeping Bill from his mother. I told Bill that he may hate him, but he's becoming him. It's too soon to see if his patterns will change.

▶ **Brandi and Colin** are divorced. I have no information on Brandi but Colin got on the singles circuit, dated a slew of women, and then repeated his pattern by getting involved with another dependent woman. That brought him back into therapy to complete his emotional work regarding standing up to his mother and older brother (he always did what they wanted him to do and then secretly rebelled which set up his passive/aggressive behavior). He's been dating a new woman who seems healthy and independent, but he still struggles with his desire to rebel. He says this is the most emotionally honest relationship he's ever been in, and he's trying not to screw it up.

▶ **Britney and Kyle.** Both Britney and Kyle got healthier, but not in time to save the relationship. Britney had given Kyle the ultimatum about getting into therapy, and he did (for a few sessions). Kyle began speaking up to Britney and asking her for what he wanted. However, he never did his deeper emotional work so Britney didn't trust him. Kyle needs to equalize the relationship with his mother by confronting her and sharing his feelings, so that he'll be able to stand up to Britney and ask for what he wants so he doesn't develop more resentment. However, Kyle wants to protect his aging mother and refuses to clean up his emotional baggage with her. After ten years without marriage and with much resentment on both sides, Britney now seems resistant to changing to meet *his* needs (to cut back on social activities and family commitments).

Britney began spending more time making herself happy, going out with friends to have fun (instead of obligation dinners), has lost fifteen pounds and is looking and feeling great. It's no surprise that she met a new man four months ago who she says is giving her all the love and attention she ever wanted.

He gave her a ring last week and Kyle was the first person she called to tell. Kyle was devastated and asked her to come back to him. Britney is very confused. She feels she's "in love" with the new man, but doesn't want to let go of Kyle because he's been her best friend for over ten years. [Britney never finished her emotional work about learning to "separate" from others.]

Kyle immediately came back to therapy and began working on his issues with his mother. He told Britney that he knows he wasn't really emotionally available before, but feels he can be now. He recently gave her an ultimatum: "Break up with the new man and come back to me now or stop calling me and leave me alone. I won't just be your 'best friend.'" She's moving forward with her engagement.

▶ **Charlotte and George** are still together and communicating better about their sexual issues.

▶ **Crystal and Brett.** Crystal filed for divorce while Brett was staying with his mother after being released from the psychiatric hospital. Once Brett was feeling better, he begged Crystal not to go through with the divorce. However, she reminded him that their relationship was not good before his psychotic break, and said she planned to get on with her life and hoped he would too.

▶ **Cynthia** has begun to date one man steadily and is confident that she'll eventually end up with the man of her dreams, whether it's the present man in her life or someone else. She's also amazed at how healthy her friendships and work relationships have become since she stopped giving so much, and now focuses on "equality" in her relationships.

▶ **Darlene and Bob** divorced after only a few sessions with me, because Bob had wanted the divorce for years. Both moved on with their lives. Neither of them worked much on their emotional issues.

▶ **Deanna and Daryl** have learned to protect their relationship by setting boundaries with others in their lives. They still both work hard, but have learned to set aside quality time for each other.

▶ **Emma and Dwayne** are still together, having worked out their babysitting issue. The twins are in school and have adjusted very well.

▶ **Gretchen and Art** are more happily married than ever and have learned to negotiate their differences. They're proud of their ability to solve problems on their own. Both worked on their emotional baggage, but both still have more work to do.

Gretchen admits that she learned to sacrifice and then complain about it from her own mother. Gretchen had a talk with her mother about this, but has trouble getting angry at her mom about her whining and complaining behavior because Gretchen, herself, still does the same thing from time to time.

Art wrote his father a confrontation letter holding his father accountable for destroying his brother (who can't hold a job and uses drugs), but barely touched on his father's domination of him, which was a big part of Art's depression. The letter was good and powerful, but Art never had the courage to send it.

▶ **Ian** (one of the two men in our stories without a mate) is still a single man. I ran into him recently, and he was flirtatious as usual. He said he's still searching for Mrs. Right, and my guess is he's probably still pining away for the one woman who rejected him.

▶ **Jane and Gary** dropped out of therapy when I pushed Jane to leave Gary because he was becoming physically abusive with her. When I checked up on her later, she said she had no access to money now (her mother had paid for her therapy) and was now seeking therapy through a battered women's shelter.

▶ **Janis and Tyler** broke up. When Tyler ended the relationship a third time, Janis no longer fell for his persistent cards and phone calls saying, "let's be friends," that used to pull her back in.

Janis worked on her emotional baggage, first handling her mother's alcoholism through boundary-setting. Then she worked on her feelings toward her deceased father, whose bad behavior she always covered up just as she did Tyler's behavior, making excuses to her friends that he was really a good guy but just confused. Realizing she was repeating a pattern helped Janis let go of Tyler completely. She recently began dating a radio announcer (she used to be in radio) who seems to adore her.

Although Tyler had four or five sessions with me, he mostly just defended his confusion and never really worked on himself.

▶ **Jennifer and Matt** are still together but living separately, sort of. (Years ago, they bought a house in Texas, and Jennifer is spending more and more time there while leaving Matt in Denver.) She admits she still has resentment toward Matt for his years of control over her, but she knows she'll never leave him since she's never worked and loves the lifestyle he's created. At least she has learned to speak her mind and get what she wants from him.

▶ **Jill and Glen** are no longer together, but Glen hasn't given up. Jill dropped out of therapy because she told me she wouldn't give Glen up no matter what he did to her. Then she called me last week and said, "I've finally had enough, and I've decided to move to Phoenix, go back to school, and start my life over far away from him. Let's talk about my new life!"

▶ **Jo-Ann and Michael** are still together. Jo-Ann did a lot of emotional work but Michael did not. Jo-Ann worked on her parental issues, and then she sent Michael in to see me to work on his passivity. However, after three or four sessions of getting in touch with his anger at Jo-Ann, he canceled his next appointment and never returned my phone calls. I recently heard they reached their goal of moving back to Boston.

▶ **Katherine and Graeme** are working out their financial issues, but Katherine will probably always have to stay in control of the family finances. Graeme has not quit gambling, although he gambles less and no longer uses family money.

▶ **Kirsten and Sheldon's** relationship ended because Sheldon was married to someone else and Kirsten finally realized he was a "no win" deal. Kirsten did some emotional work with both her parents, but continued

301

to choose unavailable men. She took a break from therapy because she decided to focus on becoming a single mother before her biological clock ran out. However, Kirsten recently came back when her attempts failed—the doctor said she's too old to conceive. She's broken-hearted, but I've asked her to look at how to have a happy "future life without baby," and finish her emotional work separating from her family.

▶ **Krista and Eugene** are still living together, but in the process of divorce. Krista's abusive stepfather died just as she was beginning to understand his effect on her. He taught her to sacrifice to win love and approval, as well as how to become abusive herself when she is resentful of Eugene. While she was away handling the family matters, Eugene came to therapy alone. He worked on his controlling father issues, realizing he has chosen women who act like his father, so he can play victim to them.

While Krista was gone, he regained his independence and felt relieved she wasn't there to bitch at him. When she came back, he told her he wanted a divorce. As if the timing wasn't bad enough already, a week later, Krista found out she has breast cancer (for the third time). Krista can't believe she sacrificed her life for Eugene and his kids and he's now abandoning her in her time of need. Eugene has agreed that they will stay together (as roommates) until her chemotherapy is completed, but is moving forward with the divorce.

▶ **Kristi and Gavin** are in the process of a messy divorce. She hired an aggressive attorney and is playing out the victim role, using the courts to punish Gavin for controlling her—keeping him from his daughter and draining him financially by dragging the proceedings on and on. I'm now involved in his custody battle working with Gavin on "how not to play victim to her."

▶ **Kyla and Brock** are doing very well. Kyla is seeing her own therapist and Brock is working with me to help him break his addictive behavior to drugs and to Kyla.

▶ **Lana and Ian** are still together and Ian has found another job, but is not making enough to pay half of the expenses. Lana has consulted with an attorney in an effort to protect the few assets she has left and prepare herself in case she and Ian don't make it.

▶ **Linda and Grant** are separated and Grant is now living in the mountains. Linda is just beginning to find her niche in her career and can't see herself giving it up. They still spend weekends together. Grant tells her about job openings in the mountains, but he still resents her decision to stay in the city to live her new life.

▶ **Lindy and Anthony** are still married. Anthony agreed to go to counseling if he could choose the therapist. (He did not choose me.) Lindy called the other day and said that the new therapist fired Anthony, but that Anthony still would not see me. At this point she believes he's actually having an affair with one of her best friends and is trying to get him to see another therapist. I recommended some ultimatums, but she wouldn't agree to them. She never rescheduled.

▶ **Lynn and Peter** are doing very well. Lynn is working and enjoying it. Peter is helping at home and learning new respect for Lynn.

Lynn realized she saw Peter as a father figure and related to him the same way she related to her real father—by rebelling. Lynn pretended to obey but secretly began hiding in her own world. Lynn addressed the emotional issues she had with her parents, which helped give her the courage to stand up to Peter instead of hiding in her own secret world.

Peter was eager to do his emotional work, but was surprised to learn that, though he was a great rescuer of others, he wasn't dealing with his own emotional issues. Instead, he intellectualized away his emotions and carried around an edge of anger. Peter began to address the emotional issues from his childhood—his father's passivity and his mother's control. The upshot to this is that Peter (wisely) cut his mother out of his life, because of her destructive ways, and has begun to develop a deeper emotional relationship with his father—as he's now building with Lynn.

▶ **Margaret and Donald** are doing very well. All they needed was to start communicating again, and now that they're rebuilding their emotional and sexual intimacy.

▶ **Maria and Carl** are finally starting to work together. It wasn't until Carl made it clear that he would no longer live with her punishing ways that Maria agreed to try to let go of her resentment from the past. She finally dropped her wall of grudges, and she and Carl began to communicate like they never had before. Both Carl and Maria worked on their emotional baggage with their respective families and this helped them to understand their own relationship problems better. The last I knew, the relationship was warming up and beginning to work.

▶ **Marilyn and Larry** broke up after Marilyn realized she was acting out the dysfunctional relationship she had with her father, a military man who ruled with an iron fist. Marilyn longed for an intimate connection with her father but never really felt his love, which left her prone to choosing emotionally unavailable men. So when Larry entered her life, his cold, controlling, and abusive ways not only seemed normal to her, but also felt like the same kind of "love" her father had given her. The reality is that both men are emotionally repressed and have difficulty connecting with others. Marilyn now knows that and can see through Larry's rejecting ways. She admits, however, that it's been hard to give up the addictive relationship because Larry still calls every six weeks or so, trying to get back together. But it helps that she has a great new man in her life who has helped bring back all of her sexual passion!

▶ **Marion and Tom** almost ended their relationship when Marion lost her job and Tom became more critical and abusive. Marion withdrew, moved to the other bedroom, and began to look for other living options. After several weeks of this, Tom told her he was embarrassed about how he had acted, stopped drinking (at least temporarily), and offered to help her financially. Neither Marion nor Tom have worked on their own emotional baggage.

▶ **Mary and Patrick** have been separated for eight months. Neither has filed for divorce, but Patrick is not participating with Mary emotionally, financially, or even with visitation of the children. Mary believes a divorce is inevitable and, although she was having difficultly accepting it, she now knows she'll be okay without him.

Mary finally understood how her upbringing played into her feelings of inadequacy in her relationship with Patrick. She was intimidated by Patrick's family money because she grew up dirt poor. Plus, he came from a stable home and she was a child of divorce, a fact that made Mary feel even more deprived. And finally—the most important influence on her low self-esteem—and a key reason she felt Patrick was better than she was because she had a deep, dark secret. Mary had been sexually abused at the age of twelve, and raped twice as a teenager—and she believed it was her fault as most victims do. She told me, "I was so starved for attention that I allowed a twenty-two-year-old married neighbor to repeatedly have sex with me for several years. And as a teenager, I always dressed slutty and probably brought those rapes on myself."

I helped Mary see how she had been truly victimized many times and that none of it was her fault or anything she needed to be embarrassed by. I also helped her understand that her parents should have protected her, but instead set her up to fail by not being nurturing, supportive, and protective. She needed to be mad at them and her abusers, not herself—and that's why she had not healed.

After much emotional work regarding her parents and her sexual abuse, Mary is getting stronger day by day and is beginning to see that her dependency on Patrick was understandable given her childhood. She is beginning to forgive herself and realize that Patrick isn't—and never was—better than she is. Now she can let go.

▶ **Melanie and Jackson.** Melanie could never trust Jackson again, and filed for divorce. She's moved on with her life back in Denver—with a new job and a new man. Jackson has never stopped begging her to forgive him and take him back.

▶ **Misty and Gordon** have moved back to California near her family. She has her old job back, and their relationship has improved, along with her power and self-esteem.

Misty began her emotional work when she realized that, although she adopted her father's controlling style, she was actually very intimidated by him, and that both her dad and Gordon had intimidating, self-righteous ways about them. Misty and Gordon had set up a competitive relationship—they were both controllers—but Gordon had won. Gordon's biggest problem was seeing every situation in their relationship as win/lose. Although he was at times able to see the role he played in his problems with Misty, he did very little emotional work on himself. Gordon had a special way of intimidating Misty much like her father's style that had worked only too well. Besides, Misty had been living on his turf. But now they're on her turf and she'll never give her power away again.

▶ **Myra and Joseph** are doing better because Joseph has learned to stand up to Myra. Each time she criticizes him, he tells her to stop and walks away when she doesn't. She asked him the other day, "Do you see us together long-term?" "Only if you learn to respect me and we start working together like partners," he replied. He's also handling his ex-wife and children better now that he's not allowing Myra to interfere.

▶ **Nancy and Mark**'s relationship will be ending soon, although Mark doesn't know it. After only two years of marriage and a two-year-old child, Nancy hates Mark. Not only did he control her time and withhold money, but he also refused to "let" her travel with the baby to see her family. She recently came back to therapy (paid for by her grandmother) to discuss and make a plan to leave Mark. She says she feels like he is her captor and she has to plot and plan her escape as such. She's seen an attorney (who helped her realize that Mark couldn't keep her from vacationing with her family), and has a plan to leave him at the end of this school semester.

Nancy did some emotional work on abandonment issues with her parents and has improved her self-esteem as a result. She has committed to finishing her emotional work once she has left Mark.

▶ **Phyllis and Keith** are still together and their relationship is improving. Phyllis had to do some major confrontation with Keith regarding his critical and controlling ways, but he "got" it and their relationship has improved and deepened, and he moved in one month ago.

▶ **Rosalind and Rod** are still together and working well together. Rod is helping out around the house and with their daughter, but is still not emotionally available. She hopes to bring him in to her next appointment to work on this.

▶ **Rose and Terry**'s relationship ended two years ago and she's now very happy and engaged with a September wedding date.

▶ **Sandy and Jimmy** are divorced and Sandy is doing very well.

▶ **Shara and Lucas** are separated and have filed for divorce.

▶ **Sharon** is over the man she felt obsessed with, has been dating a new man, and is proud of herself for not obsessing in this relationship. However, she is very protective of her family and denies that she has any emotional baggage from childhood that she needs to work on, so she is no longer in therapy.

▶ **Shonda and Lawrence** broke up because Shonda called Lawrence one too many times. But Shonda wrote a goodbye letter and got stronger. She also learned her lesson and "played it right" when she met a new man, and they've been dating successfully now for six months.

▶ **Stacey and Dean** are now divorced, even though Stacey couldn't let go. She even had her grown children try and shame him into leaving his girlfriend and coming back to her.

▶ **Sue and Ryan** have been in the process of a divorce for almost a year. Sue has been living with a man most of this time and Ryan has been dating one particular woman. However, recently they called and asked to come back in for marriage counseling and try one more time to put it back together. Sue worked on her emotional baggage by confronting her father and sexual abuser and is standing up to her mother more often, especially when she tries to interfere. Ryan agreed to look at his controlling ways, but still doesn't believe it relates in any way to his childhood.

In therapy this time, each was more respectful of the other. First, issues and boundaries regarding the others they dated were addressed. Then decisions about Cory, who is now nineteen, were addressed with a decision to help him get on his feet but not live with them. They've bought a new house together, have a plan regarding finances and getting Sue stabilized in a new career, and look forward to trying to share their lives together.

▶ **Tami and Brandon** are now happily married. Both worked on their issues with their parents and learned to protect their relationship from invasive friends and family.

▶ **Tricia and Kevin** are divorced, and have moved on with their lives.

▶ **Veronica** is divorced and dating several men, and recently testified in a trial in Florida (where another woman was raped and killed) to try and get her rapist (who is in prison) the death penalty.

My Own Deep Work

As I said in the Introduction, I've not asked you to do anything I haven't done myself. I've confronted both my parents about issues from my childhood. I've apologized to my sister for being controlling with her. I've confronted (sometimes in person, mostly in letters) my ex who damaged my self-esteem. I've stood up to, and will continue to stand up to, anyone who abuses me. I accept that I'm not always liked when I am myself. I still get controlling at times, though I'm no longer proud of it. I still secretly believe, however, that there's nothing worse than being victimized, so if and when my buttons are pushed, I still lean more toward the controlling side when I respond. I've learned that meeting my mate half way, giving him full respect, and controlling only my own behavior are the secrets to a happy, healthy, forever-passionate relationship. Changing myself changed Alan and ultimately changed our relationship into something incredibly wonderful.

About the Author

CAROLYN BUSHONG, L.P.C., is a successful psychotherapist who has maintained a private practice in Denver for more than twenty years, specializing in relationships. She is the author of two other books, *Loving Him Without Losing You* (CBPA Publications, September 2001) and *The Seven Dumbest Relationship Mistakes Smart People Make* (Fawcett, April 1999). As an expert on relationships, she has appeared on *Oprah, The View,* and numerous other national television talk shows. She has a weekly radio show that airs in Denver on Thursday morning drive-time on 92.5 FM Denver. Bushong is also a regular contributor to *Cosmopolitan, Redbook, New Woman, First for Women, US Weekly, In Touch,* and many other national magazines.

Bushong lives in the mountains outside Denver, Colorado. She conducts psychotherapy by phone for those who do not live near Denver. You may contact her to schedule an appointment by calling (303) 333-1888.